Stuart Cosgrove was a fanzine writer on the northern soul scene before joining black music paper *Echoes*, and then the *NME* as media editor. Born in Perth, he graduated from Hull University. In 2005 he was named Broadcaster of the Year in the Glenfiddich Spirit of Scotland Awards and in 2012 he won a BAFTA for the Channel 4 coverage of the London Paralympics. He co-hosts Scotland's most popular radio show, *Off the Ball*, and his most recent book, *Detroit 67*, is a cult bestseller, which was shortlisted for the Penderyn Music Prize (2016). The second book in his soul trilogy, *Memphis 68*, will be published by Polygon in 2017.

YOUNG SOUL REBELS
A PERSONAL HISTORY OF
NORTHERN SOUL

Stuart Cosgrove

Polygon

First published in Great Britain in 2016 by Polygon, an imprint of Birlinn Ltd. This paperback edition reprinted in 2017.

Polygon
West Newington House
10 Newington Road
Edinburgh
EH9 1QS

www.polygonbooks.co.uk

ISBN 978 1 84697 393 2
eBook ISBN 978 0 85790 894 0

British Library Cataloguing-in-Publication Data
A catalogue record for this book is available on request from the British Library.

Typeset by 3btype.com

CONTENTS

Foreword   v

Chapter 1 *The Amphetamine Rush* 1971   1

Chapter 2 *Locusts in the Night* 1967–1971   13

Chapter 3 *In Search of Obscurity* 1967–1973   43

Chapter 4 *The Road to Wigan Pier* 1973–1981   65

Chapter 5 *Red Riding, West Yorkshire* 1973–1981   103

Chapter 6 *The Deep Sea Where the Music Roars* 1974–1984   125

Chapter 7 *Soul Not Dole* 1974–1990   155

Chapter 8 *Ticket to the Freak Show* 1978–1986   177

Chapter 9 *The New Model Army* 1980–1985   207

Chapter 10 *London Calling* 1984–1990   235

Chapter 11 *The Twisted Wheels of Technology*   257

Glossary of Terms   279

Index   285

FOREWORD

The recent success of my cult book *Detroit 67: A The Year That Changed Soul* has convinced me that readers yearn for ideas that connect soul music to the wider society. So I have written about things than ran parallel to the rare soul scene: amphetamine abuse, police raids, the north–south divide, the Yorkshire Ripper murders, the miners' strike, the collapse of the industrial north, and the rise of new technologies, which against all expectations have breathed new life into the northern scene.

Many people have helped me with their memories and they are credited within the book itself, but I want to single out three people who gave me encouragement and personify what the northern soul scene is about. Dave Molloy from Bolton is one of the northern soul scene's great minds, and he holds in his head a repository of knowledge and perspectives. I owe him many thanks, as well as Maureen Walsh from Dewsbury who helped me to connect the big social stories of the day to the scene, and was a touchstone for what really mattered in our young lives, and my long-time friend Mike Mason who grew up with me in the same housing scheme in Scotland and has remained a great friend across many years and through numerous scrapes.

Thanks to the editorial team who helped me to prepare this book for publication – especially Alison Rae from Polygon Books and designers Chris Hannah and Mark Swan – and my immediate family and the wider soul family who I have met on the way. Thanks also to those who have helped with interviews and personal memories, knowingly or otherwise, especially members of social media groups and the daddy of the rare soul forums, soul-source.co.uk. The striking cover image is of Stephen Cootes, a painter and decorator from Penicuik, crowned World Northern Soul Dance Champion in Blackpool in 2011. Remarkably, Stephen was born ten years after Wigan closed.

It's 5 a.m. at a soul all-nighter in a local community centre in Glenrothes, Fife – The Exit Centre. A dancer entranced by soul looks up to the heavens.

1
THE AMPHETAMINE RUSH
1971

Independence is a heady draught, and if you drink it in your youth, it can have the same effect on the brain as young wine does. It does not matter that its taste is not always appealing. It is addictive and with each drink you want more.

Maya Angelou

Nothing will ever compare to the amphetamine rush of my young life and the night I was nearly buggered by my girlfriend's uncle in the Potteries. It was a lumpy bed, upstairs in a red-brick terraced house in Tunstall, near Stoke-on-Trent, a few streets away from a famous northern soul club called the Golden Torch. My would-be molester was ancient, hopelessly drunk, and in a deep sleep. His vest stank of Woodbines, stale ale and the old ways, and he had the roughened hands of a seasoned foundryman. It was obvious from his determined grasp that he had stuck his rod in hotter things than me. I clung desperately to the edge of the mattress, wheezing with asthma, as his hands groped ever closer towards me. For a few uncomfortable hours I clung on, fearful for my anal membranes, but as the night ticked gradually by it became clear I was a shifting fantasy in his drunken dreams. Through the haze of drink and hard-ons, he thought I was Emma Peel from *The Avengers*.

When he awoke in the new light of the morning the old man was visibly disappointed. Far from being a sex siren in long leather boots, I was a stick-thin teenager from Scotland with atopic eczema and an insatiable appetite for the music of the American ghettos. Soul music had consumed my life, and I was on the first stumbling steps on a journey to forbidden places. Malcolm X had a phrase for it, 'by any means necessary', and not even the humiliation of being trapped in a creaking bed with a grunting drunk could deter me from northern soul and the first all-nighter I ever attended.

Saturday passed slowly as I browsed around local market stalls. Then night slowly fell and we walked through the backstreets of Stoke along cobbled terraces. The army of leather feet resonated like a drum solo, building percussion in our speeding heads and raising the adrenaline of anticipation. A swell of people hung by the door of what looked like a wartime cinema, and a blackout curtain seemed to have closed across the north of England. It was virtually impossible to make out faces or detail; everything was sound. A pounding noise escaped through the doorway and the wild screeching sound of saxophones pushed through the fire escapes, desperate for air. We paid at the ticket booth, but even in the foyer, an intense heat much like an industrial oven scorched through the thick aggressive air, and the noise was so pure, so fearless and so commanding, it dragged you inwards into a scrum of lurching bodies: hot, wet and demonic. This was in every respect the Devil's music, and I had travelled hundreds of miles from home to sip with the deranged serpents that slithered so gracefully on the floor. There was no going back. No music later in life would ever touch its uniqueness, no rock concert could match its energy, and no rave could come close to its latent illegality. This was northern soul: the reason they invented youth.

My early life had been troubled and economically deprived. But the gods had plucked me out of ordinary life and thrown me into the most extraordinary youth culture Britain has ever produced. I had grown up in a single-parent family in a council housing scheme in Scotland called Letham. My dad died when I was an infant and so the hope of suburbia or even an ordinary upbringing suddenly vanished. It scarred me then and it hurts me now. My dad was a giant in my life, a left-wing lorry driver who had travelled to Russia as a trade unionist and had met the famous spaceman Yuri Gagarin. The week before he died, in a gesture of man-to-boy kindness, he had sent me a postcard extolling the virtues of the Soviet space race, with Yuri Gagarin resplendent on the front. It was rare, the only one that anyone in my class had ever seen, and the stamp was authentic Soviet-era philately, with a rouble sign and two space dogs on the top left corner. Before the postcard arrived on my doorstep, he was dead, killed in a car crash on a road winding through the east of Scotland. The Cold War postcard took on a near religious significance in my life. I kept it tucked away in a drawer, too precious to put a pin through or leave on the kitchen table. In the terminology of northern soul, it was 'rare', a 'one-off', a 'fucking dobber', the only Soviet postcard anyone in Letham had ever seen. Kids crowded round me to look at the stamp. It featured a wee dog called Laika, a mongrel who had been plucked from the streets of Moscow by Soviet scientists and fired into space in Sputnik 2. I loved Laika like an emotionally needy child, not realising that within a few years I was about to be plucked from the streets like a stray mongrel and thrust into the intense heat of the Torch.

In the months after my dad's death, I took comfort in making lists on pages torn from a school notebook, a list of Soviet sputniks, space-age dogs, and cosmonauts: there was Gagarin, Titov and Popovitch, but the darling of them all was Valentina Tereshkova, the first woman in space. She looked like a stern schoolteacher with her head in a goldfish bowl but she helped prepare me for the journey to come. Compiling lists and recording obscure detail is part of the everyday autism of northern soul, and it was one I had begun to master early in life. Psychologists have spent decades trying to understand why people make lists. For me, one of the most credible is the so-called Zeigarnik Effect, which is what psychologists call our mind's tendency to get obsessed with tasks we have not done rather than those we have completed. It is a disorder that I was already trapped in: every new record I bought was swamped by the lists of those I had heard, those I needed to own, and a special few that were out of my reach, records so rare that only one or two existed in the world. But those glorious days were yet to come, and while I lived in a ghetto of sorts, a grim but likeable post-war housing scheme with windows that rattled like an old washing machine, it was not the ghettos I yearned for. Around the age of fifteen, as the rawest pain of my father's death had begun to heal, I became increasingly fixated on inner city America: the high-rise blocks on the Chicago South Side, the sparse prairie ghettos of Detroit, and the graffiti-strewn subway stations of New York. It was a love affair that was rich in discovery and one that would never end.

Northern soul is a scene founded on obscure music from the African-American society and works according to codes of behaviour that baffle outsiders. It is a world I have tried and failed to explain, but rather than confuse outsiders with minutiae it is best to point to images. One is a boy and the other is a girl; both are dancing, but by their movement and style they say everything about the scene. The boy is lost in the music, caught in a trance . . . His feet, sprinkled with talcum powder, navigate a wooden floor. He is looking skywards to the heavens and his hands are clasped to his chest in a near religious experience. The implication is clear: soul is more than a music, it is a spiritual calling and a route to all-night fanaticism. The girl is more controlled. She's staring into the distance, her cropped peroxide bob cut elegantly short. Her Fred Perry-style shirt is miraculously white, her bright red lips glow through the night, and her long heavy suffragette skirt angles down to the floor. It is a timeless style that could have been worn at Blackpool Mecca or on the pier at Cleethorpes in 1975, and it screams through studied coolness. Northern soul is all of that: it is the fanatical height of spiritual cool.

A favourite game on the northern soul scene is, what was the first record you ever bought? The answer determines when you joined the scene. Was it in the Mod days of the late sixties, at the high point of Wigan Casino, or in the latter days of an all-nighter in Stafford (brazenly called Top of the World)? My answer was suitably vague. I had learned a lot from my older sister, a first generation Mod, who collected R&B imports and 7-inch vinyl discs by old bluesmen like Jimmy Witherspoon, Howlin' Wolf and Rufus Thomas, names she lovingly wrote on the brown paper covers of her schoolbooks. I was too young back then to get those cool cultural references and was so besotted by Scottish football that everything was seen through its smudged prism. I spent a baffled summer seeing the exotic names on my sister's schoolbooks – names like Wilson Pickett, Lee Dorsey and Otis Redding – assuming that they must have signed for Dundee United. Why else would they be written on a school jotter? When I was asked what my first record was, I cited 'The Boogaloo Party' by The Flamingos (US Philips, 1966), because I liked its exuberant title and its risky promise of ghetto fun. But deep inside me was a niggling act of contrition. As a Catholic lad who had been an altar boy and could still recite chunks of the Latin mass, it was not a wholly accurate account of my young life. To put it more crudely, it was a flagrant lie. The first record I ever bought, admittedly for my mum's birthday, was 'Dominique' by The Singing Nun. It was 1963, and I went into the Concorde, a record shop in Perth, to buy a record I knew fell tragically short of hipness. Rather than just take the thing and retreat in embarrassment. I stupidly asked to listen to it in one of the plywood record booths of the era. To my eternal shame I overheard two mouthy Mod girls in the next booth suppressing full-scale laughter at my choice. To this day, it is a record that makes me shiver with embarrassment. I take only a small sliver of comfort from the fact that The Singing Nun ended up as a depressed lesbian who failed to pay her taxes and committed suicide with an overdose of barbiturates. I can only hope that those mouthy Mods are now fat grannies from Muirton who smoke Embassy Regal and drink Diamond White behind the Asda Superstore.

My older sister was already going to clubs that played music on the fringes of northern soul – mostly Modernist cafés and youth clubs. The first place was the Knack Bar, a small youth club hanging perilously on the banks of the River Tay, which flows majestically through Perth. The second was the infamous Ingleneuk, an R&B haunt tucked away beneath old railway arches behind a garage forecourt. Like many of the big northern soul clubs of the sixties, it had emerged from a late night blues café called the Blues Workshop, an after-hours shebeen where musicians improvised into the early hours. 'Ingleneuk' is a Scottish term for a small inlet or corner, but the venue belied its cosy name and attracted rogues, bandits and pop pioneers, driven to hell on Lambretta scooters. It played imports and hosted R&B singers, and the local house band, The Vikings, became the nucleus of a much more famous seventies funk outfit, the Average White Band. Although it was a small town, Perth had talent. The first person I heard singing soul was a guy called Dave Amos, whose nickname Papa Stone conjured a delta bluesman plucking a box guitar by a parched cotton field; in fact he lived on a bleak council scheme called Hunters, which festered by old railway yards and had never seen the sun. Dave sang as if he had been born in a Bourbon bar and specialised in great cover versions of Chuck Woods, Otis Redding and Wilson Pickett. At a dancehall in nearby Dundee, he was once told by the Vikings' manager Andy Lothian to 'lay off the ballads' because it would provoke the crowd. 'They just fight when it goes slow,' Amos was warned.

It still gives me a daft boyish thrill that it was guys from Tayside who would become the first white band to go to number one in the black American charts. On 22 February 1975, by which time I was a regular at Wigan Casino, the Average White Band's 'Pick Up The Pieces' (Atlantic, 1974) knocked Linda Ronstadt off her perch at the top of the Billboard 100. James Brown, the egocentric Godfather of Soul, was so hacked off with AWB's success he recorded an answer record under the mysterious name AABB – the Above Average Black Band. By then, the Ingleneuk had closed down, in part due to problems with noise and amphetamine abuse, and frustrated that I had been too young to get in, I went one day with my friend Mike Mason to track it down. After a few false starts we found it tucked away down a lane to the left of a junk-ridden garage. All that was left was an intimidating wooden door with a sliding rectangular peephole. This club was gone but so many of those things lay ahead: the furtive lanes, backstreet clubs, old forecourts, railway arches – the cherished habitat of underground soul clubs.

By my late teens I was a regular at the Letham Community Centre disco, a magnet for babes and psychopaths. Every Scottish housing scheme has characters like Francis 'Franco' Begbie from Irvine Welsh's *Trainspotting*, guys with an innate and intimidating capacity for random violence. Our local sociopaths were called the Mental Pack, skinheads and periodically suedeheads who wore the fashions of the day: Sta-Prest trousers, Monkey boots and Arthur Black shirts. I can name them with trepidation to this day: Snitcher Meechan, Johnny Burns and a terrifying guy with a Crombie coat and an exaggerated limp called Crooky. His real name was Jimmy Cruikshank and the limp was real, too. In a whispered exchange under the noise of sixties soul, a mate in the know told me that he had lost his leg due to frostbite, after escaping from Polmont in the midst of a snowstorm. Polmont was Scotland's terrifying young offenders' institution, and the whispered detail only added to the climate of fear. Despite the constant worry of being 'dug up' – local vernacular for being physically threatened – Letham Community Centre became my second home, and the place I first heard ska, Motown and Stax. What I didn't know back then was that this music was only the shimmering surface of the untold wealth of black America.

Hunting for soul in Perth was limited to a few racks of cheap albums next to the pick'n'mix in Woolworths. It was there, dodging the authoritarian 'floor walkers' who had been employed to stop shoplifting, that I first encountered style: Edwin Starr dressed as an FBI agent, The Temptations in matching pink suits, and the Four Tops shimmying at a garden party, on the cover of their *Greatest Hits*. I had yet to dig deeper and discover the hidden symbols of ghetto chic: Chuck Jackson's pinkie ring, Levi Stubbs' iridescent trousers and Holly Maxwell's peroxide afro. The real pleasures were yet to come.

By the age of sixteen, I was so deeply immersed in soul music that even my dire secondary school could not stifle the joy of life. Much as I had loved my primary school, which had looked after me during childhood bereavement, I loathed the suffocating rules of my secondary school. Fortunately, in the backroom of a failing pub called the Corinna, a small soul club had opened up and I fluttered to it like a moth to a bulb. This was the Perth City Soul Club, the first real soul club I ever attended. Even in its infancy, it was following the Hezbollah rituals that define the northern soul scene. One night, a DJ was brought in front of the committee charged with playing a Bowie record; he was given a stern warning and a second chance, but there was a noisy faction on the committee who wanted him hounded through the streets in sackcloth and then burned at the stake outside H Samuel. I was among that zealous throng and I have not mellowed since. For a child raised in the church by my mother and tutored in the ways of socialism by my late father, I had discovered a new overarching ideology: the fundamentalism of northern soul. That First Commandment has stayed with me throughout my life: there shall be no other music before soul.

Childhood asthma is a gift. For reasons best left to pharmaceutical science, Perth skinheads had discovered small brown pills called Do-Dos, a legal substance dispensed to people with mild asthma or bronchial infections. Unknown to the helpful counter staff at Boots in the High Street, Do-Dos contained ephedrine, a substance similar to amphetamine, and so could be used as fake speed. Every Saturday before the football, I was dispatched to the counter at Boots to get Do-Dos. They were then doled out in the Cutlog Vennel. Perth is an old medieval city and narrow alleyways called vennels cut through the town. When my family first arrived from Galway they lived in the Meal Vennel, an old slum where my dad had been born. These tiny lanes had once been the trade thoroughfares of the old town but had become a place to hide or to dodge the law. Do-Dos were my first naive and tentative exploration of the 'Mod drug' amphetamine – you got a wee buzz and your wheezing chest cleared up – but there would be better jube-jubes to come.

By eighteen years old I was a student in Hull and prone to pretension. The poster above my bed was a quote from Italian poet Cesare Pavese: 'We do not remember days, we remember moments.' My mission on leaving home was to relish those moments, gorge on experience and dig deeper into the genius of black America. The Brynmor Jones Library at the University of Hull was called 'the Liquorice Allsort', with its six layers of black-and-white floors stacked on top of each other. The librarian was

England's most famous modern poet, Philip Larkin. You could sometimes spot him among the shelves: bald, speccy, and scurrying around in bookish disarray. I once scared him by appearing unexpectedly in the same aisle of books and he shied away like an agoraphobe who had been caught in the light. Larkin was a jazz buff and that proved to be critically important. With a huge academic budget and the power to buy what he wanted for his library, Larkin had dedicated the top floor to two subjects: theology and jazz. The rows of books were crammed with the origins of soul: books on slave songs, gospel, ragtime, jazz, ghetto poverty, the civil rights movement and R&B. Many were hardback tomes, some impenetrable to the casual reader, but I scoured the shelves tirelessly for three years, reading anything and everything about the music and the social conditions of black America. Larkin deserves my eternal respect. Famous for his line 'they fuck you up, your mum and dad', I was more taken when he drifted to jazz and blues as in the poem 'Reference Back':

> Oliver's *Riverside Blues*, it was. And now
> I shall, I suppose, always remember how
> The flock of notes those antique negroes blew
> Out of Chicago air into
> A huge remembering pre-electric horn
> The year after I was born

O

It was on Tuesday, 12 October 1971, that my northern soul voyage seriously began. The university Union ran a weekly disco and it was there that I met my mentor – an already seasoned northern soul girl called Pat Wall. Pat stood out from the crowd. She was distinctively dressed in what was known then as a Tonic suit and wore clumpy loafers adorned with leather tassels. Her hair was cropped on top, and feathered at the sides. Her accent was deep, friendly and unashamedly working-class. It was not quite love at first sight, more a moment of catatonic disbelief. Neither of us could quite believe the other actually existed: two suedeheads jostled together in a sea of hairy students. We simply moved towards each other and started to talk. Pat was from Rochdale and was studying PE at a training college next door to the university, but we never really talked about subjects or seminars or essays; we plunged straight into soul. Meeting Pat Wall was a life-changing moment. She knew much more than me, she had better records, and access to the northern soul scene in ways I'd never imagined. It was a lesson in so many ways. Mentors were meant to be older and wiser men, but Pat Wall was a teenage girl, a few months younger than me and a fund of new knowledge. She spoke of places I'd never heard of and people I wanted to meet. Her front teeth were slightly crossed at the front, and she modestly covered them with her tongue as she spoke, partly shy and partly self-effacing, but it endeared me to her all the more. How could anyone this cool be modest?

We agreed to meet again the next day, but even before we had parted on that first night, she had mentioned a Manchester club called the Twisted Wheel, which had just been closed by the police, and gave me an old C60 cassette tape that was like an initiation rite into a secret cult. In the inner sleeve, scribbled in smudged Biro, were the names of people I'd never heard of before – Alice Clark, Lenis Guess, Butch Baker – but would come to savour in years to come. Pat said that we should go to the Torch in Stoke and that she had an auntie there who would put us up. My mind was like a pinball machine, names rattling around like a steel ball. She called the next day from a coin-box to say she had spoken to her auntie and it was fine for us to stay. Ominously she warned me that it was a cramped house and that I might have to sleep with her uncle.

It was the longest night I ever spent, longer than any soul all-nighter, but it was the beginning of a great adventure and the first tentative steps in my life as a young soul rebel. I was going to one of the most famous all-nighters in the history of northern soul – the Golden Torch.

Locusts in the night: two soul boys in a photo booth hold up their Twisted Wheel membership cards. The sunglasses disguise the dilated pupils of amphetamine users; the boy on the right bears the telltale signs of 'speed bumps' on his mouth.

2
LOCUSTS IN THE NIGHT
1967–1971

They prefer the dark night to daylight, they dance like there is no tomorrow, and they spread the virus of drug abuse wherever they go. They are not of this world, they believe in very different things to you and I, and like many young people, they arrogantly believe they can make their own laws.

James Anderton, speech to the British Institute
of Management, Manchester 1975

Cyril James Anderton, the bearded Chief Constable of Greater Manchester Police, was a man of fastidious habits. Each morning he woke at 7 a.m., had breakfast in bed, brought to him on the same reinforced plastic tray and served up by his dutiful wife. The food rarely varied: bacon and eggs, and then grapefruit. A small book with scribbled notes sat next to his bed within easy reach, and Anderton would start the working day by writing down his dreams and organising them into patterns of recurrence, underlining those dreams when he came face-to-face with God. He would then rise to take a shower, where he prayed to heaven, eyes staring upwards into the jet sprays of hot water, his beard dripping on the tiled floor. For ten minutes or more, he allowed the water to wash away his sins as he held private ministry with the Lord.

According to his biographer, Michael Prince, Anderton had arrived back in Manchester on a mission to clean up the city and complete a task that had begun over ten years before. 'He came in like a storm and the wind continued to rage throughout his turbulent reign,' Prince wrote in *God's Cop*. Anderton's reach was substantial. He had seven thousand officers, covering a region of over five hundred square miles and with responsibility for a population of over three million people. Remarkably, for someone who held such high public office, he was neither bashful nor embarrassed about his beliefs. He proudly espoused reincarnation and told those close to him that in a previous life he had once been the Puritan leader Oliver Cromwell. Like the Lord Protector he used biblical language and described Greater Manchester as a city which had become 'engulfed by the forces of the night'. The once grand industrial buildings of Manchester were falling into disuse and ugly brownfield sites pockmarked the city. Anderton saw a connection. He believed that economic decline paralleled a decline in moral values and that Manchester's poverty was not only material but spiritual. On his desk was a folder crammed with arrest sheets for drug-related crimes, particularly burglaries and break-ins at pharmacies. It was not good news for the turbulent children of the northern soul scene; since his early days as a beat bobby Anderton had watched the scene grow and in his mind 'corrupt the values of a decent city'.

By 1975 Anderton had risen to the rank of Chief Constable of Manchester. For over a decade, Greater Manchester Police had been ruled by high-ranking officers whose Christian fundamentalism shaped their attitude to crime and punishment. Anderton was not unique but he became the most notorious of a lineage of Christian coppers, who the Mods of the sixties called the God Squad. Anderton had joined the force in 1953, leaving for promoted posts in Leicester and London, and then returning north to Manchester. His return came at a critical moment in the history of the northern scene. Two of the major clubs – the Twisted Wheel in Manchester and the Torch in Tunstall, near Stoke-on-Trent – had both fallen foul of the law and been closed down. The passions that they had unlocked for all nightclubs playing imported black music was not curtailed, though: on the contrary, the passions had spread unchecked across the north of England, and a new club called the Casino had opened twenty miles west of Manchester's city centre, in a decaying old ballroom on Station Road, Wigan. On a busy night, the Casino could attract up to 2,000 frenetic dancers, its popularity having spread largely by word of mouth and tiny adverts in the small-circulation soul press. By pure coincidence, the Casino had opened against a backdrop of seismic change in policing too; a nationwide restructuring that favoured scale over community meant that Wigan was absorbed into the Greater Manchester Police region, and came under the uncompromising sway of James Anderton.

Wigan Casino felt preciously close to home. Anderton had been born the son of a miner into red-brick poverty in Wigan's Goose Green and grew up as a God-fearing teenager in the town's Pemberton area. He had been drafted into National Service at the age of eighteen, having taken guidance from his great-uncle Nehemiah Occleshaw, a police officer in Wigan whose name alone conjured a Dickensian past. His parents had courted at Wigan's Empress Ballroom and married before the Second World War. The furthest the family travelled in his infancy was on an annual working-class pilgrimage to Blackpool, where they unwrapped their Pac A Macs, trudged the wet sands and ate sodden sandwiches. It was a conventional upbringing that resisted the distractions of fashion and youth culture. The passage of time had been unkind to coal miners, to the Pier at Blackpool, and to the cavernous ballrooms that had been built across Britain in the dance-band era. New patterns of entertainment had ravaged the old ways, mobile discotheques were undermining the need for live music, and big bands had given way to disc jockeys. Down-at-heel ballrooms like the Empress in Wigan were on their last legs. In a last desperate bid to stave off closure, the Empress had rebranded itself as Wigan Casino, and to Anderton's personal fury became the epicentre of the north's rare soul scene.

Anderton loathed everything Wigan Casino had come to represent: the drugs, the pounding black music, and most of all the surly and unruly teenagers who flocked to its doors. He once described them climbing off buses like 'locusts in the night', and as an advocate of the Lord's Day Observance Society he hated the way that northern soul all-nighters were eroding the sanctity of Sunday. In Wigan, a couple of shops stayed open to serve the hordes – a burger van parked close to the club and sold them a roll and regurgitation, or as they say in Wigan 'botulism on a bap' – and the local swimming baths, where Anderton had learned to swim, was where the exhausted soul dancers went to hang out before their trains home. For Anderton, Wigan Casino had become a post-industrial Gomorrah, with the Sabbath being flagrantly desecrated by teenagers who danced to obscure music and treated pharmaceutical pills as if they were the unholy Eucharist. He saw them as a weird sect – and they probably were – but whatever his views, he could not stop the weekly pilgrimage to Wigan.

Anderton's hatred of black music did not begin with Wigan. Nor did it end there. It had been ignited over a decade before when he was a beat copper walking the streets of Manchester's multiracial Moss Side, policing the illegal blues parties of the fifties. It was on the streets of Moss Side that he met his long-time colleague – and ultimately his rival and nemesis – John Stalker, then a uniformed officer about to be recruited into the plainclothes vice squad. From the forties onwards, Moss Side had catered for the night: first, African seamen that arrived by ship from Liverpool to Salford Docks, and then immigrants who came with government support to find work in the National Health Service and public transport. This was the notorious era of 'No Blacks, No Irish, No Dogs', and in the north of England it was Moss Side that hosted blues clubs, playing ska and reggae alongside American R&B. Moss Side and Hulme, near Manchester's city centre, had been particularly hard hit by economic malaise and had been razed to the ground twice in thirty years. Victorian slum housing was demolished during the sixties after the biggest demolition project in Europe. The red-brick terraced houses were replaced by high-rise flats and huge concrete crescents, which only served to foster crime, indifference and alienation. As Anderton trawled the streets of the inner city he became convinced that God was the ultimate copper and that morality was the guiding principle of good governance. He shared the unshakeable Christianity of the American Deep South where preachers described R&B as the Devil's music. He preferred the term 'beat clubs' and refused to dignify nightclubs with the word 'soul', as if it was a word stolen from the Lord. The police were tasked with policing a pocket of illegal shebeens, brothels and nightclubs, including the Reno on Princess Road and Moss Lane, which had begun its life as a Salvation Army hostel for African seamen. An upstairs bar known as the Nile Club was on their watch list, the Public Services Vehicle Club in Hulme (known as the PSV Club) was frequently raided, and another target was the Russell Club, which in a later life would play a crucial role in the evolution of Manchester's indie scene, Factory Records and the emergence of the city's super-club, the Hacienda.

Northern soul has always been an enigma. Somehow, through

its obsessive yearnings, it has managed to forge links between Britain's most forgotten industrial towns and the ghettos of black America. At its rousing best – shrieking vocals, blaring horns and sexually depraved saxophone breaks – northern soul can be traced back to early post-war Britain, when cafés emerged across the country, providing a third space where young people could escape from home and work. Back then, sociologists described a new kind of consumer – the 'teenager' – who was attractive to advertisers, and a source of delinquent concern for the authorities. It was famously in London's Soho, far from the industrial north, that a professional wrestler called Paul Lincoln opened a café called the 2i's. Situated at 59 Old Compton Street, it was a musical melting pot where jazz, skiffle and calypso were played live or via the café's jukebox. One regular session guitarist, Joe Moretti, claimed that 'in 1958 the 2i's was the fuse for the explosion that was to come in the world of UK rock and roll . . . it was just a little café with an old battered piano in the basement in Old Compton Street. But it had a soul and a buzz.' The 2i's became Britain's first recorded all-nighter, and its equivalents were beginning to spring up in towns and cities elsewhere, among them the Left Wing Coffee Bar in Manchester's Brazennose Street, which in time would evolve into the first of the great northern soul clubs, the Twisted Wheel. A lesser known northern café called the Plebeians, across the Pennines in Halifax, also prospered, hidden from the glare of attention, to become a home to jazz buffs, bohemian blues fans and eventually the scooter kids, Modernists and rare soul fans of North Yorkshire.

It was at the Left Wing Coffee Bar in March 1961, with a live jazz and blues set from John Rowland and the Jazz Unit, that the first ever recognisable 'northern soul' all-nighter took place. Classified ads in the *Manchester Evening News* used the historic words 'music from midnight to dawn'. Only coffee was on sale and no alcohol licence was required, so the event took place beneath the radar of the police. That was never likely to last. The very notion of listening to music until dawn soon attracted the attention of a clique of high-ranking senior officers at Manchester Police's Divisional Headquarters in Bootle Street and triggered a war that was as much about the cracks and divisions in post-war Britain as it was about soul itself. Chief Constable John Andrew McKay was a strait-laced Scot from Blantyre in Lanarkshire. He was military through and through, and once claimed that Manchester Police were obliged to work against the emergent R&B café culture to combat 'the moral decay of the innocents'. McKay had been a military governor in Palermo during the Second World War and was a station inspector in Gray's Inn Road Police Station during the London Blitz. He believed his wartime experiences gave him an elevated status in peacetime and often came over as a pompous man who talked down to people. McKay shared many of the character traits of his namesake, the prison warder Mr Mackay in the television sitcom *Porridge*; an officious man who marched rather than walked, he managed Manchester as if it were a barracks compound, for ever suspicious of the 'Fletchers' of northern soul and the locusts of the night. In many ways, he was unsuited to manage the sweeping progress that was changing Britain. A gulf had opened up between the police – the majority of whom had seen military service – and the post-war generation of 'baby boomers', who society readily dismissed as anti-authoritarian wasters. Anderton learned under McKay's tutelage, but was not yet senior enough to spearhead the war on nightclubs. That role went to another disciplinarian Scot, a formidable chief inspector called Alan Dingwall. More than any of his contemporaries, Dingwall harboured a deep-rooted dislike of soul clubs and made it his life's work to see them closed down. He worked tirelessly against the forces of the night and drafted a policy document on what he described as the city's 'Beat Club problem', which influenced politicians, the city fathers and other towns far from Manchester. Whatever its merits, it was not in any sense an objective document: it read like a moral diatribe and argued forcefully that clubs were not only immoral but the hub of a growing amphetamine-related crime wave.

Music and society were in flux. The precursors of northern soul lurched from jazz to skiffle, onwards to blues and R&B, while teenage 'style' evolved from beatnik to Mod. But much else was shaping Cold War Britain, not least the resistance to nuclear weapons. The Campaign for Nuclear Disarmament (CND) was in the first throes of protest. Marches to Aldermaston's Atomic Weapons Research Centre in Berkshire and the US Polaris base at Holy Loch in Scotland were annual pilgrimages, which attracted righteous fervour and a new kind of music fan fascinated by urban blues and the rhythms of disaffection coming from segregated America. In time, the Holy Loch became a gateway. Black US servicemen brought R&B music with them, setting up local clubs in Dunoon and Glasgow, playing music to those they met, and selling records on 'precious' labels such as Chicago's Chess Records.

The arrival of R&B music into Britain's dockland communities was even more pronounced in Liverpool where in underground clubs such as the Mardi Gras, the Cavern and the Jacaranda imported music was played by local DJs Bob Wooler and Billy Butler. This helped to stimulate the local Mersey Beat bands and shaped the set lists of The Beatles, Rory Storm and the Hurricanes, and Gerry and the Pacemakers. Influences were coming from Europe, too, where Parisian bohemian café culture was embracing a new beatnik underground fuelled by black music, radical theory and narcotic distractions. One café which came to influence the Twisted Wheel in a subtle but lasting way was the Bus Palladium, a beatnik all-nighter on Rue Pierre Fontaine; young kids were bussed in from the suburbs to central Paris and stayed up all night infused by jazz, blues and Captagon, an amphetamine-like substance brought to Paris nightclubs by French-Algerians (and today's drug of choice for Syria's warring factions).

Anxiety about teenage behaviour was fearfully exaggerated in the daily newspapers of the day, and one event stood out as a landmark of change. On 31 July 1960, a riot at the Beaulieu jazz festival in the New Forest made headline news, with running battles between trad jazz fans and Modernists. The stage was destroyed, lighting rigs were torn down, a building was set alight, and thirty-nine people were injured. BBC television's outside broadcast stopped six minutes before it was scheduled to end with an awkward live comment: 'Things are getting quite out of hand. It is obvious things cannot continue like this.' Nor would they. Britain was staring change in the face, and it was being driven by the young.

The Left Wing Coffee Bar in Manchester and the Plebeians café, which began its life in a disused mill in Halifax accessible from the town's Upper George Yard, became hubs for new music nearly a decade before those pioneering spaces transformed into northern soul. The duffle coats, jazz and blues sounds, and the CND badges had yet to be purged, before amphetamines and urban soul arrived in earnest. The Left Wing Coffee Bar was one of a number of cafés to fall foul of the police's moral crusade, and investigations spread out to a cluster of other teenage cafés near Manchester's Albert Square, including the Three Coins, the Kardomah and the Oasis, a cult R&B café, situated in a narrow street parallel to the original Twisted Wheel, off Manchester's Deansgate. In time it would bequeath its name to one of the city's most famous pop groups.

As society changed it brought increased anxiety about the misuse of pharmaceutical drugs. In February 1964, in an unusually perceptive article for the time, society journalist Anne Sharpley wrote an article for the *Evening Standard* on the cult of Mods. Under the intriguing headline 'Purple Heart Trip in Soho', Sharpley focused on a Soho nightclub called 'The Scene', hidden away in a mews off Great Windmill Street. 'They [the teenagers] are looking for, and getting stimulation not intoxication,' she wrote. 'They want greater awareness, not escape. And the confidence and articulacy that the drugs of the amphetamine group give them is quite different from the drunken rowdiness of previous generations on a night out.' James Brown's 'Night Train' was the club's anthem, and organ instrumentals by Jimmy Smith and Jimmy McGriff cranked late into the night. Although it claimed to be reportage, Sharpley's feature was part of an editorial partnership with the MP for North Paddington, Ben Parkin, a vocal opponent of the slum landlord Peter Rachman and by the mid-sixties an enemy of Mod drugs such as Drinamyl, or what were more popularly known as purple hearts. The racy tabloid press exaggerated society's concerns. The *Sunday People* even ran with a sensational exposé of Everton's 1962–63 title-winning football team, which the paper claimed had won games blocked on amphetamine. In 1964, Parliament passed the Drugs (Prevention of Misuse) Act, which added amphetamines to a list of previously restricted drugs such as opium, morphine and cocaine. Almost overnight, Mod clubs already under the watchful eye of the law became the subject of a determined campaign to close them down. Back in Manchester, Alan Dingwall, James Anderton and John Stalker were now front-line officers in a city-wide clampdown on nightclubs. Emboldened by new laws banning illegal amphetamines, the police focused on break-ins at chemist shops across the north of England, where the newly proscribed drugs were locked away in special cabinets. From 1965 onwards, amphetamines went underground; they became harder to get from doctors and were often only available via forged prescriptions, or increasingly by burglary and forced entry at chemists. It was this latter crime that made the Twisted Wheel a priority target for Manchester's drug squad. In a joint operation with their colleagues in Yorkshire, targeting Halifax's Plebeians café, Dingwall's squad tried to arrest a young Yorkshire Mod called Ernest Hardiman from Bradford, accusing him of breaking into a chemist's shop in Crumpsall in North Manchester and feeding an amphetamine supply chain based at the Twisted Wheel. Hardiman's alibis stacked up and he evaded arrest, but that did not ease the pressure on the Wheel when a widely circulated police report from the Salford area claimed that forty-seven local chemists had been burgled in one calendar year alone.

The Twisted Wheel changed lives. It was a soul venue like no other and most of those who went there returned with a sacrilegious fervour. By 1965, the days of the socialist reading rooms at the Left Wing Coffee Bar were long gone; it had adjusted to the prevailing winds of change and hosted more R&B nights, becoming a meeting place for record collectors bewitched by the sounds coming from the American ghettos: Chess Records in Chicago, Duke Records from Memphis and Peacock Records in Atlanta (a nascent R&B label headquartered at a nightclub in the Deep South). The venue was taken over by a group of enterprising brothers from Burnage in Manchester Southside called the Abadi brothers – Jack, Ivor and Phillip. They renamed it the Twisted Wheel and hired a bookish DJ called Roger Eagle who described himself as 'more Teddy Boy than Mod' and had been a regular at the Left Wing. Eagle was a committed anti-nuclear protestor, and, importantly, had a formidable collection of old blues records. It was through his pioneering direction that Jimmy Witherspoon, Howlin' Wolf, Muddy Waters and Bo Diddley came to be played on the Manchester club scene. Roger Eagle was destined to shape the music policy of the Twisted Wheel in its formative years until the overwhelming power of the Mod movement – with its razor-sharp style and elegant Lambrettas – drove the scene inexorably towards urban soul and the sounds of the sixties.

The Twisted Wheel became the template by which all subsequent northern soul clubs were judged: the intense atmosphere, the rare soul music and the extravagant dancers. Soul seeped through the walls of the venue on Manchester's Whitworth Street, in a forgotten edge of the city adjacent to the dark industrial arches of Piccadilly Railway Station. Ivor Abadi ran the club on behalf of his brothers, defying commercial logic by only serving soft drinks and snacks, and accepting from the outset that the Twisted Wheel was unlikely to be granted a liquor licence. As crowds flocked there from across the north of England, it became clear that its unique music policy and the forbidden allure of amphetamines was what drove the Mod clientele. The main venue was a converted warehouse, with a coffee snack bar on the ground floor and a series of rooms in the cellar. Back-lit iron wheels decorated the painted brick walls, and twisted metal in the shape of spokes and wheel rims hung around the lower spaces where a stage, a caged disc-jockey area and the main dance floor dominated. For five or six years it attracted the best of new British music: some clung to the blues, others were determined to stay in touch with American soul, some were truly original, and others were just very good cover bands – among their ranks John Mayall's Bluesbreakers, Zoot Money, The Graham Bond Organisation, Wynder K Frog, The Alan Bown Set, The Spencer Davis Group and Georgie Fame. They shared a circuit with visiting artists from Jamaica and the USA, including Gino Washington and the Ram Jam Band, Millie Small, Roy C, Jr Walker and the All Stars, and Jimmy Cliff.

By 1967 the music policy had hardened. For many dancers, the vinyl had become more important than the live acts, and the Twisted Wheel had built a catalogue of sounds many of which had been unavailable at any other clubs in the UK. Eventually blues pioneer Roger Eagle ran out of patience and resigned from his role as resident DJ, claiming that he was fed up of the impact of drug overdoses and the pressure to play soul. 'I was tired of being the one to phone the ambulance,' he told the club's unofficial historian Keith Rylatt. 'I was bored of the same Tamla requests over and over again.' The Detroit soul label Tamla Motown had surged through British pop culture with a catalogue of hit records by The Supremes, The Temptations, and Smokey Robinson and the Miracles, cementing a lifelong connection between the northern soul scene and the city of Detroit. Then, in damning testimony in his biography *Sit Down! Listen to This!* Eagle admitted that 'the first two years were fun but in the third it became boring quite frankly because the music became too similar all the time, it was just a fast dance beat to keep dancing all night'. Eagle's impatience with his devoted following had soured into contempt. 'They were blocked [soul term for being up on amphetamines] out of their heads on "Blues" or whatever they were taking and you were just a human jukebox. You'd put one record on after another and if you tried anything different they would yell at you because all they were interested in was dancing.' Eagle's eclectic tastes had come into conflict with the rigid rules of a new subculture where the music had to be the rattling on-the-fours beat of classic sixties soul. The Twisted Wheel had abandoned its bohemian roots and become a fully-fledged Mod club. Soul had become a religion, one that the chosen few of the deep north would remain devoted to for decades yet to come, and as attitudes hardened the scene became intolerant of music that didn't reflect the lifestyle. Some followed the vagaries of fashion and drifted towards counterculture, psychedelia and the new hippie movement; some settled down into marriage and the straight world; and others found the scene too intense and happily joined the legions of everyday pop. Those who remained vigilant about the values of being a Mod formed the vanguard of an entirely new youth movement – one that as yet had no name but would become northern soul.

No one is entirely sure where the term 'northern' soul came from. The most likely explanation is that the term was in casual use hundreds of miles south in a record shop called Soul City on the busy Deptford High Street, in south London. One of the shop's owners, the Motown pioneer and journalist Dave Godin who became an intellectual beacon on the rare soul scene, claims the term was first used in his shop to classify up-tempo soul, the imported records that would appeal to northern customers, many of whom were fans of Manchester United, Liverpool and Leeds United down in London for away games. The shop kept a box tagged 'northern soul' behind the counter, and through Godin's journalism in the weekly music magazine *Blues & Soul* the term stuck. The explanation had long been a settled truth until a Preston-born soul fan, Stuart Raith, unearthed an old advert for a Manchester cover group the St. Louis Union, who performed at the Twisted Wheel back in July 1965. The advert described St. Louis Union as '*the* group on the Northern Soul Scene', which raises the prospect of the term having been in colloquial use in Manchester before England won the World Cup and long before even the most avid followers imagined. Whatever the truth, the term confused the uninitiated and visiting soul artists. How could records forged in the studios of the Deep South, in Memphis and New Orleans, suddenly defy geographic logic and be classified as northern soul? It is an anomaly that remains fiercely difficult to explain.

One thing that Dave Godin was adamant about was that the north and London were different places. He visited the Twisted Wheel in the winter of 1970 and became the club's greatest journalistic advocate, often arguing against his London-based colleagues. Many years later, in a deeply honest interview with the Ormskirk-born northern soul collector Pete Lawson, in his short-lived fanzine *The Gospel According to Dave Godin*, Godin set out a key difference. 'One of the things that maybe bound the Northern Soul scene together is it's a similar sort of thing to the black American experience,' he commented. 'It's almost ghettoisation, because the Northern Soul scene was so scorned by the majority of the people in the south, and in people who had access to the media.' Godin ploughed a lonely furrow. For nearly ten years he was the only serious journalist who saw value in the underground north; most commentators – trapped in a metropolitan bubble – saw it as a distant irrelevance, while the Manchester police saw it as a festering problem on their doorstep.

The Twisted Wheel had many enemies. As far back as 1964, in an excoriating Annual Report, Chief Constable John McKay condemned the rise of teenage cafés and nightclubs in Manchester and linked them to a parallel rise in burglaries of chemists and doctors' surgeries. The report was distributed to politicians and compliant journalists. Police briefings singled out the Twisted Wheel, making exaggerated claims about local teenage deaths – most of which had nothing to do with nightclubs, or even amphetamine abuse – and local journalists at the BBC and the *Manchester Evening News* helped to fuel anxieties. McKay admitted that his senior staff had been demonising clubs in the press and impeding licences wherever they could, and in turn the vigorous war on soul music gave shape to new legislation in the form of the Manchester Corporation Act. In Westminster, Lord Parker of Waddington raged against the nascent northern soul scene from the benches of the House of Lords:

> Before turning to the Bill itself, may I spend a few minutes dealing with what I am convinced makes legislation along these lines a matter of urgent necessity today . . . It was in 1964 that entertainment clubs of a kind were introduced in Manchester. They go by different names – coffee and dance clubs, beat clubs, jazz clubs and the like. They are clubs at which refreshments of the coffee, snack and soft-drink variety are available, and they offer evening and often all-night entertainment in the form of 'pop' music . . . These clubs naturally attract the young, and those of a more disreputable nature, in particular those with no fixed abode, abscondees from approved schools and other institutions, as well as those who desire to escape supervision by their parents, and indeed supervision by any adult control. They wander about from so-called club to club. It was quite common to find a girl sleeping in a different club every night, and even during the day, when the clubs were supposed to be closed. Many clubs were, in fact, really nothing more than common lodging-houses . . . it was found that dangerous drugs were being sold, distributed and taken on such premises. True, most of these were of the Indian hemp, 'purple heart' and other drugs of the amphetamine class, but activities were certainly not confined to those and extended to heroin, cocaine and morphia.

The Act of Parliament gave excessive new powers to the police, delivering them the whip hand over local licensing regulations.

Henceforth, no one could now own a club without the prior permission of the police, and opening hours were framed in a way that curtailed the concept of the all-nighter. One recommendation meant that the police could restrict the opening hours of clubs that extended into the next day, whether they sold alcohol or not. It was a law deliberately scripted to curb the popularity of all-nighters. Many clubs simply closed; others ducked and dived by moving to new premises and re-emerging with a new name. The Twisted Wheel tried to tough it out, but the club's notoriety weighed against it. Before McKay's campaign, there were over 220 nightclubs across the Greater Manchester area. By 1967 it had become a few dozen, and by 1971 only three major nightclubs survived. One of those was the Twisted Wheel. However, with new laws and a crusading police force stacked against it, the Wheel was isolated and ultimately doomed.

The Twisted Wheel hosted many famous nights. On a smouldering summer night in June 1966, Ben E King, a former member of The Drifters, sang his evergreen hit 'Stand By Me' on the Wheel's cramped stage, setting the gold standard for intimate performances. The dancers could reach up and touch him, or shake his hand from the floor. On Saturday, 1 April 1967, Mary Wells, freed from her onerous contract with Motown, sang her great soul trio 'The One Who Really Loves You' (Motown, 1962), 'You Beat Me To The Punch' (Motown, 1962) and her signature hit 'My Guy' (Motown, 1965). On Saturday, 11 May 1968, the effervescent Edwin Starr, dressed in his gangster hat and white coat, acted up to his role as soul music's secret agent by lifting the Wheel's roof with 'Backstreet' (and 'Agent Double-O-Soul', Ric-Tic, 1965). But the most revealing night came when electric-guitar god Jimi Hendrix dropped in to the Wheel, only to be apprehended by the Manchester drug squad in an operation overseen by Dingwall and John Stalker. It was 7 January 1967, and the Wheel was playing host to another stellar soul group from the USA, The Spellbinders from Newark, New Jersey, whose frantic song 'Help Me' (Columbia, 1966) was a northern soul favourite at the time. Hendrix was performing nearby at Manchester's New Century Hall on Corporation Street and after his forty-five minute set, which included a nascent rendition of the spaced-out psychedelic anthem 'Purple Haze', the group headed for the Wheel. Hendrix knew The Spellbinders from his period in Teaneck, New Jersey, when he had toured with them as lead guitarist with The Isley Brothers.

The police had already infiltrated the Wheel. Two undercover female officers affecting a Mod style had insinuated themselves into the club's inner circle, dancing, chatting and hanging out with DJs. Some combination of Hendrix's brazen personality, the whispered grapevine and the undercover officers alerted the drug squad to his movements. Hendrix and his group were apprehended on their arrival at the venue and taken to a nearby police station. According to drummer Mitch Mitchell, 'four middle-aged men jumped on us, knocked me around and broke Noel Redding's glasses. They were plain-clothes men.' While Manchester Police have never released details of the attempted bust, it is almost certain that Alan Dingwall and John Stalker were among the four, although it is unclear if James Anderton was in their ranks (he was already being fast-tracked for bigger things and a few months later joined the Chester Police Force as a chief inspector). 'We walked over to the car, and suddenly Noel and I were grabbed and slung against the railings of the police station,' Mitchell remembers. 'We got slapped around a few times and I was going, "What the fuck's going on?" They were the police, but we didn't believe it at first – they were all in plain clothes. They took Hendrix's passport off him, but left him alone because he was American.' Myth has clung to Jimi Hendrix like rust to an old viaduct. Some claim that bassist Noel Redding was hung up on a cloakroom hook and humiliated by the drug squad; others have claimed that Hendrix blew smoke in their faces; and one outlandish suggestion was that as Hendrix and his band were being questioned outside the club Mods gathered around the mêlée backdropping in front of the frustrated police officers. It is almost certainly exaggeration, but the image speaks to another growing feature of the northern soul scene – the power of myth – and the ability of the scene's young soul rebels to spin yarns and etch their scene into history, turning clubs into cathedrals, records into all-time classics and obscure soul singers into legends. It was a scene which attracted people who had turned their back on the ordinary world.

The morning after the Twisted Wheel drug bust, Jimi Hendrix and bleary-eyed band members were released from police custody. They headed to the next stop on their UK tour, which ironically turned out to be another emergent northern soul club – Sheffield's King Mojo, a converted family home on the city's Pitsmoor Road. The King Mojo was driven by local music impresario and one-time soul DJ Peter Stringfellow, whose contacts and charisma managed to attract the cream of new R&B bands such as The Yardbirds, Manfred Mann, The Isley Brothers, The Who, Wilson Pickett, The Drifters, Jimi Hendrix, Ike and Tina Turner, Edwin Starr, The Animals, The Spencer Davis Group, Small Faces, Stevie Wonder and Pink Floyd. Away from the Christian policing in Manchester, Stringfellow claims the police were rarely a problem: 'There was no such thing as capacity in those days. We'd just cram them in. Never saw a policeman in the Mojo. We knew we were really full when the Spencer Davis Group played and the coffee-bar floor collapsed.' Although the Mojo never reached the mythologised heights of the Twisted Wheel, it became a Sheffield landmark and demonstrated that passion for the music of black America was alive across the industrial north.

As the music intensified, the clock ticked more loudly on the Wheel's future. Jazz had been replaced by blues, which in turn gave way to R&B, and the raw sounds of the American ghettos finally begat soul. Pioneering DJ Roger Eagle was eventually replaced by more enthusiastic new recruits such as Brian Rae and a generation of apprentice DJs which included young Mods like Paul Davis and Phil Saxe, who were closer to the Mod lifestyle of the northern scene. They made up-tempo sixties soul – the DNA of the northern scene – and soon added another dimension: 'obscurity'. At first they played new releases available to the cognoscenti via UK labels, but increasingly by 1966, collectors and DJs were digging deeper into the US import market and finding music that had yet to come to the attention of the London-based record companies. Bypassing London was to become a proud feature of the northern soul scene for years to come, and with imports arriving weekly, people started to come from further afield – from Scotland, the West Midlands, and even London itself – to hear music that was unavailable at local discos. One DJ, Brian '45' Phillips, took his name from his signature tune, 'Do The 45' by The Sharpees, a Chicago harmony soul band on the One-derful! label. Released in November 1965, due to the sluggish pace of international mail and UK Customs, it did not hit the Wheel's turntable until nearly a year later, by which time it had slipped into obscurity, even in Chicago.

Pat Wall from Rochdale, the girl who first accompanied me to northern clubs, was a young teenager when she first went to the Wheel. She had plans to become as PE teacher and was already a gifted member of the City of Manchester Swimming Team who followed a punishing early morning training regime. Naturally reticent and uncomfortable in the limelight, she describes being 'overwhelmed by northern soul at first', and remembers standing reluctantly outside the Wheel, scared to go in. It took her a while to pluck up the courage to dance, and she spent hours by the side of the floor mesmerised by the dancers thrashing around in front of her. Most of the club's acrobatic dancers were men, and as journalist Dave Godin has famously claimed, he had never seen their like except in the ghetto clubs of Chicago. In his inimitable portentous way, Godin claimed in *Blues & Soul* magazine that 'the dancing is without doubt the highest and the finest I have ever seen outside of the USA – in fact I never thought I'd live to see the day where people could so relate the rhythmic content of soul music to such a skilled degree in these rigid and armoured Isles'. Pat Wall watched them go through their routines: spins, backdrops, splits and even headspins. Most newcomers were content (or too intimidated) to watch from the sidelines, but she knew that if she mastered their gliding and side-to-side technique, then the acrobatics would be easy. She kept her own shoebox of singles back home in Rochdale, most of which had been bought at Spin Inn on Cross Street, and among them were Little Hank's 'Mr Bang Bang Man' (Sound Stage 7, 1966), The Dramatics' 'Inky Dinky Wang Dang Do' (Wingate, 1966), Mickey Lee Lane's 'Hey Sah-Lo-Ney' (Itzy, 1966) and Rex Garvin's 'Sock It To 'Em JB' (Atlantic, 1966). While swimming, she would imagine the body turn at the end of a length as part of a dance routine and would simulate the northern soul 'swallow dive'. She often practised in the kitchen of her mum's council house, mastering the smooth sliding style across uneven linoleum, and within a matter of weeks she could compete with any of the Twisted Wheel's young men. Her dance tricks were mesmerising and her unassuming smile, whispering the lyrics as if she were praying, as if there were no greater music in the world, made her stand out in a crowd of older and brasher men.

Ironically it was closure at the hands of the law that gave the Twisted Wheel its final seal of approval, like the rock star who dies young, drugged in a bath, or the film star who crashes through the windscreen of a car. It died young and beautiful, and so passed into legend. It became the club against which all other northern soul all-nighters would be measured: the music, the atmosphere, and most of all the tense feeling of lawlessness. Ideological policing, local bylaws and urgent legislation hustled through the Houses of Parliament brought the Twisted Wheel to an end. The club shut down in early 1971, snagged by a new requirement that stopped premises from staying open more than two hours into the following day, but not before it ignited a passion for black American music the like of which no previous generation had ever experienced. Its closure left a huge vacuum that seemed nigh on impossible to fill. For a time, that challenge was taken up by a wave of new Mod clubs across the north, including the Metro in Wakefield and Hernandos (aka 'Hernie's') in Harehills Road in Leeds, but they too fell foul of drug raids and were closed down. The Metro made national headlines when a Yorkshire drug squad, fortified by the success of their Manchester colleagues, swooped on the club and arrested over a hundred young soul fans, provoking exaggerated reports in the following week's papers. The *News of the World* claimed that a dealer had been caught outside the Metro selling rat poison, but in fact he had been attempting to pass off the anticoagulant drug Warfarin as amphetamines. Hernies was next to meet its fate. A raid there in May 1971 was accompanied by even more dramatic press reports, describing a sinister sect of soul fans who wanted to see the liberalisation of illegal drugs. Pete Dillon, a northern soul diehard, was working the espresso coffee machine on the night. There were 'no bouncers, just a locked wooden door with a peephole. If you weren't wanted they didn't open the door, hence [the reason] the drug squad took so long to get in.' Julian Bentley, a familiar face on the early Leeds soul scene, was the DJ there. He remembers that 'when the "squad" raided the club, to get to the DJ area you had to remove some vertical wooden poles – it took the coppers quite a long time to figure this out while I continued to play sounds'. As Yorkshire Mods danced on, enraging the drug squad, arrests followed. Yet again the press demonised the club and forced its closure too. One news report in the *Yorkshire Evening Post* featured a charmingly naive description of the raid: 'As the night wore on, it was apparent that the drugs were taking hold of some of them. Their dancing became less inhibited in some cases, and a number of them were wandering about aimlessly with glazed eyes.'

Replacing the Twisted Wheel proved to be a challenge, but eventually the baton was passed to the Golden Torch Ballroom, a converted cinema in Tunstall, near Stoke-on-Trent. The interior of the Torch also told a story of change, not least the collapse of traditional religion and the rise of youth culture. It was a small hall with marble pillars and a balcony overlooking the wooden dance floor. It had started out as a church, before becoming a roller-skating rink and, in the immediate post-war period, morphing into the Little Regent Cinema. Local soul fan and businessman Chris Burton changed its use again and it became a Mod club, and then eventually an all-nighter whose influence stretched across the Potteries, to Lancashire in the north and the Midlands to the south. Like the Twisted Wheel it had its own unique iconography – a blazing torch – which came to dominate posters, flyers and ultimately woven badges, setting the style for rare soul club iconography to come. Every new club needed its logo. A pair of clasped hands adorned the badge of Leeds Central Soul Club, the red rose of Lancashire featured in the Wigan Casino badge, and the clenched fist of the Black Power movement appeared on countless northern soul club badges across the decades. The Torch had another feature that became important in the years ahead too: atmosphere. While rock venues measured atmosphere by decibels, northern soul measured it by condensation – the small droplets of water that fell from the roof onto the dancers below. Condensation may be an unscientific way to measure a great club, but the prison-like rooms of the Catacombs Club in Wolverhampton had it, the Torch had it, and the toilets at Wigan Casino cascaded like a northern Niagara. Condensation, rusting droplets of water and the percussive soul-clapping that greeted classics like Gloria Jones's 'Tainted Love' (Champion, 1965) became northern soul incarnate.

As major all-night soul clubs began to emerge across the north of England, new patterns of club culture grew up alongside them. Best described as 'hot spots', the big clubs reached out to a radius of fifty miles and beyond, creating northern soul strongholds which had midweek nights, local venues, import record shops and a tier of collectors and local DJs who carried the torch of rare soul to their communities. These were clubs in every sense of the word, often membership-based, locally managed by enthusiasts, and held in venues that were willing to tolerate young people. Many of them aped the patterns of older working-class institutions – electing committees and treasurers, and holding nights in fading workers' clubs, bowling clubs, miners' welfares and industrial social clubs. While future generations of dance music fans would pursue the 'pop-up' approach, running their events in warehouses, derelict buildings and secret rave venues, northern soul stuck more closely to working-class towns and familiar venues such as old decaying ballrooms, working men's clubs and rooms above local pubs. The most successful rare soul club in the Midlands, the Catacombs in Wolverhampton, was in an old lead-smelting plant and the dance floor was within old furnaces knocked into alcoves. Another popular all-nighter held throughout the seventies at Wakefield Unity Hall used premises that originally belonged to the co-operative movement in the Victorian era, and had an unbroken link back to the origins of nineteenth-century socialism. Likewise, the Social and Reform Club, a rare soul venue in Grimsby, dated back to electoral reform movements of the nineteenth century.

Hot spots grew up around the main clubs. The Twisted Wheel drew its core membership from urban Manchester and eastwards out to Rochdale, Oldham and beyond. The Plebeians in Halifax reached out to emergent soul communities across Calder Valley to smaller towns such as Hebden Bridge, Sowerby Bridge and Todmorden, the hometown of a pioneering DJ duo called Ginger and Eddie, and one of the scene's major rare soul aficionados, Tim Brown, owner of Anglo-American Records. The Broken Wheel, a canal-side club held in an old rubber warehouse in Retford in Nottinghamshire, drew Mods and soul fans from

Mansfield, Worksop and South Yorkshire. The Compass Club opposite the Harbour Clock in Torquay was the venue frequented by northerners working the holiday season in Torquay. The Torch in Tunstall drew its members from far and wide but particularly the Potteries and the Black Country, creating a constituency that survived into the eighties, and fed another significant venue, the Top of the World in Stafford. These places each had their own local idiosyncrasies but they agreed on shared sounds and musical heroes unknown to the wider society, such as Phillip Mitchell's 'Free For All' (Shout, 1970) and songs that seemed to speak in coded ways about the amphetamine drug culture, such as Roy Hamilton's 'Crackin' Up Over You' (RCA, 1966).

One of the most remarkable hot spots of all grew up around a rare soul club in Droitwich in Worcestershire, called Chateau Impney, which broke the mould by forgoing old dance halls, industrial warehouses and working men's clubs in favour of a French-style château, which dated back to 1875 and was in part modelled on the Palace of Versailles. The mansion had been built for a local industrialist who had made a fortune in salt mining and built the château to appease his homesick Parisian wife. It was an unlikely place for the Mods of mid sixties Britain to congregate. Club regular Stuart Russell recalls: 'The Chateau's discotheque was in the darkened basement, and every Sunday afternoon from four until seven o'clock, it became a favourite rendezvous for teenagers.' Mods from across Worcestershire would congregate at the Chateau, drawn by the emerging reputation of a colourful rare soul DJ, 'Farmer' Carl Dene, who took his nickname from his headwear – hats normally worn by farmers and tractor drivers. Carl Dene was a pioneer of tracking down rare records and would take out adverts in the music industry press, hassle record labels and distributors, and write frequently to America in the hope that DJ demonstration records would be sent over the Atlantic. Through a local friend and contact, Richard Selwood, the owner of Hot Wax Records in Gloucester, 'Farmer' Carl and a local collector, Graham 'Docker' White, discovered an imported 7-inch single that had been lying unloved on the jazz shelves of Ray Avery's Rare Records in Glendale, California. It was sent by airmail to Hot Wax and within months was destined to become a historic record on the northern soul scene. Leon Haywood, formerly a keyboardist with the legendary Sam Cooke, and latterly a successful jazz funk artist, had recorded a frenetic song called 'Baby Reconsider' on an under-funded Los Angeles label called Fat Fish. It had all but faded from sight but found its way via Chateau Impney onto the decks of the Twisted Wheel. 'Baby Reconsider' (Fat Fish, 1967) became the first truly rare northern soul record. Other copies were near-impossible to find, and so its value escalated. Famously it sold for £40 at the Twisted Wheel, an extortionate sum of money at the time, and the equivalent of around £700 today. It is far from being the most expensive northern soul record, nor is it one of the best, but the song set the rules for what was to come. Rare soul prices became inflationary and an aura grew up around hard-to-import discs. Within a matter of a six months, 'Baby Reconsider''s reputation soared again, when it was bootlegged and fake copies flooded the rare soul market that had grown up in and around the Twisted Wheel. New rules had been set, obscure black American labels from the sixties became the holy grail, and original copies as opposed to reissues, or the vilified bootleg copies, came to define the scene. A principle had been established that has been adhered to by DJs and collectors down the years – northern soul was all about OVO, original vinyl only. Breaking this cardinal rule remains a heinous crime to this day and is anathema on a scene that can be unforgiving about the standards of soul. Others quickly followed. Jackie Lee's 'Darkest Days' (Mirwood, 1967), Dobie Gray's 'Out On The Floor' (Charger, 1966) and the San Remo Strings' effervescent instrumental 'Festival Time' (Ric-Tic, 1966) became cherished rarities, but this was only the beginning. Rarity and price inflation were both to intensify in the years to come.

O

Meanwhile, James Anderton was rising through the ranks and had learned from his Scottish Presbyterian bosses. By 1967 he was zealous in his opposition to late-night entertainment and an adherent of observing the Sabbath. He believed that crime was ultimately connected to the decline of morality and that in the clubs much of that could be attributed to the abuse of amphetamines. When Anderton finally became the new Chief Constable of Manchester in 1975, he looked back on the closure of the Twisted Wheel as a triumph and imagined that a zero tolerance approach to all-nighters was the only credible approach to stemming drug-related crime. Despite the evidence of widespread social change around him, Anderton was adamant he was right, and in his many public outbursts seemed to prefer the past to the present. He was convinced there was unfinished business in Manchester's club culture. Behind the old premises of the Twisted Wheel, along the dilapidated banks of the old Rochdale Canal, a new dance music community was gathering.

Manchester's gay community had been on the periphery of Anderton's attention until the mid seventies, but the more they came to occupy city bars and run dedicated late-night clubs, the more the homosexual lifestyle came to repulse the police chief. Before the Canal Street gay village flourished, bars and clubs like Napoleons, Clone Zone and New York had all been along Bloom Street. Other gay pubs and clubs were spread out across the city centre, including two of the most pioneering: Stuffed Olives and Heroes near South King Street. Andrew Berry, one of the first people to DJ at the legendary Hacienda in Manchester, had gone to Heroes, 'entering by the back door', and frequently made comparisons with northern soul: 'Heroes on King Street was another gay club but this time more hardcore – a real clone club, San Francisco, almost like Skin Two, slightly fetishy, druggie, a bit seedy with rent boys and old men,' he claims. 'The music was amazing: DJ Les Cokell who had come from the northern soul scene and had got into hardcore hi-energy. It was open every night and was always packed. I met Diana Dors there! And Quentin Crisp.'

Les Cokell was the ultimate connector. He had been a DJ at the Twisted Wheel and a near oracle at Blackpool Mecca, where he was one of the northern soul scene's best known collectors. He had come out as gay many years before his untimely death in a car accident in Manchester in 1998, by which time he was an underground dance hero. Cokell's career had begun as a local DJ at the Falcon Manor in his native Settle in the Yorkshire Dales where he threw now legendary soul parties in the village that attracted fans from Blackpool Mecca and Plebs in Halifax. The area was so remote that hundreds danced in the rural roads free from police and the drug squad's attention. In the mid seventies, as northern soul was splintering and Manchester's gay clubs were in their infancy, Les Cokell learned of a new underground – the New York loft scene – and through friends made contact with David Mancuso, whose downtown Manhattan loft parties were the roots of gay disco. Cokell became aware of the so-called 'priests of the night', DJs Michael Cappello at Café Francis and David Rodriguez at the Limelight, and it was through him that Blackpool Mecca's Ian Levine visited 12 West, a gay club between 12th and Jane Street in New York's Greenwich Village. It was there that Levine met DJ Tom Savarese, a connection that transformed Blackpool Mecca and provoked a major split in the traditional constituencies of northern soul.

James Anderton was now fighting a nightclub war on two fronts: a campaign to silence northern soul and a specially commissioned vice squad whose role was to raid Manchester's gay clubs. According to lesbian city councillor Mary Murphy, 'the biggest perpetrators of hate crimes in the city were the police'. That was not how Anderton saw it. He was unsophisticated about music, and all he could see were clubs, licence breaches and a moral demise. In the early days of the AIDS pandemic, when sensitivity would have been a better policy, he addressed a police training event in Manchester, telling the audience that HIV and AIDS patients were 'swirling around in a human cesspool of their own making'. At a stroke, he became headline news and the most reviled police officer in Britain. Only the covert intervention of Prime Minister Margaret Thatcher saved his career. Anderton's anti-gay rhetoric fortified his reputation as 'God's Copper'. According to one of his own officers, Deputy Chief Constable Trefor Morris, 'he was an influential member of the Christian Police Association, heavy with evangelism bordering on militancy . . . He could get carried away.' It was Anderton's comments on AIDS that made him a hate figure for the liberal left for years to come, but ironically it was not the gay clubs that stoked his greatest anger; that was reserved for a club which was showing open contempt for Christianity and betraying the Sabbath. It was an all-nighter that was desecrating the very ballroom where his mother and father had first met. Many years after its name had changed, he still clung to the past and insisted on calling it 'the Emp' or 'the Empress Ballroom', unable to budge from his childhood memories. The place he had grown to hate more than any other late-night club was the underground cathedral of northern soul – Wigan Casino.

3
IN SEARCH OF OBSCURITY
1967–1973

We can only see a short distance ahead, but we can see plenty there that needs to be done.

Alan Turing

By the spring of 1973, obscurity had taken over my life and I had become adept at cracking codes. I learned the basics at a record shop called Ralph's situated near the gaping mouth of Manchester Victoria Station. This was northern soul's answer to Hut 8, the wooden shed where Alan Turing led the cryptographers that finally cracked the German Enigma machine. Ralph's Records was a tight and claustrophobic shop with rows of vinyl banking up to the tills. It had curious homemade devices that stopped shoplifting: four thin brush shanks were driven through the holes of imported records and then padlocked at the counter end. It prevented records being secreted into a bag or simply grabbed in a dawn raid. I spent months of my life in Ralph's, looking at labels, gazing at credits and listening in to conversations. Those who were trusted or who intended to buy were allowed to actually touch and inspect the records. Calloused hands carefully held them up to the light, and blemishes debated, arcane information openly shared. I had seen this tenderness before. The 'doo men' of central Scotland, their hands battered by industry and hewn with hard work, would gently stroke the light-grey feathers of a prize pigeon and then kiss its beak.

I quickly learned how to differentiate rare from commonly available, and original from bootleg. I felt I understood these records – it was the men's tattoos that mystified me. Crude Indian ink etched into the forearms and knuckles spoke in hieroglyphics: SKF, ZTSC, 2648, CEN1179 and RIKER. I learnt that 2648 was Motown's address in West Grand Boulevard in Detroit, that CEN1179 was the Twisted Wheel's phone number, that SKF was the abbreviation for the pharmaceutical company Smith, Kline & French who manufactured the amphetamine drug Drinamyl, and that Riker was a rival company who manufactured Durophet. The term 'Riker-Liker' was commonly used back then to describe someone blocked on amphetamine, and it was a phrase often tattooed on forearms. That left the greatest mystery of all: ZTSC. What did it mean, where did it come from, and why would it be injected with smudged Indian ink into the knuckles of a grown man?

For a brilliant hot summer in 1973 we had rented a flat on the corner of Lightbowne Road, in Moston in north Manchester, above Dr Iqbal's surgery. Pat Wall, my mate Mac from Scotland, his girlfriend Linda from Derby, and Pat's old school pal Linda Spencer from Rochdale would huddle together in two box rooms, or on the front-room settee where the pooled records were kept. It became a stop-over flat after all-nighters, and each weekend the human debris from the night before would be slumped untidily around the rooms, either coming down or fast asleep. During the week, we were joined by crews from Oldham and Rochdale, often talking until dawn about soul or travelling to midweek venues in the area – Motown in Shaw near Oldham, the Seven Stars in Heywood and Sale Mecca. Everything was subservient to soul. I had taken a summer job as a message boy with Railway Control in a dreary office block overlooking the old concourse of Piccadilly Station. From the corridor at the back, towards the lifts, you could see the old Twisted Wheel building on the corner of Whitworth Street. Mac had also moved down from Perth to be closer to the northern scene and had just packed in his job at Rowntree's in York, which had brought our free supplies of KitKats and Polo mints to a tragic end. Although he had failed at school, Mac was a self-taught graphic artist, who had an uncanny ability to replicate any image we could throw at him – clenched Black Power fists, obscure label designs, or the Road Runner cartoon character in full flight with sparks hurtling from his feet. Mac always added propelling pills flying from Road Runner's triple-claws.

It was on the corner of Lightbowne Road that I first saw James McGuire, his lower lip chewed to a cud. He was perched on a wall sifting through a small 7-inch record box outside our flat. Mac had agreed to decorate the box for James, so we all sat round the kitchen table, watching him using an old ruler and a box of Saxa salt to measure the height and width of the letters – ZTSC. He traced the letters in pencil first and then, with silver paint, he carefully completed the job. It was James McGuire who told me that ZTSC was a secret northern soul code etched into the inner wax of soul records, adding a piece of inventive nonsense that desperate exploited soul singers scratched the letters into their records hoping that they would be picked up at all-nighters, a bit like a message in a bottle but northern soul-style.

James was a regular at the Pendulum, a basement nightclub in an old Sports Guild building opposite Manchester's Victoria

Station. In the aftermath of the Twisted Wheel, it became the place where the city's displaced northern soul refugees congregated. He described his first night there, standing nervously on the corner of Long Millgate trying to pluck up the courage to go through the doors. 'I was still shaking going down the stairs into the crowd,' he told me. DJ Barry Tasker was playing records that he had never heard before, but they came one after another with such a liberating force that he described it as akin to a religious conversion. 'Like those kids getting thrown in the river in America,' he said, descriptively throwing his hand into the air as if in a trance. The Pendulum had a concrete dance floor – not perfect for dancing – but those who took to it like a second home seemed undeterred. Barry Tasker, and latterly the enthusiastic Richard Searling, bossed the turntables, playing records that eventually made their way to the forefront of the all-nighter scene. It was a place that seemed to give license to collectors and encouraged their taste for the esoteric, the rare and the unheralded. James McGuire had taken to scribbling down the names of records in a small referee's notebook, listing as many as he could decipher – Duke Browner, Lou Johnson, Roy Freeman . . .

Lists are an essential part of the culture of northern soul: play lists, wants lists and discographies of the rare labels that populate and give shape to the scene. The most important list of all came every Thursday from John Anderson's Soul Bowl, the rare soul warehouse in King's Lynn. Rather than wait for it to be delivered to his home, James would rise early and head for the Royal Mail sorting office on Mirabel Street. 'I used to speed-read the list as I ran back towards Victoria Station to a long line of telephone boxes,' he explained. 'I always made sure I had a pile of coins and would begin phone bashing Soul Bowl. On a good day you were straight through and you'd get records from the front page . . . If your luck was out, some twat from Stoke would get their first.'

When I met him in the spring of 1973, James kept returning to the myth of ZTSC. I had my doubts, but it was such a charming story and one he so emphatically believed that I never argued. To prove his point, James asked a Stockport lad hovering by the turntables at the Pendulum to show me the hidden scribbling. He lit a match and shone the flame on the grooves of a white demo of Laura Lee's 'To Win Your Heart' (Ric-Tic, 1966). Sure enough, there were the letters ZTSC. I had seen them before, and over the years to come would see them hundreds of times more, sometimes scratched with a pin, often stamped into the vinyl. The ZTSC myth became the northern scene's version of the Enigma code, however the truth was more prosaic. ZTSC was the manufacturing code for a Columbia pressing plant serviced by record company offices in Detroit and Chicago and a pressing plant in an old furniture factory in Terre Haute, Indiana. Many independent labels from across the American Midwest bore the ZTSC code; a sweep that included great Pendulum standards such as Darrell Banks's 'Open The Door To Your Heart' (Revilot, 1966), Duke Browner's 'Crying Over You' (Impact, 1966) and Tamiko Jones's 'I'm Spellbound' (Golden World, 1966).

Mac and I were friends who were already pursuing different myths. I was ZTSC and he was SKF. Or put more simply, I had become obsessed with collecting rare records and Mac had become more intrigued by the drug scene. When Mac casually told me that James McGuire's mum Nettie was 'a hefty big woman', his eyes twinkled like a winter star. It was conspiratorial code for someone who, unknown to them, might be a route to a prescription for Tenuate Dospan, the pharmaceutical name for 'chalkies'. Chalkies looked like little white tombstones, were hard to digest and had wicked after-effects, but they kept you up and running. Most amphetamines were prescribed to suppress appetite, or as Mac more crassly put it, they were 'drugs for fatties'. The ruse he had worked out was simple but brilliant. Mac had a Polaroid camera which dispensed instant shit photos. One day he took a photograph of Mrs McGuire on Kenyon Lane sitting on a small wall with her shopping bag spilling out in front of her. He then showed the photo of the overweight woman to Pakistan's finest mind, our landlord Dr Iqbal, claiming it was his auntie back home in Scotland. Mac faked concern for her weight and asked the good doctor what he would advise. Dr Iqbal duly obliged and listed several options, which he naively wrote down on a medical pad for Mac. The next steps were meat and drink to Mac. He had already stolen a book of prescription slips from the surgery's office supply cupboard on the landing below our flat, and with his finely tuned graphic skills he forged prescriptions for a range of amphetamines. It was a sight to behold: a young man with no previous interest in the European metric system happily conjuring up milligrammes in front of my eyes. He'd perch at the kitchen table like the blind guy from *The Great Escape*, carefully copying down key words in a flowing legible text – Tenuate Dospan, dexamphetamine, Drinamyl. Bit by bit, he learned to copy near perfect scripts and with a gleeful flourish would forge Dr Iqbal's signature from our rental agreement. The fake scripts were cashed in chemists across Manchester, and for months to come, Mac boasted that he had pulled off the perfect crime. Perfect except for the stomach cramps. Chalkies were a notorious beast when it came to a settled digestive system.

One of the cardinal rules of the northern soul scene is a respect for obscurity and those who die young. Strange as it may seem to outsiders, the northern scene prefers heroes who are unknown to the wider world or those who left us tragically early. Failure says something important about the cruel serendipity of fame, and most of the records played on the northern soul scene are there because at some stage the commercial vagaries of the recording industry have stacked the cards against them. Throughout much of the sixties, the music of black America was under-capitalised, under-promoted and often produced away from the commercial centres of New York and Los Angeles. Local releases remained local, narrowly distributed and largely unknown. Northern soul cherishes its role as a saviour of the neglected – rescuing some acts from being almost wholly forgotten while plucking others from semi-obscurity and giving them the status of gods.

One woman stands head and shoulders above the rest. Linda Jones was born and raised in Newark, New Jersey. She recorded her first single as a nineteen-year-old and was mentored by producer George Kerr, who in 1967 secured her a contract with the Warner Brothers subsidiary Loma records. Linda was blessed with one of the great voices of the gospel heritage, but her only significant national hit was the blistering ballad 'Hypnotized', which grazed the outer reaches of the pop charts. Unable to crack the conundrums of African-American music, Warner Brothers closed down Loma in 1968, leaving great soul records by The Apollas, Larry Laster and Ben Aiken languishing in the obscurity of thrift shops and ghetto record stores. Linda Jones returned home and signed to a series of tiny East Coast labels, but again success evaded her. However, her outstanding voice was cherished on the northern scene where it was presumed she was too good for success, too talented for the charts and too special for the uninitiated. It was an attitude sprinkled with an inverted snobbery, but for northern soul fans Linda Jones was too good to be famous.

Jones had suffered from diabetes most of her life and was prone to debilitating fatigue. Appearing at the famed Apollo Theatre in Harlem she travelled home to her mother's home to rest and fell into a diabetic coma. Tragically she never recovered, and passed away leaving a rich catalogue of relatively unknown classics behind her – 'I Can't Stop Loving My Baby' (Loma 1967), 'My Heart Needs A Break' (Loma, 1968) and 'I Just Can't Live My Life (Without You Babe)' (Warner 7 Arts, 1969) – each of which had been played at rare soul clubs across the north. Jones's death brought revered status in a scene that was uniquely vulnerable to young death, one in which drug abuse was widespread, travel from place to place was the norm, and defiance of the real world was admired.

The journalist Dave Godin, the man often credited with coining the phrase 'northern soul', had written respectfully of Linda Jones; in his regular columns for *Blues & Soul* magazine, he campaigned on behalf of her pleading and tortured ballads, and through his recommendation she won the approval of the soul cognoscenti. Godin described her in celestial language always deploying the same canonising phrase – 'the late great Linda Jones'. This phrase came to be passed on reverentially by others. In his collector's guide to Wigan Casino, record dealer Tim Brown claimed that her name 'should be whispered with reverence whenever true fanatics meet, due to the range, the sheer melisma of her powerhouse vocals'. Richard Searling, a major DJ on the northern soul scene and at the time the resident DJ at VaVas, a northern soul all-nighter in Bolton, was another influential figure who lifted Linda Jones onto the pedestal of greatness; he too always introduced her music with the phrase 'the late great Linda Jones'. But it was at Blackpool Mecca, the Harvard of northern soul, where she was most revered. The Mecca was a Saturday nightclub in the Highland Room situated on the top floor of what was a mainstream nightclub aimed at tourists and day-trippers. The legions of northern soul fans who flocked there were required to wear shirt and tie, then had to travel by escalator to the top floor where they entered a *Brigadoon*-themed room. Claymores and tartan kitsch adorned the walls and soul music seeped through the speakers. It was here that the myth of Linda Jones was given its fullest exposure. When DJ Ian Levine introduced her gigantic song 'I Just Can't Live My Life (Without You Babe)' it was always with a profound respect. The song was an agonising rollercoaster that combined high-energy dance beats with melancholy vocals: 'Sad and lonely, since you went away, I can't live my life without you.' Not even opera could compete with the wave of emotions her music let loose in fans: respect, loss, appreciation of her genius, a betrayed talent and the lifelong pursuit of soul, one that cruel fame had casually bypassed. When the song ended, something spontaneous and remarkable happened: dancers would simply stop dead and clap, a resounding applause that would continue until the next record began. Over time, applauding great singers and great records became common on the northern soul scene, with hundreds of young people, mostly white and working-class, proudly respecting the memory of the dead and the unknown. More than the amphetamines, or the acrobatic dancing, this was the true spirit of northern soul – a deep and heartfelt love affair with obscure and overlooked music.

The death of Linda Jones coincided with the triumphant height of the Torch all-nighter in Tunstall, Stoke-on-Trent, a club that in part filled the vacuum left by the closure of the Twisted Wheel. Resident DJs Keith Minshull, Alan Day, Martyn Ellis, Colin Curtis and Tony Jebb launched many northern classics including Tony Clarke's 'Landslide' (Chess, 1967), The Invitations' 'Skiing In The Snow' (dynoVoice, 1966) and a perky Linda Jones B-side called 'You Hit Me Like TNT' (Blue Cat, 1965). It was a song whose title alone could have been written for the club. The Torch was an arsenal of sound, overcrowded and dripping with sweat. By the time I went there, it was facing pressure to close its doors. Club manager Chris Burton told northern soul historian Mike Ritson that it was complaints about the noise rather than the perennial problem of amphetamine abuse that extinguished the Torch. 'We regularly had attendances of over a thousand on Saturday nights. It wasn't that big, but when we had fifteen or sixteen hundred in there it was just hell,' he recounted in Ritson's book *The In Crowd*. 'All the drinks labels would peel off the bottles on the bar due to the heat. We couldn't have coped with that every week, but I think it had its part to play in the northern soul thing. For a time it carried the torch, I suppose – the northern flame.' Next door to the Torch was a hay merchant's yard. The owner complained vociferously to the local council that his horses could not sleep due to the racket – a story so bizarre and unlikely that it captured the attention of the local press and brought on a flood of complaints. Paradoxically a dance-craze record by Pennsylvania musicians Cliff Nobles & Co. called 'The Horse' was regularly played by the Torch DJs (its coded references to heroin probably going over the heads of the restless equines next door).

As the clock ticked down on the Torch's future, the rare soul scene continued to unearth young singers who had died tragically young, among them two Detroit vocalists, Tony Clarke and Darrell Banks. Born in New York, vocalist Tony Clarke was christened Ralph Thomas Williams, and raised in Detroit before he relocated to Chicago to join the famous Chess Records. It was there that he adopted the pseudonym Tony Clarke, but like a criminal or an absconder he also called himself by the aliases Ralph Williams and Ralph Ferguson. His restless talent was first recognised on the turntables of the Twisted Wheel, where a mid-tempo song, 'The Entertainer' (Chess, 1966), became a club favourite. Clarke's success was short-lived. He moved on again, this time to Hollywood, where he appeared fleetingly as a bit-part actor in Sidney Poitier's *They Call Me Mister Tibbs!* His next release was the brilliant 'Landslide' (Chess, 1967), an out-of-control dancer which replicated the mass movement of an actual landslide, and helped introduce the word 'stomper' into the lexicon of rare soul. A huge record in the final days of the Torch, it carried with it the portents of pain and misery to come in Clarke's own life. The introductory lyrics – 'Misery is rushing down on me like a landslide' – summed up the singer's own tumbling experiences. Separated from his partner and travelling between cities to stay in touch with his estranged children, he returned home to Detroit where he broke into his partner's home armed with a tyre jack. The love that had brought Tony Clarke and Joyce Elaine Williams together had soured into bitter acrimony, and there had been a long history of spousal abuse and custody disputes. Clarke's wife had banned him from her home and as security had armed herself with a pistol, fearing he might return. When Clarke appeared uninvited, she shot him dead. Such was Tony Clarke's heightened status at the Torch that details of his death were only sketchily shared. I was told at the time that he had been the innocent victim of gun crime in Detroit; another story had him killed in a bank robbery; another that he had been shot at home by an intruder. The misleading stories sealed his reputation, and it was many years after his heroic status was assured that the hidden history of his violent past came to light.

The singer Darrell Banks was similarly precocious. His young life was also cut horribly short. Again, the dramatic circumstances of his death contributed to his cult status. In February 1970, he was shot and killed by a Detroit police officer. At the time he was presumed to be an innocent victim of a racially motivated murder. It subsequently transpired that Aaron Bullock, the police officer who shot him, was off duty, and a dispute had flared up over Banks's ex-girlfriend, Marjorie Bozeman. Banks was born Darrell Eubanks in the industrial town of Mansfield, Ohio, to a single mother. In June 1966, Detroit's Revilot Records released his debut record, and it became one of the great 'double-siders' of the rare soul scene: the top side a haunting mid-tempo soul classic, 'Open The Door To Your Heart', the powerhouse B-side 'Our Love (Is In The Pocket)'. Both songs were of such enduring quality that they have been played at almost every northern soul venue over the last forty years, first at the Twisted Wheel and subsequently at the Torch, Wigan Casino and beyond. In 1967, Banks headed south, hoping for greater reward with Stax in Memphis. Another release, 'Angel Baby (Don't You Ever Leave Me)' (ATCO, 1967), joined his two Revilot songs on the evergreen roster of rare northern soul, but despite his initial success as a soul singer Banks received precious few royalties or reward for his music. 'Open The Door To Your Heart' became caught up in a copyright dispute with soul rival Donnie Elbert, who claimed that it was derivative of his own composition 'Baby Walk Right In'. Elbert believed that Banks had fraudulently claimed sole writer credits on the song, and after bitter exchanges in public and in private, the courts found in favour of Elbert. Ironically Donnie Elbert had only become aware of the similarity between Banks's 'Open The Door To Your Heart' when another cover version by British R&B singer Chris Farlowe was released in Europe. Elbert was by then living in London promoting his own hit 'A Little Piece Of Leather' (Sue, 1966), which had been broken at the Twisted Wheel. With a chequered history, a failed copyright case, patchy relationships with his record labels, and a reckless attitude to life, Banks died penniless. He was buried in an unmarked pauper's grave at Lot 539 in Detroit's Memorial Park Cemetery. A headstone was subsequently laid many years later. David Meikle, a first-generation Mod from Glasgow who had first heard Banks's songs at the Twisted Wheel in Manchester, had motivated soul fans from around the world to help fund the headstone by donation. The inscription on the new headstone simply reads 'Open The Door To Your Heart'.

In December 1972, the Torch made history. The converted old picture house tucked away in the backstreets of Tunstall attracted the biggest northern soul crowd ever, at the live recording of an entire show by a visiting Chicago soul singer, Major Lance. It was an odd venue. A Roman chariot hung over the entrance, glass-panelled double wooden doors led into a cinema foyer, and the ticket booth harked back to the post-war period. Inside was the dance floor: once the home of gently waltzing couples, it now swarmed with energetic dancers, none of whom danced together or had any intention of taking a partner. The dance band had long since surrendered to the sound of rare soul music and a group of DJs who included two local youths, Keith Minshull and Colin Dimond, a skinny shaman with the stringy hair of a rock guitarist, who worked under the stage name 'Colin Curtis'. Chris Burton told *Blues & Soul* magazine that 'when the club was first opened back in 1965 it was called the Golden Torch: it was a semi-ballroom with all the delicate awnings painted golden to add to the effect. And let's be honest, the Golden Torch sounded better too! Then, when we went over to soul we had all the bits and pieces removed, hung a few torches up, and everything was painted black . . .'

The faithful faced intense extremes of heat and cold. Outside it was freezing cold, early morning frost was already settling on the cluttered rooftops and fog was descending on the low-rise residential streets. Inside it was as hot as the furnaces that powered the potteries. It was an intense and brutal heat that seemed to increase with every great sound – 'Quick Change Artist' (Karen, 1967), a power-pop soul record by The Soul Twins out of Ann Arbor in Michigan; 'Just Ask Me' (SPQR, 1967), a hectic dancer by Lenis Guess, a local soul impresario from Norfolk, Virginia; and 'Just Like The Weather' (Constellation, 1967), a storming Chicago soul song by gifted vocalist Charles Davis, working under the pseudonym Nolan Chance. The heat refused to recede and each new song cranked the mercury higher. Although surviving the night was a northern soul rite of passage many hardcore soul fans have admitted to leaving the Torch early to find comfort in the freezing streets outside. When Major Lance came on stage it was bedlam. The Torch had an official capacity of only 500 but up to 1600 northern soul fans packed the event. Lance's long, sleek frame shimmied across the stage, taunting the audience and pointing the microphone towards them as if they were his backing singers. The Torch was a scrum. Bodies crushed together, hands soul-clapped upwards to the dripping ceiling and from time to time the crowd surged forward more like an unruly football crowd than a concert. DJ Ian Levine who was appearing for the first time that night described it as 'the most electrifying night of my whole career'. 'You could not have squeezed one more person in that club,' he told DJ historian Bill Brewster. 'They were hanging off the rafters. It must have been a hundred-and-twenty degrees. It was so hot and packed, the sweat was rising off people's bodies as condensation and dripping back on to them from the ceiling.'

Major Lance was already known to the initiated for a string of up-tempo soul sounds, many of which were standards on the northern soul scene; among them were 'The Monkey Time' (OKeh, 1963), 'Um, Um, Um, Um, Um, Um' (OKeh, 1963), 'Investigate' (OKeh, 1966) and 'Ain't No Soul Left In These Old Shoes' (OKeh, 1967). The songs all had their memories but none came close to rivalling the mystique of the label that recorded them – the Chicago-based black music label OKeh Records. OKeh released records on a vivid pink label; the name was written like a signature and so distinctive that it was imitated as graffiti, on woven badges and in tattoos, crudely etched by mystified tattoo artists in the cities of the north. This was the era when gang culture and the early days of football hooliganism had colonised the words 'OK' and 'Rules' in graffiti slogans. For the football fans of the northern soul scene it was a simple adaptation – 'Burnley Rules OKeh'.

OKeh's Chicago-period soul was urban, up-tempo and (unintentionally) obscure. For over forty years, OKeh has been an imprimatur of northern soul, like a wax seal of approval, and artists like The Vibrations, The Triumphs and Major Harris, who are mostly unknown to the mainstream, are godlike characters to the initiated.

Few knew at the time just how iconic the OKeh Record Corporation actually was. It had been founded during the First World War by a German mechanical engineer called Otto K E Heinemann. He emigrated to New York and set up a company that produced machine parts for the infant recording industry. Using his own initials, he contrived the name 'OKeh'. His business included a recording studio, a pressing plant and a label producing old 78rpm discs. Unknown to the collectors of the northern soul scene, OKeh had already attracted a collectors' market of its own: retired white American men who were searching for rare 78rpm discs. In 1920, OKeh recorded the African-American blues singer Mamie Smith, and had an unexpected smash hit with 'Crazy

Blues' (OKeh, 1921) that secured their reputation with the urban blues scene for decades. In 1922, OKeh hired Clarence Williams as director of what was then known as 'Race Records' and opened a studio in Chicago, in turn hiring a local R&B powerhouse Carl Davis as A&R head of their Chicago operation. Connections are everything in musical production. Davis identified one of the city's most creative minds, the now legendary Curtis Mayfield, as his second-in-command, and in turn Mayfield secured the services of a local teenager he knew from his days at North Chicago's Wells High School. His name was Major Lance.

For a period in the mid sixties, OKeh attracted Little Richard into its ranks, but most of its releases only sold locally or quickly faded from sight. Two collaborators, Larry Williams and Johnny 'Guitar' Watson, were recruited to produce Little Richard and they hustled studio time to cut their own 1967 album *Two For The Price Of One*. On the cover, Williams and Watson stand astride a Cadillac, holding on to rodeo ropes as if they are taming wild horses. One particular track – the hectic 'Too Late' (OKeh, 1967) – became a northern classic and has withstood the test of time, gracing the turntables of all the major clubs and becoming a beacon of the oldies scene. OKeh became a substantial part of northern soul mythology, and lent its name to a massively popular club in the rugged textile town of Keighley in West Yorkshire, which has now survived over thirty years of rare soul nights, and to the OKeh Soul Club in Bathgate in central Scotland, a town devastated by the collapse of the motor manufacturing industry in the eighties.

The smell of northern soul was not only youthful sweat, it was scented with a refined understanding of obscurity. The way the recording industry had marginalised OKeh elevated it above the rest. One young woman, Sandi Sheldon, became an enigmatic classic. Her only song – 'You're Gonna Make Me Love You' (OKeh, 1967) – plunged into obscurity; no one could find her, she had no trace of previous recordings and appeared to have disappeared. It was only many years later that her identity was revealed. Sandi Sheldon's real name was Kendra Spotswood, and she hailed from Englewood, New Jersey, where she had once competed in local talent contests against 'the late great Linda Jones'. 'You're Gonna Make Me Love You' had died a death, only to be resurrected and held in the highest esteem in the north of England.

On my first night at the Torch, sporting tinted wire-rimmed glasses, I tried desperately to imitate the cool cadence of a Black Power intellectual as I sauntered around the cramped dance floor. It was like navigating a cauldron. The DJ, Martyn Ellis, who had a big and bombastic personality, and urged dancers to do more with an enthusiastic barrow boy-style of delivery, was the first person I heard saying the name 'Sandi Sheldon' but he would not be the last. The New York producer Van McCoy had cast Sandi Sheldon in a new guise, this time as lead singer of a group called The Vonnettes, a less than subtle nod to The Ronettes. Another obscure northern soul record called 'Touch My Heart' (Cobblestone, 1968) was released to even less success. Sheldon's relationship with McCoy floundered, and she relocated to Atlanta, Georgia, where she retired from the music industry still only twenty-five years old. As she hustled a living in Atlanta in a variety of poorly paid jobs, she was a heroine on the northern soul scene – brilliant, energetic and, most of all, obscure.

The lifespan of the Torch roughly parallels the history of another legendary label, Ric-Tic Records of Detroit. Ric-Tic's soul output had begun in earnest back in July 1964 when the Golden Torch was still trading as a fleapit cinema. The first significant soul record on the label's roster was 'Gino Is A Coward' by Gino 'Whirlpool' Washington (Ric-Tic, 1964), followed over the next six months by two songs by Freddie Gorman, a Detroit mailman whose daily delivery round took him through Detroit's Brewster Projects, the original home of The Supremes. But it was in July 1965 – the year that the Torch opened as a soul club – that Ric-Tic tasted their first success. Edwin Starr's 'Agent Double-O-

Soul', a secret agent soul song from an era fascinated by spies and FBI agents, broke into the local charts in Detroit and set the pace for a phenomenal year of creativity to come. Berry Gordy, Jr's Motown Corporation took Detroit's feelgood bubblegum soul sound to the world. The output was seismic: Stevie Wonder's 'Uptight (Everything's Alright)' (Tamla, 1965), the Four Tops' 'Ask The Lonely', 'I Can't Help Myself (Sugar Pie, Honey Bunch)', 'It's The Same Old Song' (Motown, 1965), Kim Weston's 'I'm Still Loving You', 'A Thrill A Moment' and 'Take Me In Your Arms (Rock Me A Little While)' (Tamla, 1965), Martha and the Vandellas' 'Nowhere To Run' (Gordy, 1965) and The Supremes' 'Stop In The Name Of Love' and 'Back In My Arms Again' (Motown, 1965). Never in the history of African-American music had an individual city made such an impact. Motown's success unintentionally forced small labels like Ric-Tic and its sister label Golden World into the shadows, despite their roster of artists being world-class. JJ Barnes, Laura Lee and The Fantastic Four all recorded for Ric-Tic, and two internationally distributed pop hits from Edwin Starr, 'Stop Her On Sight (SOS)' (Ric-Tic, 1965) and 'Headline News' (Ric-Tic, 1965), enjoyed reasonable success. A deal was struck in the winter of 1966 that brought Ric-Tic under the influence of Motown, but despite what many on the northern soul scene thought and said at the time, it was a largely benign deal, securing Motown another recording studio to cope with demanding recording schedules. Much as they were lionised at the Torch and across the northern soul scene, Motown were less interested in the roster of talent they had inherited and more focused on the studio they had acquired on Detroit's West Davison Street. This simple misreading of Motown's motives led to another myth on the northern scene. When Ric-Tic's artists dispersed or disappeared, it became to many a Motown conspiracy. Edwin Starr frequently told fans and journalists that he felt marginalised by Motown and that he had been 'starved of attention'. He also spoke on behalf of a then less well-known label mate JJ Barnes, whose songs 'Please Let Me In' (Ric-Tic, 1965) and 'Real Humdinger' (Ric-Tic, 1966) were Torch standards and laid the groundwork for a myth that grew in scale and intensity with time. Barnes was an exquisite singer; at his height, his voice bore a resemblance to the smooth yet raspy crooning delivery of Marvin Gaye, who in the mid sixties was already a major Motown artist (and the brother-in-law of Motown owner Berry Gordy). Barnes was led to believe by several people in the gossipy world of Detroit soul that he was being deliberately sidelined by Motown because he was perceived as a threat to Marvin Gaye. His career in Detroit stalled, and Edwin Starr invited him to travel to England where they worked closely with the growing northern soul scene in the years to come. Comparisons with Marvin Gaye grew as Motown's reputation soared, but the cult of obscurity that was shaping northern soul offered a new interpretation: that Motown was deliberately suppressing the careers of lesser artists for their own international gain. These conspiracy theories grew and festered: earlier Motown artists such as Singing Sammy Ward and Hattie Littles had been dumped from the label and left to a life of near poverty; that the Ric-Tic artists were signed to shut them up; and latterly that the tragic Detroit singer Carol Anderson was snubbed by Motown because she was clinically obese. Much of it was fanciful exaggeration, but on an underground scene harnessed to the cult of obscurity, low-level paranoia was common.

Meanwhile, the Torch was careering headlong towards trouble. In November 1972, owner Chris Burton was asked to attend a meeting at Burslem Police Station to discuss drug abuse, over-crowding, and neighbourhood complaints about noise. A short-term strategy was thrashed out that would keep the Torch's fragile licence in place, but only if the doors were closed when capacity was reached and if the management co-operated by advising police when amphetamines were being sold on the premises. Burton was required to keep photographic records of people he had expelled from the club and refuse them entry in the future. A stricter regime of re-entry was introduced and exit doors were padlocked (in violation of fire regulations) to prevent dealers gaining entry, but it all proved to be too little, too late.

On 16 March 1973, when the Torch came to renew its licence after sturdy opposition by Stoke-on-Trent's quasi-legal Environmental Health Department, it was refused. One by one, complaints against the Torch were read out by Mr David McEvoy, the lawyer representing the police. There were incidents of under-age customers; poor hygiene standards had been reported by environmental officers; the Torch had supposedly tolerated customers with a criminal record; and drugs had been seized on numerous occasions, most infamously when Stoke's tiny seven-man drug squad staged a raid on cars leaving the M6 motorway and arrested several soul fans for possession of prescribed amphetamines. In fairness, the Torch's licensing hearings were free of the Christian ideology that had dominated policing in Manchester. Chris Burton was allowed to speak in defence of his club and call witnesses to its good character: they included John Abbey, publisher of *Blues & Soul* magazine and the owner of Contempo Records, who had funded the Major Lance *Live At The Torch* album. Others who spoke up for the club were promoter David Daniels, local journalist Frank Elson (a columnist with *Blues & Soul*) and the singer Charles Edwin Hatcher, better known as Edwin Starr. However, the weight of evidence was stacked against the Torch. A report presented to the licensing board by Detective Sergeant Ernest Gardiner claimed that up to seventy per cent of the Torch's clients were illegally using amphetamines; it was a statistic that stuck and almost certainly sealed the Torch's fate.

Drugs had brought the Torch notoriety – and in part brought about its downfall – but the council were responding more to local neighbourhood complaints. Even on my first night at the Torch, I remember walking up crowded backstreets, with houses right and left squeezed on top of each other and windows at a level you could peer in to. The noise of footsteps, laughter and often heavy coughing ricocheted around the streets, and the percussive beat of loafers, brogues or Solatio 102s, the crossed leather shoes worn by dancers, sounded like tap dancers' shoes or miners' clogs from the industrial past. From miles away you could hear the pounding sound of Detroit's bass guitars and driving saxophones, a noise sublime to some and a wild cacophony to others.

A 'For Sale' board went up outside the building and the premises that had once housed the Golden Torch were eventually bought by a camping equipment business. 'I was upset,' says Chris Burton, who for a few brief but remarkable years had turned the place into the greatest club in Britain. 'It was one of the saddest days of my life.'

It had a bittersweet memory in my life, too. The first northern soul all-nighter I had ever attended was closed, but it left a legacy that has never faded; like the divine voice of Linda Jones its tragic end brought a new immortality. Years after the scene had moved on, the building that housed the Golden Torch was devastated by fire, its old interior laid to waste, and the remains of the gutted building were finally demolished. Northern soul's second super-club had gone, and the torch was about to be passed to the biggest of them all – Wigan Casino.

WIGAN CASINO

Soul Club LADIES

4
THE ROAD TO WIGAN PIER
1973–1981

As you walk through the industrial towns you lose yourself in labyrinths of little brick houses blackened by smoke, festering in planless chaos round miry alleys and little cindered yards where there are stinking dust-bins and lines of grimy washing and half-ruinous w.c.s.

The Road to Wigan Pier, George Orwell, 1937

Even today, the people of Wigan have not fully forgiven the socialist writer George Orwell. In 1936, he spent three weeks there, studying the lives of coal miners and their families. His description of one house trapped in 'indescribable squalor' and another in which a 'sewer runs under the house and stinks in summer' left an indelible mark. 'One woman's face stays with me,' Orwell wrote, 'a worn skull-like face on which was a look of intolerable misery and degradation.'

Orwell's diary of Wigan left a stigma. Wigan is a word you say in inverted commas, a place where the past still lingers. One of Orwell's intentions when he first set foot in the town was to discover the mythical Wigan Pier, and in a radio interview in 1943, he admitted failure: 'Well, I am afraid I must tell you that Wigan Pier doesn't exist. I made a journey specially to see it in 1936 and I couldn't find it. It did exist once, however, and to judge from the photographs it must have been about twenty feet long.' The original 'pier' at Wigan was a coal-loading jetty, where wagons from a nearby colliery were unloaded onto canal barges. It was demolished in 1929, but the international success of Orwell's book and his intriguing failure to locate the mythical pier had strange consequences. *The Road to Wigan Pier* burned a scar on the face of the town that has not completely healed; it took soul music and one of the greatest underground clubs of all time – Wigan Casino – to give the town a different image.

Wigan had a unique characteristic that helped make the Casino the most popular northern soul club of the seventies: it had two railways stations. From this seemingly banal fact its popularity grew and grew. Wigan North Western served the main line from Glasgow to London, and so stretched from the populous Central Belt of Scotland to the south, making Wigan accessible to millions of people from Motherwell to Rugby within a couple of hours. A couple of hundred yards from the mainline station was Wigan Wallgate, a local station that serviced lines from Manchester, Southport and Kirby. It spread out to a radius of 300 miles and thus accessed a population of ten million or more. The only rare soul club that enjoyed the same accessible rail network was Up the Junction in Crewe, which was tucked away among narrow streets of red-brick terraced houses at walking distance from Crewe railway junction, a powerhouse for steam locomotives and a virtual byword for the British rail system. For the northern soul scene, travel mattered. In an era when cars were scarce, reaching all-nighters by train and coach became essential to the young and largely working-class subculture. At least one rare northern soul song owes its popularity to the rail network. Don Thomas's 'Come On Train' (NUVJ, 1973) was an up-tempo, light funk dancer whose lyrics were often sung by soul fans, much like a terracing chant, as they waited for trains to take them to Wigan Casino, the Pier at Cleethorpes or Blackpool Mecca. (The song was not about railways at all, but the symbolic train of social change that had shaped black American aspiration since slavery – but it had 'train' in the title so that was enough.)

Wigan Casino was the brainchild of Russ Winstanley, a mobile discotheque DJ with a droopy moustache that would have shamed a Mexican gaucho. He was born and raised locally, had visited the Torch sporadically, and ran a successful midweek venue at Newtown British Legion Club. With the closure of the Torch, he convinced the owner of Wigan Casino, Gerry Marshall, that there was a gap in the market and a glaring opportunity for a new all-nighter. Russ was determined and ambitious. He already owned a successful record shop, ran a market stall, and hired out disco equipment to parties and weddings. He was first and foremost a salesman, and from the outset divided opinion on the northern scene. Unlike most soul fans, who had grown up religiously devoted to black music and the styles of the post-Mod era, Winstanley had a more 'chequered' past. He began his musical life as a rock fan and worked as a roadie with Wigan group The Kibbos, who in the early seventies morphed into the pop rock band Rainbow Cottage. Winstanley claims to have sung backing vocals for the band, helped them backstage, and lugged their equipment. His early career as a DJ had spanned the subcultures, too, from heavy metal to glam rock and inevitably to soul. Eclectic tastes were rarely tolerated on the northern soul scene, which by the mid seventies was hardening into a zealous sect with its own strict rules. Russ was undoubtedly in the right place at the right time, but he also had three redeeming features: he was a grafter; he had a natural instinct for what filled a dance floor; and he had found premises that were perfectly suited to northern soul.

At 2 a.m. on Sunday, 23 September 1973, Wigan Casino opened as a soul all-nighter. It was huge, atmospheric and bristling with potential. The wooden floors were made for the sliding harmony of leather shoes, the gigantic balcony provided a unrivalled vantage point where fans could look down on the athletic show below, and the warren of adjoining smaller rooms and bars was a perfect marketplace for record dealers. A decent crowd of 652 was attracted to the opening night via a full-page advert in *Blues & Soul*, but over the weeks a mixture of word of mouth and the accessibility of Wigan via the rail network meant that the Casino attracted crowds nearing 1,500. On the opening night, Russ Winstanley was the only named DJ; when he took short breaks for a piss or a coffee he was replaced by a friend, Ian Fishwick. It was an inauspicious, even amateurish, start to a club that quickly became a legend. Realising he could not continue on such thin resources, Winstanley recruited the ebullient Martyn Ellis, a former Torch DJ, and then Kev Roberts, a precocious teenager from Wirksworth in Derbyshire, who had built up a phenomenal rare soul collection. Ultimately Wigan made its biggest and best DJ booking when Richard Searling from the Pendulum joined the fray. Searling was a connoisseur of rare soul, preferring the rich female vocals of Linda Jones, Lorraine Ellison and Millie Jackson to the careering instrumentals that blared through the night. Searling, from Tonge Fold in Bolton, was already a successful DJ at VaVas, a short-lived all-nighter in Bolton memorable for its mirrored walls and the paranoia they induced in the blocked-up dancers. Bolton had also staged one of the most notorious all-nighters of them all; when the Torch closed, many headed to a tiny venue called Troggs in Farnworth, but the venue could never hope to hold the throng of Torch refugees. A riot ensued and police were called to clear the streets.

Wigan Casino was an electric charge which ignited a key chapter in the story of British youth culture. For some it came to define what northern soul was all about, but for others it did interminable damage by dragging the scene kicking and screaming out of the underground into the garish lights of *Top of the Pops*. However, no one disputes its unique chemistry. Writing in his book *Soul Survivors*, Winstanley described it as 'the special place'. 'People would clap in time with the music at certain points,' he explained. 'When you had a couple of thousand people who clap at a key moment, it sounded like a pistol cracking.' The music was frantic and came with such relentless power that within a matter of a few months the Casino had forced its way to the forefront of the northern scene, attracting dancers – and dealers – from across the north of England.

The Casino was not one club; it was at least three. After a few months, a smaller ballroom located at the front of the balcony led to a dirt box of a room known as Mr M's, which became a venue within a venue, and attracted lesser known DJs playing mostly old sixties soul. It was ferociously hot, like a colonial jail, and was accessed by a small corridor about which many had anxieties. Like the men's toilets downstairs, it was an intimidating place where rip-off merchants and drug gangs congregated. Crews from Wolverhampton, Manchester and Preston were among the most feared, and it was not uncommon to hear of people being 'rolled' – having their money, drugs and even their full-length leather coats ripped off. Ian Melia, a collector from Merseyside and a long-standing northern soul loyalist, often rages against the way Wigan's memory has been sanitised, and is sceptical about the scene's much vaunted 'friendly camaraderie'. 'It might be now,' he argues. 'But I was there [in the seventies] on the scene when record collections were robbed, many people ripped off for their gear, and good hidings given out.'

In his book *Nightshift*, Pete McKenna describes the Wigan toilets as resembling a war zone – 'an absolute fuckin' disaster area

. . . full of people pissing and dealing with water running down the walls and always half an inch of piss covering the tiled floor.'

Looking down from the towering balconies, you felt as if you were looking through a net curtain or through steamed-up glasses – nothing was quite in focus. It was a blur of sheer excitement. At the far end of the main hall was a record bar where collectors gathered to share the latest news about bootlegs, rare records and obscure songs. It was rather like Venice's Rialto, a trading place where genuine dealers, shysters and more than a few passing Shylocks came to swap, barter and sell. Every rare soul record worthy of the name found its way into rows and rows of cardboard shoe boxes and orange crates. It was also an academy of sorts where knowledge was exchanged, history was woven, and great soul singers were praised. Next door to the Casino was yet another venue, the Beachcomber, a place where soul fans went to chill out in the morning. It was a cavernous room – in many respects a holding camp to prevent the asylum seekers of the night from drifting off and causing an uproar in town.

Arriving at Wigan was an energetic scrum. The all-nighter was preceded by a 'normal' disco where the 'divs' fervently danced to Gary Glitter, unaware of the underlying creepiness, and then dispersed, incoherent with drink, to look down on the druggies outside. By 2 a.m. our numbers had swelled, as trains arrived from Scotland, Manchester and the Midlands, along with car pools and hired coaches. By 1973, a small cluster of motorway service stations on the M6 were used as places to change clothes. Over time, they became makeshift clubs with music blaring from cassette recorders, largely gash recordings from famous all-nighters past and present. Places such as Birch Services, Charnock Richard and Knutsford became meeting points for small crews of northern soul fans to mingle and forge friendships that would last a lifetime. Like the convoys of cars that travelled to underground and illegal raves in the eighties, the rituals of northern soul fans often bewildered onlookers and mystified the police. When the doors of the Casino opened, a huge surge of anticipation pushed people forward, all hugging tartan holdalls and old bowling bags to their chests and dragging pals with them as they fought their way up the stairs. Others hung back, coolly, sheltering in shop doorways and in the car park opposite, passing time, dealing drugs, and speaking in a coded language that was sometimes about pharmaceuticals and sometimes rare American labels. It was a rainbow of colours: there were green and clears, blue Stax, Purple Haze, white labels, black bombers, the Detroit Emeralds, red and browns, Laura Greene, Blue Cat Records and purple hearts. It was outside Wigan that I bought a black ivory fist, a Black Power choker that many wore round their necks. I kept it threaded round the handles of my sports bag as a discreet icon of faith, still too stuck in the old ways to wear a necklace.

David Nowell, from Chorley, described Wigan in near photographic accuracy in his book *The Story of Northern Soul.* 'The image lives with me today just like a photographic negative,' he wrote. 'It will hopefully stay locked in my brain until the day I die. Mere words cannot convey the atmosphere, the emotion, the sounds, and the smells. Nor can they adequately explain the passion for the Casino and zest for life that emanated from the dance floor. It was as if everyone was completely locked in to having the greatest night ever.' Once the first few hundred were in, following their preferred routines, rushing to favourite areas of the floor, getting close to the DJs or arranging their boxes in the collectors' room, I would take my place among them. It was always the same place – to the left of the main hall just in front of the DJs' stand, where the acoustics allowed you to hear the sometimes garbled intros of the main DJs, men with thick Lancashire accents who were more interested in breaking new records than improving their elocution.

At the front of the stage, in the land of a thousand dances, friendships developed that in many cases lasted a lifetime. There was Caesar from Leeds, a great dancer with an impeccable taste for fine soul; Guy Hennigan from Skipton, a furtive collector who would be promoted to one of the scene's most revered DJs in years to come; Gaz Kellett, a blocked young diehard from Preston, who went on to lead a rare soul cadre called The Cybermen. Mary Sowter, a petite young beauty, and her friend Ann from Hyde, who both looked too young to be out all night, and probably were. There was Dave Evison, a garrulous ex-soldier from Stoke with an infectious love for old-school, rough-house soul. Dave had a distinctive dance style, and somehow managed to use his leather shoes to clap against the dance floor to the beat of a big tune. There was Lorraine Davies from Stretford, a woman of such elegance she could have been on a fashion shoot and in the genteel words of soulful femininity 'glowed' but was never known to sweat. She had an entire cellar in her family home dedicated to the northern scene with a 'Prescription' counter sign hanging tantalisingly from the ceiling. There was Julie Pender from Heywood in Lancashire who I knew from the Pendulum; Yogi Haughton, a Manchester collector who reversed the path I had trodden and set up home in Scotland; Lesley and Adele from York whose enthusiasm for all-nighters was unbounded and who defied their families to travel far and wide; there was Geoff Grindall from Dumfries, Dave Withers from Manchester, and the legendary Dave Molloy from Farnworth, who was one of a swarm of 'swallows' who hung around near the DJs. Whenever a new record hit the decks, the swallows swooped, straining to gain any detail of what the sound might be – label, artist, colour or even the dialling code in America, which would signify the city the rare soul sound had come from. The atmosphere was unprecedented and knowledge was king, but something profound had happened, too. At Wigan, friends became a new family and in my case they were drawn from all over England, a place I had benignly considered a foreign country.

The Casino's first few years reflected music in flux. Sixties soul was still dominant but the music was fragmenting. The first record ever played at the club was The Sherrys' faux-Motown song 'Put Your Arms Around Me' (J.J. Records, 1967), a home-made soul song produced by a Philadelphia patriarch called Little Joe Cook. His daughter and nieces shared the vocals. The group had gone through several manifestations and in the early sixties had once featured a family friend, the legendary Tammi Terrell. Another familiar play was a brash saxophone-led song called 'Psychedelic Soul' (Thomas, 1968), executed with unruly brilliance by a Chicago taxi-driver called Saxie Russell. It was cast in a style reminiscent of the great Detroit saxophonist Jr Walker and had the same rasping saxophone and gruff hoary voice. 'Psychedelic Soul' was an anthem – a dark acid explosion which was ideally suited to the blocked and belligerent atmosphere of the Casino, and pointed to an underlying tension within soul itself. The sound of the sixties, the platform on which northern soul was founded, was being disrupted by new forms of African-American music: funk, psychedelia and upfront dance music.

Next up was a gifted musician called Leland Michael Postil. He had adopted the name 'Mike Post' and was a Grammy winner for his work with 'Classical Gas', a global hit for classical guitarist Mason Williams. Mike Post went on to a career as a television composer, creating music for *The A-Team*, *The Rockford Files* and *Hill Street Blues*. An unlikely figure to be accepted into the secret brotherhood of northern soul, he was white, bespectacled and raised in the campus town of Berkeley, California – a far cry from the ghetto. His own album *Fused*, released in 1969, stiffed and disappeared from sight, yet tucked away in the deleted album was a high-impact track aimed at the *National Geographic* TV market called 'Afternoon Of The Rhino' (Warner Brothers, 1969), a tune which replicated the stampeding sounds of a crash of rhinoceroses in flight. The sound was perfect for the 'stomping' dance beat that was to become Wigan's trademark. Next was Tony and Tyrone's 'Please Operator' (Atlantic, 1969), a charming piece of novelty sixties soul, in which a frustrated guy asks for a refund from a telephone operator after he has been dumped by a distraught girlfriend. The song was produced by Aretha Franklin's husband, Ted White, who managed to hustle a deal on the back of his hugely successful wife. But it didn't work out for Tony Johnson and Tyrone Pickens; their record only found love on the floor at Wigan. Next, Stanley Mitchell's 'Get It Baby' (Dynamo, 1968) from the conveyor belt of underground soul in Detroit, a filthy get-down R&B record with an intimidating beat which never lets up. And then there was Gloria Jones's 'Tainted Love' (Champion, 1965), an iconic Wigan record made internationally famous by synth pop group Soft Cell, whose members, David Ball and Marc Almond, met at Leeds Polytechnic and were in part brought together by their shared love of northern soul. Gloria Jones's song had everything: a big open sound, siren vocals and group clapping. It had bombed on its release, and, in any case, it was a B-side, but such were the gems of northern soul – overlooked, under-funded or just downright obscure, but always with a careering beat and an enormous sound. Jones witnessed early death and pop myth close up in 1977 when she crashed her Mini near a humpback bridge in Barnes, South London, killing her boyfriend, glam rock star Marc Bolan.

Wigan rapidly became the epicentre of northern soul, and with Russ Winstanley keen to promote it as the biggest soul club in the UK, Station Road, Wigan, became the address most synonymous with the northern scene. Ian Cunliffe disagreed: he was convinced that the centre of northern soul was 29 Cranham Avenue, Lowton, Lancashire. 'Cunny' was a collector, who for two manic years between 1973 and 1975 hired a bungalow in a nondescript street in Lancashire, which to the bewilderment of the neighbours became an unofficial embassy for northern soul. The house was strategically placed for the biggest and best all-nighters: six miles from Wigan Casino, ten miles from Manchester and the site of the dearly departed Twisted Wheel, and fortuitously close to the M6 motorway and clubs across the north. A whole week of rare northern could be reached daily: the Carlton in Warrington on a Wednesday, the Blue Rooms in Sale eight miles away on a Thursday, the Pendulum in Manchester on Friday, and then back to Wigan at the weekend. Soul ruled Cunny's bungalow. It was a gathering place for the waifs, strays and aristocracy of northern soul. It began with a household of four, and before the landlords objected seventeen people were in residence, northern souldiers drawn from the frontline of the rare soul scene. Major DJs often stopped by to rest between all-nighters, but with time the bungalow's notoriety drew the attention of the serious crime squad who targeted the premises after a spate of burglaries at local chemists. One regular visitor was a local man with a reputation that preceded him – Frankie 'Booper' New – by most people's reckoning the best dancer on the northern soul scene.

Northern soul dancers have often been described by the media in condescending terms such as 'the Brut-soaked masses' or the 'all-night throng', as if they were indistinguishable, and known only for their acrobatic style, but they were always individuals with a special status, the equal of DJs and collectors. Booper was as close as it gets to aristocracy. A car mechanic from Widnes, he had acquired his own classic Jaguar and often turned up at Wigan in a dinner suit and briefcase, like a latter-day James Bond, before stripping off to reveal a navy vest and muscular arms. His image could easily have been interpreted as the ultimate pose, but Booper had a night job as a doorman at a 'div club' in Lancashire and came to Wigan directly from work. Booper had won several northern soul dance contests dating back to the Twisted Wheel and had a fearsome reputation on the floor. It was as if NASA had invented a device that could drill into the surface of the moon, and the device was a sixteen-stone guy from Widnes. His spins were achieved by a slight leap in the air, then he'd land like hard metal drilling downwards into the core of the floor. Those who danced near him talk of feeling drops of sweat as he spun furiously through an entire record. Periodically he would acknowledge the sweat by swatting it away without breaking step. He seemed otherworldly – and there was always a hint of menace – but by all accounts he was a decent man whose dancing was more intimidating than his personality. According to Wigan DJ Ian Dewhirst, 'he was one of those guys who had a strong physique, and he used to be one of the guys who would run up to the wall and do back flips off it. He'd do things of such astounding athleticism. Frankie was the king at the Torch.' Dewhirst once told DJ historian Bill Brewster that he'd witnessed a guy dying on the floor at Cleethorpes after a bout of intense spinning. 'They twirl round faster than the eye can see,' he told Brewster. 'I once saw a guy at Cleethorpes get locked into doing one. And when he came to a standstill, blood was coming from his eyes, his nose, his mouth, his ears. He blew up. It was upsetting, because it was right in front of the DJ stand.'

Others followed in Booper's footsteps, often young working-class men who combined dancing with martial arts. Sandy Holt from Bolton became a Muay Thai boxing instructor, and when he won a dance contest in the latter days at Wigan he was on his way to 5th Degree, the equivalent of 5th Dan black belt. Keb Darge from Elgin was a Scottish martial arts champion before he joined the northern soul scene, first as a dancer then subsequently as a major DJ in the eighties. But neither were contemporaries of Booper and never went head to head with him. That job fell to another legendary northern soul dancer, a tiny thin bespectacled guy called 'Matchie' from Rotherham whose real name was Ian Clowery. He had won the Torch's esteemed dance contest, and although he was Booper's physical opposite, he grabbed attention with an array of gravity-defying tricks that featured backdrops, swallow dives and elegant spins driven by purpose rather than power. Others followed the athletic Gethro Jones from Wolverhampton and the elegant Steve Caesar from Leeds, who won the first Wigan Casino dance contest in 1974, turning his back on extreme athleticism for a style that became known on the scene as 'floating' – a more nuanced and inspirational style of dancing that anticipated the shifting musical patterns of modern soul. To those outside the scene the most famous dancer ever was a petite blonde who regularly travelled on a Derby bus to Blackpool Mecca – Jayne Torvill – and would go on to win a gold medal at the 1984 Winter Olympics in Sarajevo with her ice-skating partner Christopher Dean. There she described her world-famous 'Bolero' routine as 'the dance of my life' but that had already happened nearly ten years earlier on the floor of Blackpool Mecca's Highland Room.

If the beginning of the night was hectic, the end was emotionally more subdued: it was regretful, solemn, almost elegiac. By 1975, it had become established practice that all-nighters would finish with '3 before 8': these were three soul songs to mark the end of the night, played as the clock reached 8 a.m. and the morning light sliced through the skylight windows in the decaying roofs of the Casino. The three songs all have a story to tell: they were Jimmy Radcliffe's 'Long After Tonight Is All Over' (Musicor, 1965), Tobi Legend's 'Time Will Pass You By' (Mala, 1968) and Dean Parrish's 'I'm On My Way' (Laurie, 1967). The trio captured the emotional narrative of all-nighters: moving on, the passage of time and reluctant departure.

Jimmy Radcliffe is an unsung hero of African-American progress. In the early sixties he became the first African-American to compose and sing commercial jingles for the burgeoning Madison Avenue advertising industry. It was an industry that was almost entirely white, with a creative power base at the Brill Building on 1619 Broadway, the epicentre of music publishing. Radcliffe worked in a building bustling with creative energy. The singer-songwriter Carole King once told sociologist Simon Frith that it was the intense competition that marked the building out as special: 'Every day we squeezed into our respective cubby holes with just enough room for a piano, a bench, and maybe a chair for the lyricist if you were lucky.' She said in the book *The Sociology of Rock*, 'You'd sit there and write and you could hear someone in the next cubby hole composing a song exactly like yours. The pressure in the Brill Building was really terrific.' The corridors were alive with action: Jewish impresarios rubbed shoulders with Italian-American crooners, and poets worked with hucksters. Few if any were black, and the one that stood out was Jimmy Radcliffe. Fighting a weight problem, Radcliffe knew that the real deal was intellectual copyright and he could make more money writing songs rather than touring on the 'Chitlin' Circuit' of low-value ghetto venues. Radcliffe became the first person to try to combine the burning social messages of the civil rights movement with the output of the Brill Building, and according to his contemporaries he brought Harlem to Broadway, shaping poignant political stories about life in the ghettos. His best compositions – 'Three Rooms With Running Water', 'My Block' and 'Deep In The Heart Of Harlem' – were radical and well before their time. Radcliffe refused to pull any punches, and by the late sixties he had returned to live performance, appearing in residence at the Greenwich Village club Casbah and sharing a stage with The Last Poets. He was increasingly drawn to the politics of Black Power and went on to write protest songs such as his commentary on poverty in Brooklyn, 'Inside Bedford Stuyvesant', and the psychedelic funk protest song '1969'. Changing social attitudes were not lost on Wigan, where some dancers had appropriated the black leather gloves of the Panthers and most soul club badges featured the black fist of solidarity. Tragically Radcliffe did not witness his northern soul success, or even know that 'Long After Tonight Is All Over' had achieved cult status at the Twisted Wheel. He developed complications after a kidney operation and died on 27 July 1973, two months before Wigan Casino opened.

The second last song before 8 a.m. was Tobi Legend's 'Time Will Pass You By' (Mala, 1968), by some distance the most impressive and, in northern soul terms, the rarest of the three. It was unusually poetic for a three-minute pop song and, according to author and journalist Laura Barton, who was born and raised in Newburgh near Wigan, it was a song about 'the preciousness of life'. Writing in the *Guardian*, she said that 'like many pop songs, there's something of the sonnet about "Time Will Pass You By"; it's there in the song's intention of course, but there is something about Legend's track that has always reminded me specifically of Shakespeare's "Sonnet 60".' Putting aside the risks of pretension in comparing northern soul to Shakespeare, Barton quotes the song's memorable refrains: 'I'm just a pebble on the beach and I sit and wonder why/Little people running around/ Never knowing why.' For the dancers of the northern soul scene, a subculture that attracted some phenomenal egos, there is no question that they saw themselves as the 'little people', the 'pebbles on the beach', ordinary people who happened to be in an extraordinary club at an extraordinary time.

Wigan traditionally ended with Dean Parrish's 'I'm On My Way' (Laurie, 1967), an atmospheric pop song about departure and the fleetingness of life – 'you're here today and gone tomorrow'. It was the one I liked least of all, and came not from soul music but from New York's Italian-American lounge bar scene. Dean Parrish was born Phil Anastasi, and might better be described as a crooner rather than a soul singer. Unquestionably a very good record of its kind, it provoked divisions within the scene's deepest purists. Parrish was a white artist and was never someone who militant soul fans at Wigan universally endorsed. Since my days reading African-American history and the story of the blues on the top floor of Hull University library, I was of the unshakeable belief that pop should never be played on the northern soul scene. Much as I love the way that 'I'm On My Way' has gained its status as the 'final record' of the revered '3 before 8', it is not a record I own or really care that much about. Call it snobbery or reverse racism, call it bull-headed purism, but it is great atmospheric pop. It is not great soul. I was not alone, either. In the record room at Wigan, where some of the world's most knowledgeable soul fans gathered, an artist being exposed as white was a near-fatal comment. Any record that was less than good was often met with the reverse racist put-down, 'He's white you know'. It was a criticism often meted out to the discoveries of the club's principal DJ, Russ Winstanley, a rock and pop fan who came to exert a powerful but inconsistent place within the inner sanctums of the scene.

The Lord's Day Observance Society was by now at its angry height, and Wigan was in its sightlines. The society was an organisation with one doctrinaire objective: ensuring that the Sabbath was respected. They targeted places of entertainment from sporting venues to nightclubs, and lobbied them energetically to discourage Sunday opening. The society was losing the long game, but its members were sufficiently organised to lobby MPs, influence local councillors and picket clubs that were undermining Christianity. By 1974, the Casino was high on the hit list. Not only did it open in the small hours of Sunday, it crashed through the Sabbath like a stomping backbeat. Cyril Anderton, Chief Constable of Greater Manchester Police and a keen member of the Lord's Day Observance Society, met routinely with Harold Legerton, the society's General Secretary, and Leslie Yates, their north-west organiser. All three shared the view that 'only acts of necessity and mercy should be permitted' on a Sunday. Anderton loathed all-nighters and had been a prominent figure in the small clique of Christian police officers that had forced the closure of the Twisted Wheel in 1971. Now he was in charge of a sprawling urban area that reached out from central Manchester to Wigan, and he had the final say on police policy and manpower deployment. Ironically his own daughter, Gillian, had attended the Blue Rooms, a short-lived rare soul club in her native Sale, but was forbidden from going to all-nighters; and of course the depraved Wigan Casino was out of bounds.

Initially at least, Anderton's biggest concern was not the Casino but another local institution, Wigan Rugby League Club, which was gearing up to play matches on a Sunday. He had supported the side since his childhood and could recite by heart their greatest teams. He had been at Central Park back in 1952 when a clash with Wakefield Trinity became the first league match to be broadcast on television; he had been at a famous game in 1959 when over 49,000 people packed into the ground to see a game against St Helens, and he regularly travelled on the northern exodus to Wembley to the Challenge Cup Final (once taking off his jacket to assist police quelling crowd trouble). Anderton lobbied Wigan Rugby League Club via the offices of its then Chairman Freddy Pye; their fathers had been close friends and worked on the same shift at a now derelict pit. As his police career took off, Pye made his fortune in the detritus of a dying industrial landscape – scrap metal. Pye had once presented Anderton with a polished miner's lamp engraved with the club's insignia, which was on display in the offices of Greater Manchester Police. Anderton willed Wigan not to succumb to Sunday sport and frequently wrote discouraging letters to other club chairmen in the Rugby League. Paradoxically it was the so-called 'Winter of Discontent' in 1974, rather than an attack on the Sabbath, that forced some football matches to be played on a Sunday. When the national fuel crisis and power cuts hurt hard and fuel had to be rationed, Cambridge FC were forced to entertain visiting northern club Oldham Athletic in a Sunday cup match on 6 January 1974 after power cuts prevented a Saturday kick-off. The floodgates had opened, and all to the detriment of protecting the Sabbath.

In the week that the Twisted Wheel was closed down, the Westminster Parliament debated the Sunday Entertainments Bill (1971), which aimed to make it easier to trade on a Sunday, but the bill was narrowly defeated. The 'distinctive character' of a Sunday was to be protected by law, and so everyone who entered Wigan Casino was required to carry a membership card – a small passport which was coyly marked 'Gents' or 'Ladies' and was sent on application through the post to a home address before entry could be secured. It was cash at the door but only on submission of the card. Such was the scrum to get in, this technicality was frequently overlooked as the young guns of northern soul fought to climb the steep stairs. The impact on Wigan in the early years was measurable. With Anderton driving overall policy in what was known as L-Division, from his HQ in Manchester, police presence at Wigan Casino increased. Officers were regularly stationed at Wigan North Western and Wigan Wallgate stations to intercept northern soul fans as they arrived by train. A team of drug squad officers habitually took up their positions at the top of the stairwell at Wallgate, swooped from shop doorways and randomly targeted club goers. They were dragged in different directions, isolated from each other, and then body-searched, the contents of their holdalls scattered onto the streets. This was not a one-off occasion; it was a ritual. Some took to hiding their amphetamine in stashes inside the station, which they could return to when the squad disappeared. Others hung back at motorway service stations until it was time to drive the final few miles to the Casino. And some took a more pragmatic approach, arriving blocked out of their minds and incapable of being caught in possession.

A local drug squad officer with the barely believable name of Detective Constable Swallow claimed at the time that ninety-eight per cent of the people who attended Wigan were abusing amphetamine; it was an exaggeration but it talked to a wider truth, that speed was rife at all-nighters and it was northern soul's drug of choice.

Dr John Benstead was a Home Office pathologist and a keen golfer. He had little time for the Lord's Day Observance Society and earmarked every Sunday as a day for golf. He had a friendly disposition, lit up rooms with his garrulous smile, and greeted everyone he met with a warm firm handshake. Dr Benstead's social life was conducted in Southport's well-heeled and wealthy society, and he knew next to nothing about Wigan Casino. He was of the considered view that Royal Birkdale was Lancashire's most celebrated club, arguing that it had hosted the Ryder Cup and several open championships, and that he had shaken hands with Arnold Palmer, Lee Trevino and Tom Watson there. After many years as a decent club player, Benstead rose to the hallowed offices of club captain of Royal Birkdale, and when he was on duty there he often wore a carnation in his club blazer – an elegant presence as he strolled through the white art deco clubhouse that looked out like a lighthouse to the Irish Sea.

It was a chilly Monday, 19 May 1975, when Dr Benstead first came across the name of Wigan Casino. He was on Home Office duty, examining the body of a twenty-year-old girl who had been found dead in a house in Widnes. It was a relatively routine examination and he duly reported that the girl had died due to morphine poisoning. For the parents of the dead girl, the death confirmed what they had already suspected: that she had died of an overdose, and that the fatal trail led back to Wigan Casino. The Coroner's Court were unambiguous, too. Her Majesty's Coroner John Hibbert of Cheshire singled Wigan out for special criticism and vowed to investigate the club for himself. Hibbert was a substantial figure in local legal circles who would go onto act for forty years as the region's most senior coroner, eventually presiding over the victims of the IRA bombing of Warrington. Like pathologist Benstead, the Coroner was also an accomplished golfer, frequenting the Astbury Club, in leafy south Cheshire. He was astounded that a club like Wigan Casino could be so lacking in basic rules and regulations, and once asked a colleague if he could see the Casino's articles and memorandum of association, a charmingly naive perspective on northern soul.

The Coroner's Report fanned local reaction; letters of complaint flooded in to the *Wigan Observer*, and police were once again told to intervene. Readers claimed that the local paper was in part to blame, having given too much positive publicity to the all-nighter and acting as a cheerleader for the club's growing fame. In the week that the Coroner's verdict was reported, an anxious parent wrote to the *Wigan Observer*:

Recently I have been disgusted at the articles on the soul nights at the Wigan Casino. These articles have been written in such a manner as to imply to teenagers that they are missing the major event of the year, instead of conveying the much truer picture to them and their parents of the likelihood of being introduced to the drugs scene. I recently have become involved via a very close friend in the horrors of this practice, he having lost approximately three stones in weight in as many months. My fear of his involvement was heightened only recently by the tragic death of a young girl barely out of her teens after a trip to the Casino.

Only this evening were we treated to a nauseating article in your newspaper. I read that the people at the Casino are angry at the imputations of drug taking at their club. I'll bet they aren't as angry as the friends and relatives of the teenagers involved in drug taking.

I only hope that that the police inquiries being started can manage to get this and other places like it closed down.

Andy Wilson kept all the cuttings. He was busy rebuilding his own life, and through a deft mixture of theory and practice went on to become a senior lecturer in Criminology at Trent University and Britain's leading expert on amphetamine abuse. Andy was a northern soul pioneer from Harrogate, who spent much of his formative years at Wigan Casino, and is now a world expert in drug subcultures. He always was.

I first met Andy at a midweek club called the Ebor Suite in York and then again at Wigan. His cropped frizzy hair barely concealed a brilliant mind, and we often spoke through racing tongues at my flat in Rochdale, or in railway stations in the Manchester area. Unusually for an academic, Andy Wilson had more than passing practical experience of his subject. He was a northern soul diehard, a decent dancer and a young man who travelled weekly to Wigan where he rubbed shoulders with some the scene's least savoury characters. He has since traced a challenging narrative of drug abuse on the northern soul scene, one which cites Wigan Casino as a key staging post. In the early years, Mod drugs such as Drinamyl or the so-called 'purple hearts' were under the control of pharmacists, but Wilson claims that further draconian controls had dramatic and unforeseen consequences. He knew from his nocturnal field research that chemists who followed the letter of the law usually locked amphetamines in secure cabinets, and tended to store them alongside other banned drugs such as heroin and other opiates. When chemists were burgled to access amphetamines, the raiders inevitably also stole opiates. Wilson then traces a frightening scenario where 'cranking' – injecting and mainlining drugs – enters the once 'pristine' pill-popping northern soul scene. He personally charts the death of more than ten northern soul fans from across the north of England who he claims were 'mixing the medicine'. Wigan's toilets and the doorways along Station Road were testament to the theory: discarded needles or 'works' were often abandoned by 'crankers' with little interest in concealment.

The police inquiry into Wigan Casino lasted for months. New pressure was put on the management to improve scrutiny, but by April 1975, Wigan had over 100,000 members and the management had to temporarily suspend membership because of complaints about overcrowding and heightened police pressure. New door staff and security were employed, and the Wigan drug squad insisted on being kept in touch with the Casino's all-nighter plans. Coroner John Hibbert was true to his word and visited the Casino, taking notes as he watched from the balcony, mesmerised by the dancers on the floor below, but pathologist John Benstead filed his notes and moved on to his next case. Later in the winter of 1975, he was called away from Royal Birkdale to Preston Royal Infirmary where the bludgeoned body of a twenty-six-year-old alcoholic woman had been admitted. Her corpse had been found in a lock-up garage near Preston town centre, and it was presumed she had been battered to death. The dead woman was Joan Harrison, an early victim of Peter Sutcliffe, the Yorkshire Ripper, whose psychopathic reign of terror was casting a dark shadow over the heartlands of northern soul.

Hundreds of northern soul fans began their Saturday night at Blackpool Mecca and travelled on to Wigan all-nighters on free coaches provided by the Mecca organisation. The company laid on the coaches to shuttle people to and from the Mecca, and the returning coaches to Wigan Casino were frequently packed with soul fans hustling a free ride. The Casino and the Mecca had much in common, but such was the intensity of the northern soul scene, they came to be compared unfavourably with each other. Wigan ran all night and had a lawless and atmospheric reputation; the Mecca closed early and came to be known as a place for connoisseurs – it was a pint of bitter versus a glass of fine wine.

By 1975, the two clubs were seemingly at war. To understand what lay behind the disputes you have to understand one of northern soul's most complex and talented characters, DJ Ian Levine. Ian Levine always stood out. In a scene that was principally working-class, he had grown up the son of a Blackpool casino entrepreneur and had access to considerable personal wealth. He travelled extensively to America where his family had business interests and holidayed every year in Florida, spending his spare time miles from the beach searching down old record shops, hunting through warehouses and striking deals to buy deleted vinyl. Levine was a fanatic. The record dealer John Anderson, who had a trove of great records stored in his purpose-built farmyard in King's Lynn, Norfolk, tells of nights when he would wake up, look out through the curtains to remote rural roads, only to see Ian Levine slumped in his car, waiting for the dawn to break.

As a teenager, Levine embarked on the near impossible task of collecting every African-American soul record in the world, and from childhood was a world authority on the BBC science fiction drama *Dr Who*, devoting a lifetime to collecting scripts and television memorabilia, and tracking down lost episodes of the show. He rarely approached anything half-heartedly and had a savant's capacity for storing information, listing records and keeping tabs on rare records. He began as a collector at the Twisted Wheel, and briefly had a DJ slot at the Torch, but from the tender age of seventeen, it was at Blackpool Mecca that he stood out. Levine was the polar opposite of Wigan's Russ Winstanley in terms of their attitudes to what was best for northern soul. Winstanley was a pop fan who unsurprisingly assumed that the DJ's job was to fill the floor and keep the maximum number of dancers happy; Levine saw his role as an educator, breaking new sounds, digging deeper for classics and staying loyal to records that needed time to make an impact. He was not afraid to 'clear the floor' and allow a great record to play even when no one was dancing. It was a policy that needed bull-headed determination, and to this day his legacy lives on in several DJs who take a masochistic pride in clearing the dance floor.

Two distinct trends were beginning to emerge: Wigan was a citadel of great sixties soul, while the Mecca was favouring newer and more recent seventies sounds. At the turn of the decade, soul music had gone through profound change; the synthesiser was in more common use, the traditional on-the-fours dance beat was being displaced by funkier and edgier beats, and the roots of what became disco were springing up. It was against this background of change that Wigan invited Ian Levine to join them as a guest DJ. It was a controversial decision, and there was tangible tension on the dance floor. Some dancers booed Levine, and others wore hastily produced badges declaring 'Levine Must Go'. It was often described much like 'the shock of the new', but it was never a simple schism between old and new. Among Levine's records at the time were releases that pointed forward to the many tributaries that soul music would follow in the years to come. One record by the Delreys Incorporated, 'Destination Unknown' (Tampete, 1971), a thundering indie record from Miami, looked forward to street funk; Valentino's 'I Was Born This Way' (Gaiee, 1975) was one of the first ever gay disco records; Oscar Perry's 'I Got What

You Need' (Peritone, 1975) replicated the sweeter soul sounds of Philadelphia International; and East Coast Connection's 'Summer In The Parks' (New Directions, 1976) was the earliest example of Washington Go-Go. The band impersonated Kool and the Gang, Earth, Wind and Fire, and 'D.C.s own Soul Searchers' in a pounding piece of whistle funk which stretched northern soul into a new and much disputed era.

Some at Wigan resented the new directions; others understood that to stay alive the music needed to change. DJ Colin Curtis, who shared the decks with Levine at the Mecca, has described their partnership as overseeing 'a mammoth period' in the progressive history of northern soul. Battle lines were drawn. Wigan's Russ Winstanley instructed the club's DJs that two particular Mecca records were to be banned from Wigan's turntables. They were Boby Franklin's 'The Ladies Choice Part 1' (Fee Records, 1973), a modern record from a small local Detroit label struggling to survive in the first city of soul, and Snoopy Dean's 'Shake And Bump' (Blue Candle, 1974), a Miami funk rarity which tried to cash in on the US ghetto dance craze, the bump. Another Wigan DJ, John Vincent, has since claimed that he was discouraged from playing a third record, The Pointer Sisters' 'Send Him Back' (Atlantic, 1972). It was a curious state of affairs and smacked of soul censorship, but many supported the ban, preferring a life of unfettered sixties soul. Another petition tried to ban the DJ Martin Barnfather, aka Soul Sam, from the Wigan roster, too. His crime was playing 'too much funk'.

Paradoxically Miami funk was to feature in one of Wigan Casino's most memorable nights. On 26 April 1975, Miami singer Betty Wright was booked for a live concert featuring a visiting fourteen-piece band. The traditional all-nighter was to be extended by two hours until 10 a.m. the following day and a forty-piece soul show band was to back the singer. April showers broke and rain poured down on the massive crowd outside. One by one, the drenched dancers took to the floor, gradually edging forward to get closer to the stage and creating a log jam of bodies as if it was a punk gig. A mosh pit clustered at the front edge of the stage, and many more unable to get a good view streamed up the two stairwells to watch from the balcony.

Betty Wright wore a stunning full-scale afro which seemed to exaggerate her size. She was born Bessie Regina Norris in Miami and had been singing under her stage name since childhood. Wright had recorded for several Miami labels such as Alston and Dade, both already known to northern soul collectors, and finally recorded for TK Records, a Miami institution owned by local executive Henry Stone. A bearded white man who had the demeanour of Colonel Sanders of the Kentucky Fried Chicken chain, Stone had relationships that led back to northern soul; he had sold records in bulk to the celebrated English soul dealer John Anderson but he also knew DJ Ian Levine, who since adolescence had been knocking on doors in Miami. Stone enjoyed success. Betty Wright had introduced him to George and Gwen McCrae. George McCrae's global hit 'Rock Your Baby' had been released the previous year, and Stone's warehouse man and sometime receptionist KC Casey – who had dealt with a demanding Ian Levine on several occasions – formed a band called KC and the Sunshine Band, who bagged an international hit with 'Blow Your Whistle'. Casey has since admitted that music gave him a good living but he would have been richer if he had a dollar for every time a northern soul collector had walked into the warehouse asking for a copy of the Twans' record. Obscure local group The Twans had long since been forgotten, but their record 'I Can't See Him Again' (Dade, 1967) was a reckless Motown-style dance record with all the ingredients of classic northern soul: up-tempo beat, gospel chorus and dog rare. Worth thousands of pounds in years to come, it was already a near impossible record to find for even the most intrepid and resourceful collectors.

Betty Wright took to the stage in the early hours. It was a memorable performance and every bit as historic as Major Lance's live show at the Golden Torch in 1972. Many hundreds were locked out. Michael Hutchinson from Sale had left it late and spent the night wandering around a Wigan housing scheme; others had been accommodated in the spill over at the Beachcomber. When a live group came to Wigan – something I was never keen on – I would go upstairs to look down on the crowds and the stage below. The place I normally danced – and where I was photographed with Julie Pender from Heywood – was by now rammed with people. Julie had travelled on 'the Fearless 400', Selnec's Trans-Pennine Express, a bus route that brought hundreds to Wigan from East Lancashire. Now a grandmother, Julie describes it as 'the best night ever' and remembers Betty Wright 'bringing the house down'. It was phenomenal, certainly the best live act I have ever seen. Her tour came on the back of a stunningly good modern soul album called *Danger High Voltage*, which spawned three different songs all played at Wigan – 'Love Don't Grow On A Love Tree', 'Where Is The Love' and the electric 'Shoorah! Shoorah!', later covered by Joss Stone. The big songs from Betty Wright's set were already known to the fanatical crowd and the response was evangelical, too raucous by far for the Lord's Day Observance Society but a religious experience of sorts. It was a personal triumph for Russ Winstanley and secured the Casino's reputation as the UK's most passionate soul venue, but it also proved Ian Levine's point. Soul was changing. Betty Wright's brand of Miami funk was one of the new strands of a soul heritage that simply refused to settle. In the 'hidden' music of Little Beaver, Timmy Thomas and Clarence Reid, there was more to come. Betty finally left the stage exhausted and triumphant. She had looked out on a crowd almost entirely white and working-class. Off stage, she was lost for words. Drifting into her own satisfied coma she could only say a single word – 'Wow!' It was the greatest live show of her life too.

Something had changed. As much as there were people within the northern soul scene who wanted time to stand still in the glorious soul of the late sixties, that was never likely to happen. In the aftermath of Betty Wright's show, the term 'modern soul' entered the bulging vocabulary of the northern scene; its advocates would grow confidently with time and the new style would become the core of more disputes yet to come. Rather than allow emotions to cool down, Ian Levine continued to proselytise on behalf of the new music, and his personality – never less than emotional – often led him to overstate his case. He refused to pour oil on troubled waters and at the mountainous peak of the scene declared in his own inimitable style that northern soul was dead, saying infamously that 'the Casino was a wonderful place, but the longer it went on, the worse the music became . . . some of the stuff they played at Wigan had nothing to do with northern soul.' It was a putdown that harboured some truths but provoked Russ Winstanley, a more conservative and bluntly straightforward man. Protective of his achievements, Winstanley argued a rearguard defence of the atmospheric sounds of the Casino and damned Levine with faint praise, claiming in his later years that when people came up to him in the DJ decks they never asked for Mecca sounds, only the sixties stompers of Wigan Casino. Within ten years, Russ Winstanley was a nostalgia DJ playing at oldie venues and Levine, pursuing his passion for metropolitan disco, was a DJ at the infamous gay nightclub Heaven and a pioneer of hi energy dance music. They were men destined never to agree.

By 1977, the shimmer of Wigan's brilliance shone less brightly. It still had the lead as an all-nighter, but something of its unique charisma was fading, and in the words of one of its most cherished rare soul DJs, Richard Searling, the Casino had become guilty of 'dumbing down'. Russ Winstanley was proud of Wigan and proud of his definitive collection of 45s on the famous Cameo-Parkway label. Based in Philadelphia, the label was closely connected to the American network television show *American Bandstand,* which became a route to commercial success for its artists. Cameo-Parkway was a promiscuous label; across time it released doo-wop, rockabilly, garage rock and novelty records. Soul was part of its story, but it was a musical ragbag and never consistent in its approach to black American music. Bizarrely Cameo-Parkway's biggest international hit came courtesy of a local poultry-farm worker, Ernest Evans aka Chubby Checker, whose novelty record 'The Twist' spearheaded the greatest dance craze ever. It was Chubby Checker's less well-known stormer 'You Just Don't Know (What You Do To Me)' (Cameo-Parkway, 1966) that attracted attention on the northern soul scene. Russ Winstanley had a formidable record collection, built in part by his connections in America, his own record stall, and his privileged access to the decks at Wigan. Alongside its soul releases, Cameo-Parkway also promoted garage rock, the raw and untutored sound rehearsed in suburban garages. The more northern soul collectors delved into warehouse crates, the more they came across obscure garage. Wigan began to promote garage rock within its increasingly bizarre play list, often prioritising danceability over pure soul. Suddenly bands like The Outsiders from Cleveland, The Avengers from upstate New York, and particularly The Human Beinz, from Youngstown, Ohio, with their explosive 'Nobody But Me' (Capitol, 1968), were featured alongside records by soul legends like Jerry Butler, Joe Tex and Sam Dees. Some saw the garage intrusion as simply great dance music with bags of attitude; others saw it as further capitulation. Back in the autumn of 1974, Russ had acquired an obscure record by The Chosen Few called 'Footsee' (Roulette, 1968). It was a bubblegum pop song launched to coincide with a craze for a Canadian toy called the Footsee (kids would jump over a rope-and-plastic device tied to their foot). The song was infantile and had nothing remotely to do with soul, but it had an irritating familiarity and became one of those tunes that stuck uninvited in your mind. Russ later wrote: 'The people who went to the Casino absolutely loved it. They almost jumped off the balconies to dance to it.' He was right, but 'Footsee''s success disguised another deeper reaction: many felt the song trivialised northern soul, and attitudes towards Wigan were now souring. Unknown to many collectors on the scene, plans were afoot to release 'Footsee' in the UK, and the plans had hit a snag when the original producer, Ken Ayoub, could not be traced. It was decided to re-record the song using car horns and crowd noises reputedly dubbed from the Everton v. Sheffield Wednesday Cup Final in 1966. In his book *Cider with Roadies*, journalist and soul fan Stuart Maconie dismissed 'Footsee' as an 'embarrassing novelty'.

There was worse to come. From his days as a roadie, Russ Winstanley met with a local white pop group called Sparkle, a cross between the Bay City Rollers and Mud, and encouraged them to record northern soul cover versions. On Thursday, 20 March 1975, a date etched like a horrific murder in the minds of northern soul fans, Wigan's Ovation appeared on *Top of the Pops* singing an old Torch classic, 'Skiing In The Snow' by The Invitations (dynoVoice, 1966). The group were dressed in exaggerated baggy trousers and T-shirts adorned with soul patch badges. It was the first time many people had become acquainted with the term 'northern soul' and unfortunately the clichés stuck like a demeaning glue. For the underground hardcore, it was a dire time – 'our Vietnam flashback moment', as Mike Mason, a Scottish northern soul collector put it. 'A fucking travesty', according to Dave Molloy. In extremis this was the night that Wigan Casino died, or more accurately the night that the club's first generation fell out of love with a place that had defined their life. Paul Mason from Leigh, who went on in life to become an economics correspondent for the BBC and Channel 4, had fallen in love with Wigan Casino before going to university and saw it as a landmark in his life. But it was not the crassly commercial Wigan's Ovation he remembered. 'Listen to Gene Chandler's "There Was A Time" [Brunswick, 1968],' he wrote in the magazine *Vice*. 'Gene is whining a filthy, innuendo-laden lament to the fact that all the old dance styles are out of fashion, when suddenly the band's trumpet player starts screaming out the top note of a major seventh chord, which never stops. We were using the black industrial music of the late sixties to say something about our white industrial lives in the seventies.'

Time was passing Wigan by. More dismal records found their way on to the turntables at the Casino, the theme tunes from *Joe 90* and *Hawaii Five-0* by The Ventures among them. The beat was right but the tone was catastrophically wrong. The more that Russ Winstanley pushed the Wigan brand, marketing badges, running anniversary nights, and overseeing more UK releases, the more the club's reputation for unearthing underground material relied on the formidable taste of Richard Searling. Searling was caught in the middle of various feuds throughout his career and tried to follow the righteous path. A rare record collector who had abandoned teacher training to DJ, he was a fan of Motown's archetypal sixties soul group The Originals, and yet was an early advocate of the big voices of seventies soul, among them Jean Carne and Loleatta Holloway. His play list at Wigan was mostly faithful to soul, and through a close relationship with master dealer John Anderson at Soul Bowl, he launched many classics: 'Heartaches And Pain' by Pages (Sunstruck, 1979), a modern indie soul dancer from Ann Arbor in Michigan; a double-sided obscurity by John and the Weirdest 'Can't Get Over These Memories/No Time' (Tie, release date unknown); and Don Gardner's 'Cheatin' Kind', a rare and long overlooked sixties song (Sedgrick, 1969).

Dave Molloy remembers the night he first heard John and the Weirdest; unlike the rest of us, it was before its debut at Wigan. He was travelling north by car with Richard Searling to a gig at Clouds in Edinburgh. Nervous that they might be stopped by the police, Richard had insisted that Dave get rid of any illegal substances, which he did in a oner. Halfway to Edinburgh, they stopped in a lay-by for a piss just as Richard played a cassette he had received from John Anderson. The opening bars of John and the Weirdest kicked in, as did the amphetamine, and Dave remembers looking up over Lockerbie at dancing clouds and a speeding sky. It was a moment of epiphany and he knew instantly that it would become a northern soul classic.

My favourite night of all at Wigan involved a transaction between Richard and his soul supplier. The date was 4 June 1977, the day that Scotland's Tartan Army tore down the Wembley goalposts and dug up England's hallowed turf. I had travelled down to the game and had spent the day before at Soul Bowl in King's Lynn buying records – one of them was sold to me on condition that I leant it to Richard to play at Wigan. The record was Othello Robertson's 'So In Luv' (Baby Luv, 1967). Handing the record over was a special moment. I had carried it with me on a drunken and rebellious train from London, and in my holdall was the record and a slice of Wembley turf that was finally planted in my mum's back garden in Perth. It is still a great rare soul record, but on that famous night in 1977 it was played at Wigan with the scent of hallowed turf and Scottish victory.

Wigan's biggest asset was its reputation. The influential industry magazine *Billboard* declared Wigan the club of the year, a scalp it took from Larry Levan's phenomenal Paradise Garage, in New York. But that reputation was gradually being tarnished by an obsession with oldies and a desire to squeeze juice from the pockets of its followers. As the seventies unfolded, what Searling describes as 'dumbing down' and 'over-exposure' began to erode the Casino's status. Unlike the Mods and rockers, the hippies and latterly the punks, northern soul shunned attention, but suddenly journalists and television producers had discovered the best-kept secret of British youth culture. Granada's television cameras came into Wigan under the direction of Tony Palmer, a multi-award-winning director who had previously made films about theatre and opera. He had produced high art portraits of Maria Callas and Margot Fonteyn, and pop documentaries on The Beatles, Cream and Jimi Hendrix. Palmer was a graduate of Cambridge and an apprentice to the notorious film-maker Ken Russell. He loved music but was mystified and intrigued by northern soul in equal measure. In a gesture of democracy, Mike Walker, the Casino's manager, interrupted the all-nighter and asked the dancers at Wigan for a show of hands – did they want cameras at Wigan or not? It was a simple referendum, far from scientific, and hands were hard to count in the dark. Many had not heard the question and still more were in another room in Mr M's sweating away to great sixties soul. On balance, the vote was against the cameras being allowed in but after overtures from Granada executives a documentary on the Wigan Casino phenomenon was given the green light. Hypocritically, for someone who was to go on and build a career in television, I was among the most vociferous to not admit cameras. The media had been unkind to other subcultures including the skinheads, Mods and punks, and it was not to be trusted with the more precious metal of northern soul.

Steve Whittle, a DJ at Wigan's famed oldies room Mr M's, has since claimed that the film was a diabolical mistake. 'The TV show was a bad decision on the management's part. They went back on their word not to let the cameras in.' It was a compromise too far for some. *This England: Wigan Casino* was broadcast in prime-time on Monday, 12 December 1977, and predictably divided opinion. For those who had never seen northern soul dancers it was a revelation. For the northern soul fans who had watched cringing through their fingers Wigan's Ovation on *Top of the Pops* it at least offered genuine insights and familiar faces; but for the people of Wigan, long tired of Orwell's dark satanic imagery, it was another stab in the town's heart. To flesh out his tight shooting schedule, Palmer had leant heavily on Granada's archive and added smouldering furnaces, decaying coalfields and derelict canals – overwrought historical imagery that the citizens of Wigan had long since tired of. Only when the relentless beat of The MVP's 'Turning My Heartbeat Up' (Buddha, 1974) took over the soundtrack could fans recognise Wigan's seething dance floor. Bolton rare soul collector Dave Withers appeared to emphasise a point that is often missed about northern soul: 'To get enjoyment out of life,' he said, 'people have to build more or less an alternative society just to enjoy themselves.' What he did not say was that the more Wigan was dragged into the mainstream of prime-time documentaries and chart shows, the more that alternative society began to behave like any other pop culture.

Wigan was in mortal danger of compromising its integrity by trading its 'secret' reputation for fame. Soul Sam, another of northern soul's big-name DJs, had grown to loathe the way that Wigan was dominating the scene. In a candid interview, he told the Wolverhampton collector Dave Shaw that Wigan had betrayed the north's core values. 'The Casino management thought that the way ahead for the scene was to bring it to the attention of the nation. This may have been financially successful, and indeed might have brought new blood onto the scene, but in my opinion it was bad for northern soul. What happened was the people being attracted to the scene through its media coverage began to turn it into a dance scene, not a soul scene.'

Wigan's heyday coincided with worldwide recession. Britain's economy was fragile, unemployment rose above the million mark, and the government was forced to call in the International Monetary Fund for a humiliating bail-out. According to Russ Winstanley, it was the economy rather than musical policy that forced the closure of the Casino. 'The club had suffered tremendously from the recession,' he told the local press. 'On Saturdays we once had over a thousand regularly turning up, but recently it's dropped to around six hundred.' Winstanley said he could not see the economic recession lifting and that it would be 'impossible to carry on in the present circumstances'. Whatever the underlying causes, overexposure was suffocating the Casino, and so too was the overbearing policy of oldies revival night. The venue had extended its reach to include Friday all-nighters and frequently announced self-serving anniversaries, mostly driven by revenue rather than reputation. Then, damagingly in 1979, it tried to cash in on the Mod revivalist boom triggered in part by the release of the film *Quadrophenia*, and continued to plumb new depths of obscure pop, some passable as faux soul, others truly execrable, such as the inexplicable decision to play Barry Gray's 'Theme From Joe 90', which might have worked at a kitsch fancy-dress party but was a demeaning moment for the collectors of northern soul. Dave Shaw raged against the betrayals in his short monograph *Casino*: 'I will never forgive Russ for playing reggae and ska during a regular Saturday all-nighter, just to appease a bunch of time-warped posers in fancy dress. To us it was like finding a McDonald's at the top of Mount Everest, it cheapened the experience of getting there.'

New faces arrived on the scene – not all of them committed to the unwritten principles of northern soul and the term. 'Purists not tourists' were an unflinching hardcore, set against those hitching themselves to the latest bandwagon. Wigan had run out of steam and its brilliance had come to a stuttering end. When the local council announced plans to build a new civic centre and placed a compulsory purchase order on the building, many had already drifted away to family life, to the jazz funk scene, or to other all-nighters like Yate near Bristol, a much loved venue in Gloucestershire. Wigan Casino was by now struggling to make money and the days of all-night brilliance were over. At times, only a few hundred diehards turned up; others, furious with perceived betrayals, refused to return. A last night was advertised under the banner 'The End of an Era' and most people who had the club at their heart returned. I travelled north from London with Steve Caesar, Simon Andrews and Lorraine Davies – all now exiled in London – but it was a journey with mixed feelings: nostalgia for a great place, which at its early height was the best northern soul club ever, but also frustration at the way it had been abused by the management. There was also a distinct sepia tone to the proceedings. Wigan had become fixated with oldies, playing great records from the past too often and to the detriment of new discoveries. The legendary Mecca DJ Colin Curtis had the same feeling. Several years before, outside Mr M's, which in an act of cringing deference had been named after the Casino's boss Mr Gerry Marshall, he recalled feelings of doubt. 'I remember sitting there on its opening night, and saying, "This is the beginning of the end of northern soul." I felt that regurgitating all this stuff again for people who didn't want to move on was such a retro move.' John Williams, hardcore soul fan from Anglesey in North Wales, wrote furiously to the weekly newspaper *Black Echoes*. 'What an anticlimax . . . I believe the people who run the place are now only interested in ripping people off and pocketing as much money as they can before the place finally closes on October 2, and that Wigan Casino will be remembered as a great all-nighter, not as a venue associated with ripping off as it is now beginning to appear.'

The Casino's reputation deteriorated with the building itself, and when it finally closed it was deemed a serious health risk. After several false endings, the final Wigan Casino all-nighter in December 1981 ended with the now overplayed but insurmountable 'Do I Love You (Indeed I Do)' by Frank Wilson (Soul, 1965). Much like the final days of the Torch, a fire devastated the derelict Casino, and the building was finally demolished in late 1981. Wigan Council never did build the new civic centre, and the site became a car park, then a faceless shopping centre. Wigan had survived hostile policing, drug deaths and local complaint but it could not survive its own overexposure. Now, the ground that was once the hallowed floors of northern soul's super-club is a sad café, with tacky memorabilia adorning the walls.

Late in 1981, a new club opened in Wigan, carrying the provocative George Orwell-inspired name – Wigan Pier. Greg Wilson's weekly jazz funk club featured two of the northern soul scene's top DJs, Colin Curtis from the Mecca and Richard

Searling from Wigan, both of whom remained lovers of modern soul in all its forms. Northern soul was in crisis; the scene was staring oblivion in the face. Many moved on, others gave up completely, and some like myself drifted south to London – already a different country – where job opportunities were greater. But some of the scene's most prominent personalities stayed firm and believed that the only way northern soul could survive was by returning to its underground roots. And so it proved. The challenge of rebuilding northern soul fell to the Top of the World in Stafford, which not only became the home of the new underground, but in time the club that resurrected northern soul from the dead.

Second-generation skinheads call for the
Yorkshire Ripper to be hanged, Dewsbury, 1981.
© ANL/REX/Shutterstock

5
RED RIDING
WEST YORKSHIRE, 1973–1981

The rivalry between Leeds and Bradford, two cities whose western and eastern suburbs have long been hopelessly entangled, is so ancient and so fierce as to preclude either place surrendering its identity to the other. Both prospered from worsted and woollen manufacturing throughout the nineteenth century, and vied with each other to erect the grand houses and prestigious civic monuments that, even a hundred and fifty years later, still loaned them the same air of unshakeable Victorian solidity.

Somebody's Husband, Somebody's Son, Gordon Burn
(Faber & Faber, 1984)

Steve Caesar had won the first Wigan Casino dance contest in 1974 and it gave him a sprinkle of fame in a closed community. His approachable and charismatic personality set him apart from some of the more surly stars of the scene, and our friendship would stretch over decades. Now a security officer at ITV in London, he remembers holding on to the cash prize the next morning, exhausted and vulnerable, in the Beachcomber, fearful he would be robbed. Caesar was a young black man from Leeds, a lithe elegant guy with a welcoming smile and a taste for fashion, who had taken to wearing a ghetto cap borrowed from the cover image of Curtis Mayfield's *Back To The World* (Curtom, 1973). Although he lived in Leeds, and was on the pitch at Wembley to celebrate Don Revie's 'Damned United' winning the centenary cup final over Arsenal, he had been born in St Kitts in the West Indies. He was passionate about the tiny Caribbean island, which has a population of only 45,000, and it proved to be an important source of identity for him. Caesar was raised in a prodigiously talented family; his brother Pogus is a major social photographer in Birmingham who has catalogued the reggae scene and the city's multicultural community better than anyone; and another brother, Imruh Caesar, is a celebrated afrocentric film director.

Steve Caesar was a well-known face at Wigan, Blackpool Mecca and Cleethorpes Pier, but it was at his local club, Leeds Central, that he was best known. He'd discovered rare soul at Leeds Mecca where DJ Hunter Smith departed from the mainstream to play sounds by Syl Johnson, Jerry Butler and Maxine Brown. Throughout his teenage years, he lived in a respectable Christian household in Reginald Place, in the heart of Chapeltown, the biggest multicultural neighbourhood in the city. The Caribbean-born population in Britain as a whole had grown from 17,218 in 1951 to peak at 304,070 in 1971. The neighbouring city of Bradford had been a magnet for immigrants, too, but it had a different social composition: in the sixties, about a third of Bradford's workforce were employed in the wool textile industry, and the biggest single immigrant group were from West Pakistan (many from a single region, Mirpur District in Kashmir). There followed an era of chain migration which brought extended families to Yorkshire, too, and by 1970 the electoral wards of University and Manningham had the highest concentration of immigrants in the north of England. Most were from the Asian subcontinent and many of them were Muslim. These two cities, merging into each other and sharing a regional airport, were to become the stalking ground of the most infamous serial killer in modern Britain – Peter Sutcliffe.

Sutcliffe operated in the red light areas of the decaying old mill towns, and his span of attacks, which stretched from 1969 to 1981, paralleled the heyday of northern soul. The resultant fear that gripped Yorkshire had a profound impact on the lives of thousands. The police launched an ultimately chaotic murder inquiry headed by West Yorkshire's Chief Constable, Ronald Gregory, who in the months before the Ripper's first murder had infiltrated a gang of Huddersfield soul boys accused of transporting amphetamine to Wigan Casino. At the time Gregory was one of Britain's most respected police officers but the Ripper inquiry would lay waste to his reputation and those of the overstretched detectives under his command.

Leeds Central Soul Club was tucked away in a basement near the Lower Briggate in the city centre. Like the Pendulum in Manchester and the Catacombs in Wolverhampton, it had the feel of a speakeasy; more intimate and claustrophobic than the superclubs at Wigan Casino and Cleethorpes Pier, it was important enough to set fashions that spread to the bigger clubs. The tight steps led steeply down onto the dance floor, which had the character of a Manhattan loft. Industrial pillars propped up the roof, and in a patch in front of the DJ some of the best northern soul dancers met and 'trained'. One fleeting member of the dance alumni at Leeds Central was a stunning mixed-race girl called Helen Rytka, who went there for a short while with her twin sister Rita. They would dance together at the bottom of the

Central's steep staircase: thin, young and vulnerable. Within a matter of a few months, their names would dominate newspapers throughout Britain as the hunt for the Yorkshire Ripper reached frenzied proportions.

Leeds Central faithfully followed the evolution of black dance music in Britain from early Mod-inspired R&B through commercial sixties soul, to northern soul, to modern northern, to underground disco, and ultimately to jazz-funk. It survived nearly two decades in the UK alternative club scene and was variously a Friday all-nighter and feeder club that sent soul missionaries to the Twisted Wheel, the Golden Torch, Wigan Casino and Cleethorpes. Many northern soul clubs came and went, some burned brightly for a few years and then sputtered out, but few lasted the pace quite like Leeds Central. It was the north's great soul survivor, and if its heavily varnished wooden walls could talk they would be a towering authority on soul.

In a sense, the art of being a DJ started in Leeds and dated back to the declining days of the old ballroom era. In the early forties, the local dance-hall manager was one Jimmy Savile. He was born in the city in 1926 and was a 'Bevin boy', one of the young men conscripted into employment under the instructions of Ernest Bevin, Minister of Labour with the wartime coalition government. Savile was sent to South Kirby Colliery thirty miles south of Leeds and lived in pit barracks there. At the time, record players were uncommon but they were becoming commercially available in high street shops and soon became cheaper than hiring a dance band. At the Grand Records Ball at the Guardbridge Hotel in 1947, Savile made history when he became the first entertainer to 'double-deck', using two turntables and a microphone. The night was billed 'Jimmy Savile introducing Juke Box Doubles' and it was the blueprint on which subsequent northern soul clubs were based. As Savile's reputation grew, he became a performer at the Old Mecca in County Arcade, which at weekends hosted a club called the Spinning Disc. By 1965, it was opening on Saturday mornings, replicating the successful Saturday morning cinema sessions for ABC minors. Savile's flamboyant personality made him a star attraction and children innocently flocked to him. By the afternoon, the Spinning Disc grew up and became a teenage venue with Savile handing over to Pete 'Tamla' Brent. Brent remembers the venue attracting live acts from the black American touring circuit, including Gino Washington, Edwin Starr, Eddie Floyd and Ben E King. Steve Luigi, who went on to be a Leeds Central DJ, was a regular and told me: 'I was a Mod and used to go there on my scooter [a Lambretta] and dance to the "Motown" that was played there, I particularly remember The Isley Brothers' "Behind A Painted Smile", which was played every week. This was the first nightclub I ever set foot in, and it led to me being smitten, to the point of spending the next fifteen years being into northern soul.'

Savile's career blossomed, and national bookings took him inexorably away from Tamla Motown in Leeds towards the pop mainstream and eventually on to darker stardom. But other venues resisted the pop path and dug deeper into the mines of blues and soul. The Three Coins, an R&B and early Modernist hangout, tucked away in Albion Walk amidst a warren of old mill buildings, played imported records on primitive DJ decks and attracted live acts such as Memphis Slim, John Lee Hooker, Dave Berry and Georgie Fame. Tony Banks, an influential record collector in the city, was the DJ at the Three Coins and graduated to become one of the founding DJs at Leeds Central. In patterns much like Manchester, younger Modernists met and mingled in a network of Italian café bars in the centre of Leeds, including the Del Rio in Lower Basinghall Street and La Conca D'Oro, known to the scooter crowd as the Conc. Another infamous coffee bar of the time, Lulu's, attracted harder Leeds Mods and later skinheads, eventually feeding football hooliganism rather than northern soul. Lulu's was one of the nascent gathering points for the mob that eventually became Leeds United's Leeds Service Crew.

Youth subcultures were fragmenting and music was becoming a matter of faith. Ironically the Central had begun its life as a rocker venue. In 1968, it was dominated by motorcycle gangs from Armley and Wortley, but after a series of stand-offs and fist fights, the rockers retreated to the old Star and Garter pub nearby, leaving the Central as a Mod and later northern soul garrison. By 1971, Tony Banks had transformed the Central from a Mod hangout to a rare northern soul all-nighter, following the model set by Manchester's Twisted Wheel. He played major northern soul records which had been broken at the Torch or at the Catacombs in Wolverhampton. Among them were P P Arnold's 'Everything's Gonna Be Alright' (Immediate, 1967), Lou Johnson's 'Unsatisfied' (Big Top, 1967), 'Quick Change Artist' by The Soul Twins (Karen, 1966) and Garnet Mimms' 'Looking For You' (United Artists, 1965).

Leeds Central quickly became a breeding ground for the next generation. Ian Dewhirst lived with his family in Mirfield on the road to Huddersfield. 'The Central was a total inspiration to me as a sixteen-year-old,' he claims. 'It was the most important and influential club in my musical education.' It turned out to be a formidable education – he went on to be a major DJ on the scene and enjoyed a lifetime career as a music producer and compiler of underground black music from rare soul to underground New York club sounds. In his teenage years, Dewhirst scoured Bradford Market: 'When I was fifteen I got a job at a clothes shop in Bradford, and there used to be a market stall called Bostock's. They did twenty records for a quid, American imports, with no centres in. At this time I used to buy records even if I didn't know what they were.' Bradford Market had become a treasure trove that attracted collectors from across the north. In the early seventies, Bostock's took delivery of boxes of discounted deletions from otherwise mainstream American labels like Verve and MGM Tunes but it was the cast-offs that the collectors were looking for. Among the discounted boxes were a generation of northern soul discoveries

– April Stevens 'Wanting You' (MGM, 1967), The Superiors 'What Would I Do' (Verve, 1966), The Shalimars 'Stop And Take A Look At Yourself' (Verve, 1967) and The Triumphs 'Walking The Duck' (Verve, 1966). 'Every Saturday for about a year I used to go to Bostock's in my lunch hour, come back with a bag of forty records,' Dewhirst remembers, 'and my entertainment for that night was sitting down and playing the A- and B-sides of these records and having my parents moan at me about saving money.'

Dewsbury was alive with soul. The writer Keith Rylatt remembers hearing Arthur Conley's 'Sweet Soul Music' (Atco, 1967) at the Earl's Heath Youth Club. 'It changed my life,' he claims, and he was not alone. Lives were changing at youth clubs across Yorkshire. Across the fields from Dewhirst's home in Mirfield, in a more traditional working-class neighbourhood, lived a teenage girl called Maureen Walsh, who was also drawn to market stalls. At thirteen she was working on Dewsbury Market selling shirts and sweets. Too young to go to Dewsbury's Mod club, the Bin Lid, in Union Street, she spent much of her time trying to get past her formidable mother and escape to all-nighters. When I first met Maureen, she was already an articulate and self-confident young woman. Our lives had many overlaps; she, too, had gone to university and had been brought up on a council scheme in a socialist household with parents immersed in politics. Her mother and father went on to become Labour Party leaders of Dewsbury Council. In 1975, she won the Cleethorpes northern soul dancing competition, dancing to The Pointer Sisters' 'Send Him Back' (Atlantic, 1972), and was presented with an engraved silver trophy, which is still on display in her flat in Lewisham in South London, where she now works as a youth education worker. The Walsh family were Irish immigrants from Sligo who came to the coal mines of Yorkshire and subsequently found work in local mills. First, they lived in a small Irish enclave known as Daw Green, where Maureen's father founded Dewsbury's National Irish Club. Maureen speaks candidly of growing up in an area 'that has always been dependent on migration'. She can vividly remember the first wave of Pakistani immigrants into Dewsbury and is hugely defensive of her hometown, which is frequently demonised in the press as the home of Islamic fundamentalism. She was part of a gang of teenage skinhead girls who went to nearly every youth club in the area – the Parish, Club 70 in Batley, and the Gilder in Mirfield, where they played Motown, the soft drug of ghetto America that led the innocent to mainline on northern soul. Maureen admits that as a teenager she was in awe of older skinhead girls at her school. One skin girl, Glenys Straddling, was so cool and intimidating she would insult other girls in rhyming couplets, quoting from obscure soul songs such as The Flamingos' 'Boogaloo Party' (Philips, 1966): 'See that girl dressed in red, I don't think she heard what I said.' It was in this intense environment of tough girls and musical obsession that Maureen Walsh gravitated towards northern soul. She has known DJ Ian Dewhirst since their teenage years. 'He was posher than us,' she says, recalling the finely nuanced politics of class from an era when central heating, Venetian blinds or a small family car made you posh. 'It was a working-class scene, but some people had cars, others didn't; some could afford rare records, others couldn't.'

From his bedroom beginnings, Ian Dewhirst had fallen in with a gang of hardened northern soul Mods from Cleckheaton, a market town south-east of Leeds, who were regulars at the Golden Torch and the Bin Lid. 'The Cleckheaton lot' wore the fashionable uniform of the day – fitted Mod blazers with a Torch soul badge adorning the pocket. He had first heard the name Leeds Central from his new friends and was determined to get there. 'So I went down with them,' he told DJ historian Bill Brewster, 'and it was like everything I'd been looking for. All of a sudden, this sort of underground secret world. I didn't know ninety-five per cent of the records, but they all sounded fantastic.'

Leeds Central dominated Friday nights. It had eclipsed the

meagre income that the management were generating from ballroom dancing lessons, but success brought familiar problems. With northern soul now epidemic across Yorkshire, queues snaked out into Duncan Street, and overcrowding led to complaints. Then, the Central attracted a reputation for illegal drugs. Ian Dewhirst, working under his stage name DJ Frank – a nod to Huddersfield football anti-hero Frank Worthington – worked the decks. With his DJ partner, Twink, they opened up another night called the Taurus Soul Club on Venn Street in Huddersfield, a venue that would become embroiled in the Yorkshire Ripper inquiries as the area buckled beneath the social strain of different immigrant communities. For a brief period of time, from 1974 to 1976, the Central was forced to draw back. It was never a full retreat from soul music, but the Friday night northern soul events were discouraged by the police as the owners came under legal pressure. One raid ended with police officers dramatically prising leatherette seats away from the walls while looking for hidden bags of amphetamine, effectively bringing the Friday soul sessions to a lamentable end.

At the time, the northern soul scene was passing through one of its many internal disputes. DJ Frank, in particular, had started to play more modern soul and had become disillusioned with the spiralling price of unknown rare records. Competition between DJs and collectors had become furious and had led to hyper-inflation. Dewhirst had also befriended a controversial character on the Leeds scene, the Moroccan-born shyster Simon Soussan, a record dealer and notorious bootlegger. In 1975, Ian moved to America to hunt down rare records, and within weeks he had discovered troves, including Willie Hutch's 'The Duck/Love Runs Out' (Dunhill, 1968) and another northern classic Judy Street's 'What' (Strider, 1968). After dabbling in music production, Dewhirst returned to England and teamed up with fellow collector Paul Schofield. Together they approached the management of the Central to revive Friday nights, but this time playing the new music: jazz, funk and indie disco. By the mid seventies, jazz-funk was challenging the authority of northern soul, and underground southern clubs such as Caister, and all-day events in the heart of the stockbroker belt in places like Purley, were providing serious competition to the traditional northern soul scene. The Central adapted by accommodating both. Friday night was more focused on modern sounds and Saturday nights were pure northern, driven by another of the city's major collectors, Pat Brady, a talented amateur boxer and long-time advocate of rare up-tempo northern soul. As the newer funk sounds took over on Friday nights, the Central attracted a new generation of black kids from Chapeltown and Harehills, while the Saturday night northern sessions still drew on the white working class of West Yorkshire. The atmosphere on Fridays was an elegant combustion, and it was not uncommon to see steam rushing up the stairs as hundreds of sweating bodies danced in the dungeon-like room below.

Steve Caesar moved comfortably across the genres – from northern to funk, to modern soul and back again. He had grown up with most of the new clientele, who reshaped dance styles driven by jazz, forming the internationally famous Phoenix Dance Company. Among the nucleus of the company were Leo Hamilton, Donald Edwards and Villmore James, all of whom attended Harehills Middle School in Leeds, where an enlightened curriculum made dance a compulsory subject.

Soul had never been more diverse, and Leeds stood in the centre of it all, sending core members like Maureen Walsh and Steve Caesar on pilgrimages to Wigan Casino and the Pier at Cleethorpes, and others down south to the Goldmine, Canvey Island, or locally to newer jazz-funk clubs like Primos and Leeds Warehouse, where the cloakroom attendant was a polytechnic student called Marc Almond. Almond's college course had brought him under the tutelage of anarchist beat poet Jeff Nuttall and into the brutal world of Yorkshire bluntness. Almond's first short experimental film *Zazou* was reviewed by the *Yorkshire Post* and curtly dismissed by the reviewer as 'one of the most nihilistic depressing pieces that I have ever had the misfortune to see'. Almond was a periodic visitor to Leeds Central. It was there that he first heard the northern soul anthem 'Tainted Love' by Gloria Jones (Champion, 1965) and when he set up synth-pop group Soft Cell, with Blackpool Mecca regular David Ball, they recorded a cover version of the song. It became an international hit, and for a spell Soft Cell's version of 'Tainted Love' was the single that spent the longest time in the Billboard Top 100 chart in the US, selling an astounding thirty-four million copies worldwide.

O

None of this mattered to Peter Sutcliffe. His job as a lorry driver for T & WH Clark in Bradford gave him a near photographic knowledge of the motorway slip roads, red light districts and brownfield parking spaces of West Yorkshire. He was obsessively drawn to the rundown areas of Manningham in Bradford and Chapeltown in Leeds where the majority of his victims were murdered.

Late on the Saturday night of 26 June 1977, I was in a car with Steve Caesar and Simon Andrews, who at the time was working as a bank clerk for the Yorkshire Bank. He was a well-dressed kid who liked to boast that he was the only person to get into Wigan Casino wearing a cravat. We were parked up at the junction of Reginald Place near Caesar's front door, just passing time. Simon made a casual remark about the Ripper inquiry, saying that he regularly drove through Chapeltown late at night but had never been stopped or questioned. At around 2 a.m., as we talked into the night, Peter Sutcliffe was following a blonde teenager called Jayne MacDonald along Chapeltown Road. She had been in town socialising in a few bars, including the Bierkeller and the Ostler's, a feeder pub for Leeds Central Soul Club, where we had also been drinking that evening.

About thirty yards into Reginald Street, near an adventure

playground and less than half a mile from where our car had been parked, Sutcliffe attacked sixteen-year-old shop assistant Jayne MacDonald with a hammer and stabbed her to death. Two children rushing to play in the park the next morning discovered her body. According to an inappropriate and much criticised police statement, Jayne MacDonald was the 'first innocent victim' of the man known as the Yorkshire Ripper. Steve Caesar would periodically see her father on his way to work in the months following her murder. Railwayman Wilf MacDonald died two years later 'of a broken heart', according to Caesar.

Whatever the rights or wrongs of the notorious police statement, the death of Jayne MacDonald heightened fears about women's safety. Anxiety swept across the nightlife of West Yorkshire, touching pubs, clubs, bingo halls, taxi ranks and, inevitably, the world of northern soul. Steve Walwyn from Chapeltown describes his feelings at the time as 'a nightmare, road blocks everywhere, [and] being a young hairdresser at that time we cancelled all late-night appointments because we had to put client safety first'. Playwright Alice Nutter of anarcho-punk band Chumbawamba described the period as a living nightmare: 'I remember that time, the fear that permeated everything and made you look at the world askew. If you don't know who it is then it could be anyone.' Jill Taylor, then a regular at Leeds Central Soul Club, and a young nursing student at Leeds Central Infirmary, remembers walking to and from college down the middle of the street, fearing alleyways and doors. The Ripper had a distinctive gap in his front teeth, and she remembers her brother reporting a local man who fitted the description. David Peace, author of *The Damned United*, the tale of Brian Clough's brief reign as manager of Leeds United, claims he was scared into life by the murders. 'I was a lonely ten-year-old boy who was obsessed with Sherlock Holmes, who wanted to be a detective, who converted a garden shed into a private eye's office, who scoured the streets for apple thieves and missing pets, searching for crimes. Then, in 1977, I was a lonely ten-year-old boy who found the Yorkshire Ripper,' he wrote in an article for *The New Yorker*. 'In the early hours of June 26, 1977, I was five miles away and sound asleep in my safe little bed when sixteen-year-old Jayne MacDonald was subjected to repeated violent blows about her head with a blunt instrument in a playground in Leeds, a hundred yards from her own bed.'

Nurse Jill Taylor, who spent each weekend at soul clubs, was living in a flat in Headingley at the time, less than 400 yards away from where the Ripper's last victim was killed. Sutcliffe was sitting in a parked car outside the Arndale Shopping Centre eating Kentucky Fried Chicken and chips when he saw student Jacqueline Hill. He followed her up Alma Road through Headingley. It was around 9.15 p.m. on a Saturday night in what is a busy student area, punctuated by halls of residence and student bedsits. Young people were preparing to go out, and it was a group of students heading into town who found the blood-stained raffia bag Jacqueline had dropped due to the ferocity of the attack. Fear gripped the student community, but the need to go out overwhelmed everything. 'Everyone I knew was talking about it and on the alert,' Jill Taylor reflects, but 'we didn't stop going out, we were out all the time, clubbing.' The dedicated hardcore still filed into the Central, Primo's and the Warehouse, but other pubs and clubs saw a decline in customers and a rise in women pre-arranging cabs to take them home or simply staying in.

The Rytka twins, Rita and Helena, were born into an unstable family. Their mother was Polish-Italian and their father a Jamaican who drifted between unemployment and low-paid labouring. They lived in a rundown red-brick in Leopold Street in Chapeltown, and it was no great surprise when social workers became concerned that the twins and their other siblings were not being looked after. The girls were non-identical twins who attended St Charles' Roman Catholic School, an old Victorian primary school under the guardianship of Sister Joseph. In a previous era, the school had drawn its pupils from the Leeds

Poorhouse, and it was well known to local social workers. Although they were average pupils and had no record of truancy, the school became aware of the twins' domestic circumstances and they were eventually taken into care in a Catholic children's home called St Theresa's on Thistle Hill, in the quieter and more wealthy town of Knaresborough. By the time they were in their teens, the Rytka girls had become fascinated with dance music: first pop, then soul, reggae and disco. Rita had taken to arranging her hair in a fashionable afro style and was at least in a primitive way starting to explore her Afro-Caribbean roots. Helena, who chose to call herself Helen, was a talented dancer and had ambitions to be a soul singer; she often sang along to the radio into a hairbrush-microphone, in the small bedroom they shared at St Theresa's.

Adulthood was staring the Rytka twins unfairly in the face. They were aware that sooner or later the system would not look after them. At the age of around fourteen, they found out they would have to leave their children's home at sixteen, the legal age of adulthood. Desperate for meaningful role models and a home they could call their own, the girls embarked on a touching plan to attract foster parents, or someone who would adopt them full-time. Rita wrote a letter to the local press which was published in the *Yorkshire Post*.

Dear Sir/Madam,
If my twin sister and I got fostered out together it would be like winning £1,000 on the football pools . . . To get fostered out together means to us a place of love and care and it is then that you feel wanted, because someone somewhere realises what love really is and get fostered out is part of love itself. We can only hope and pray to get fostered out together, but some day I hope we will.

Rita had also composed a poem, hoping it would touch the hearts of *Yorkshire Post* readers and induce Kirklees Borough Council into prioritising their case for foster care. Although it has the clunky sentimentality of a teen poem and was written with a purpose in mind, it is also an emotional declaration of loneliness, a Christian plea for succour, and a damning indictment of the parents who had neglected them.

> Loneliness is to live in a world
> Where people do not care
> Loneliness is to go outside
> To find no one is there, and
> You fall down in despair,
> Falling on your knees in prayer
> Asking god to rescue you . . .

The poem had a measure of success. It was circulated by Kirklees Borough Council, and a couple in Dewsbury who were already on the foster care register felt compelled to respond immediately. Weeks went by as all the necessary paperwork was completed, but eventually the twins left their girls' home and took up residence in a comfortable house with a bedroom each. That, at least in the short term, was the closest the girls came to being settled. After leaving school, Rita, the brighter of the two, won a place at Batley Art and Design College, and Helen took a job at a confectionery packaging plant in Heckmondwike, where Lion's Midget Gems were boxed. Helen's quest to become a singer took her to soul clubs across West Yorkshire, to 'Ladies Free Nights' at La Ronde and Cavernes in Bradford and to soul and jazz-funk nights at Leeds Central. She was by now a strikingly beautiful young woman, aware of her elegance on the dance floor and hopeful of a career in the entertainment industry. But she had no contacts, no resources and was unable to make even the most basic demo-tape.

Circumstance struck again. Now eighteen and at an age when they could no longer be given full-time foster care, the twins drifted through a series of flats and makeshift homes. They briefly moved to a high-rise block in the centre of Bradford, to join their estranged brother and sister, Tony and Angela. Rita had dropped out of college, Helen had given up her job at the confectionery plant, and both took up no-hope jobs in and around Bradford. For a period, Helen befriended a girl she had met on the soul scene, who lived in Tanton Crescent in Bradford's Clayton district, close to Peter Sutcliffe who at the time was living in a tiny council house with his mother-in-law.

In the run-up to Christmas 1977, with no real warning, Rita packed her belongings and disappeared into the night. It was a few weeks before even her twin sister tracked her down to a shabby bedsit in Elmwood Avenue, Huddersfield, in an area of the town propped up above the M62 motorway that links Leeds to Manchester. Rita and Helen were back together, sharing a double bed in a damp and grubby room with neither warmth nor charm. No one can be sure why they moved to Huddersfield and why so suddenly. They had not lived there before and, apart from their time in foster care in Dewsbury, they had no connections with the area. It may be that they were simply drifting, hoping that the next mill town in West Yorkshire would be kinder than the one before, but one theory is that Rita had met a man who encouraged them to move there. Very soon after her arrival, Rita began working as a street prostitute. A possible scenario is that a pimp was exploiting Rita, but it is pure speculation; no individual has ever been identified or come forward. When Helen arrived to join her, it was almost inevitable that the more subservient twin would also try to earn quick money, selling sex in the grubby side streets and derelict arches by Huddersfield's railway viaduct.

One venue that provided a brief attraction to the Rytka twins was the West Indian Club on Venn Street in Huddersfield's city centre. It was a unique club with a mixed heritage in both northern soul and reggae. Ian Dewhirst (as DJ Frank) and his contemporary, DJ Twink, had played successful rare soul nights there, under the banner of the Taurus Club, earlier in the decade and remember playing dominoes with the elderly Jamaicans who frequented the area. Like Wigan Casino – and so many major clubs in the industrial north – the West Indian Club had a heritage dating back to Victorian times (and had also been called the Empress Ballroom at one time). Howard Earnshaw, editor of the northern soul fanzine *Soul Up North*, remembers going there as a child to see music hall star Hylda Baker, whose career had been rekindled by the television series *The Good Old Days*. He was a regular at the northern nights where he remembers drinking the popular Jamaican drink Nutriment in the upstairs bar. By the late seventies, Venn Street was known to local promoters as a venue that tolerated young people, turning a blind eye to amphetamine abuse at northern nights and solvent abuse at wild punk nights featuring The Damned, the Angelic Upstarts and Crass. At its height as a reggae club, where it became a meeting place for the West Indian diaspora in Yorkshire, it often outblasted London and Birmingham, in the competitive world of ska, sound systems and dub reggae. 'Gregory Isaacs, Burning Spear, Jimmy Cliff, Sugar Minott, Desmond Dekker . . . everybody played at Venn Street,' remembers Claston Brooks, aka Danman, who ended up getting a job at the West Indian Club. He told the *Guardian*: 'The artists might do one other show in Birmingham or London, but more often than not they would come from Jamaica direct to Huddersfield. They'd stay at the George Hotel . . . play their show and, *boom*, back to Jamaica. Sound systems would come over from Kingston to play Venn Street. That's how big it was.' Stephen 'Papa Burky' Burke, the first black boy to be born in Huddersfield's Princess Royal Hospital, built his first speaker cabinets out of cardboard in his bedroom and became one of the club's key figures as the boss of the town's celebrated Earth Rocker sound system.

It is hardly a surprise that the Rytka girls were drawn to Venn Street. It was a club set up to cater for the town's mixed-race community, a hive of underground dance, and a creative space where music was played and made. Tragically for the twins, it was also deeply scarred by petty crime, drug dealing and a low-life sex trade. On Tuesday, 31 January 1978, the girls left their bedsit at around 8.30 p.m. They were conscious of the risks of street prostitution and had formulated a strategy to keep them safe. Each would keep an eye on the other, and when they took a lift in a car they were never to be away more than twenty minutes, and they would always return to the same rendezvous point, a block of grim public toilets. At approximately 9.10 p.m., Rita saw her sister get into a dark-coloured car on the other side of the street. Then she herself was picked up by another client. Helen was first to arrive back at the meeting place, which is where she was spotted by Peter Sutcliffe. Rather than wait for her sister as they had agreed, she took the catastrophic decision to go with Sutcliffe to a nearby timberyard, believing it would be fast sex and easy money. Her body was discovered the next day, lying in a deserted timber-yard. She was the eighth murder victim of the Yorkshire Ripper.

Ultimately the crime which led to Peter Sutcliffe's arrest was neither murder nor violent rape. On Friday, 2 January 1981, over three years after he had murdered Helen Rytka in Huddersfield, Sutcliffe drove to a scrapyard near Mirfield and bought two bogus number plates, which he fastened with black electrical tape over the plates on his Rover car. He then drove to Sheffield's red light district by Havelock Square, where he met a prostitute, Olivia Reivers. They drove to a nearby driveway and were in conversation when a routine police car approached them. Sergeant Robert Ring and PC Robert Hydes exchanged words with Sutcliffe, and on receiving the information that the number plates were false, they charged him with a minor traffic offence. The following day, Ring returned to an oil storage tank beside which Sutcliffe had asked if he could relieve himself; concealed there under leaves were a hammer and a knife. After a sixteen-hour interview at Dewsbury Police Station, Sutcliffe confessed to being the Yorkshire Ripper.

His arrest had a curious symmetry. This was not only the epicentre of his murderous life but the heartland of northern soul, a few hundred yards from Dewsbury's infamous soul all-nighter, the Bin Lid, and only a mile from where the Rytka twins were fostered – the place where they enjoyed the only period of real domestic stability in their lives. Maureen Walsh's mother, Councillor Mary Walsh (soon to become Mayor of Dewsbury) was called in the night to put council workers on stand-by and ensure the court was clean and ready for the next morning. Maureen was by now at university in Manchester, where she had joined 'Reclaim the Night' marches to protest against the Ripper's reign of terror, but against her mother's advice and better judgement, she had spent the previous five years hitching lifts to northern soul all-nighters. With the benefit of hindsight she looks back on the risks she took. 'I would often ignore adult advice because nothing was more important to me than the northern scene – it was my life.' She admits now to feeling 'sheer sickness' in her stomach when it was made public that the Ripper's fake number plates had been acquired at a scrapyard in Dewsbury, on the link road to the M62. It was on that stretch of road where she and her girlfriends regularly hitched lifts to Wigan Casino. 'It's difficult to explain to outsiders how many risks we took and how dangerous the streets had become,' she told me. 'But it was northern soul and that was all that mattered.'

A collective wave of relief rushed through the homes of Yorkshire when on 20 February 1981 at Dewsbury Magistrates' Court Peter Sutcliffe was committed to trial, accused of thirteen murders and seven attempted murders. Such was the severity of the case, the trial proceedings were moved to the Old Bailey criminal court in London, where Mr Justice Boreham concluded by saying: 'Peter William Sutcliffe, the jury have found you guilty . . . I have no doubt that you are a very dangerous man indeed. The sentence for murder is laid down by the law and is immutable. It is a sentence that you be imprisoned for life. I shall recommend to the Home Secretary that the minimum period that should elapse before he orders your release on license shall be thirty years . . . I believe you are an unusually dangerous man. I express my hope that when I have said life imprisonment, it will precisely mean that.' It did. He was incarcerated in Broadmoor Hospital where he has remained ever since.

○

On 1 May 2011, Leeds Central was reactivated in the midst of northern soul's revivalist movement. Maureen Walsh travelled north from her home in South London to reconnect with old friends at a packed 'reunion night' in the basement club. The older clientele had been joined by a younger soul tribe from the Leeds Central Scooter Club. They had returned to the old basement – now renamed the Hi-Fi – to find that the Central's old industrial warehouse struts still bore the traces of the dark brown paint of the past. The crowd honoured all the rituals: the light dusting of talcum powder was sprinkled on the floor, bags were searched at the door, and retro boxes of records were lovingly appraised in the DJ booth. But there was one final and improbable twist in the story of Leeds in the sixties and seventies, a twist so dark that it would be rejected as too bizarre to make the disturbing pages of David Peace's fictional thriller series, the Red Riding quartet. In 2012, an ITV documentary, *The Other Side of Jimmy Savile*, exposed the Leeds-born DJ as one of the country's most prolific child abusers. Although suspicion had surrounded Savile for years, it was a bombshell programme which revealed the DJ who had worked the kids' sessions at the Spinning Wheel as a calculating narcissistic abuser. Savile had used his reputation as a charity fundraiser to ingratiate himself with the authorities at Broadmoor, where he had befriended Peter Sutcliffe. Inevitably the revelations triggered a new round of conspiracy theories. A retired West Yorkshire Police detective, John Stainthorpe, claimed that Savile had once been a suspect in the disgraced Yorkshire Ripper inquiry, a bizarre claim that was given more credibility when a Harley Street orthodontist admitted that he had been sent to Leeds to make a cast of Savile's teeth by officers investigating the death of Irene Richardson, who died in Roundhay Park in 1977. Savile's three-bedroom penthouse overlooked the murder scene and could only be accessed by a private lift. The new residents, who bought the apartment at auction, wish to remain anonymous.

Blackpool – a towering giant of seaside soul.

6
THE DEEP SEA WHERE THE MUSIC ROARS
1974–1984

There is a pleasure in the pathless woods,
There is a rapture on the lonely shore,
There is society where none intrudes,
By the deep sea, and music in its roar:
I love not Man the less, but Nature more.

'Childe Harold's Pilgrimage', Lord Byron

Blackpool has played an inordinately important role in the history of northern soul: it is the seaside town that roared. For a brief period in the mid sixties, the soul scene's first major superclub, the Twisted Wheel, had a Blackpool offshoot. It was short-lived and soon forgotten, but it heralded the first wave that broke on the shores of the Fylde coast, and for decades to come Blackpool became synonymous with northern soul. There was, of course, a deeper logic. Since the advent of the Victorian railway network, Blackpool had a reputation as the place where the industrial working class went to play. Over eight million people – many of them mill workers, miners or ancillary workers – lived within touching distance of Blackpool, and for the heathen hordes of Scotland it was a place with magnetic power. Each year, during the Glasgow Fair (traditionally the last two weeks of July), thousands of Scottish families travelled south to a wonderland of donkey rides, kiss-me-quick hats and venereal disease. Wakes Week brought textile workers from Blackburn and Burnley in search of candy floss, ghost trains and rare soul. Whole towns closed down and emptied their excited workers into the hotels and B&Bs that crept back from the seafront. The iconic Blackpool Tower looked down on the mayhem with a steely grandeur – a bit like Paris's Eiffel Tower, but with the pungent smell of fried onion and chips.

The story of northern soul could be told without ever leaving England's decaying coastal towns: Blackpool, Cleethorpes, Scarborough, Bridlington, Morecambe, Whitley Bay, Southport and Prestatyn, each in their own way played host to rare soul venues. First, midweek nights, then all-nighters, and then as the scene matured, weekend soul spectaculars that spread like a virus through hotels, old holiday camps and along rusting piers. But, like so much of northern soul's history, the first real signs of change happened not on the wind-blasted sands of England but in the city of Detroit.

In the mid sixties, Ric-Tic Records, a Motor City indie set up by Joanne Bratton and Ed Wingate, was on the cusp of being bought up by the burgeoning Motown Corporation. Ric-Tic had become a cult label on the northern soul scene, with major dance floor releases by JJ Barnes, Edwin Starr, Laura Lee and Rose

Batiste. None of the releases was a hit and the majority slid into obscurity, ripe for discovery by the collectors of the north. What set Ric-Tic apart from many other under-capitalised labels in ghetto America was the access it had to musicians of the very highest quality. Bratton and Wingate had hired members of the Detroit Symphony Orchestra – many of them Jewish émigrés from Eastern Europe who had found refuge from Soviet communism in Detroit – and they worked as makeshift studio musicians, on a twilight cash-in-hand basis. To give the studio musicians an identity, and to cover their tracks, they became known as the San Remo Golden Strings; no one has fully explained the name, but it is rumoured that Joanne Bratton had been to the Mediterranean on vacation and returned to Detroit raving about her days in Sanremo. Another explanation came from the musicians themselves; at the time, the Sanremo Song Festival was one of Europe's most prestigious live music events, attracting classical and jazz musicians from across Europe, and many had performed there. Whatever the real reason, the San Remo Golden Strings became a byword for great Detroit instrumentation: 'Hungry For Love' by the San Remo Golden Strings (Ric-Tic, 1965), 'All Turned On' by Bob Wilson and the San Remo Quartet (Ric-Tic, 1965) and 'Festival Time' by the San Remo Golden Strings (Ric-Tic, 1966) were all featured at the Twisted Wheel and the Torch, and as oldies at Wigan Casino, and beyond. The final track was also the instantly recognisable backing track to another northern soul classic, 'To Win Your Heart' by Laura Lee (Ric-Tic, 1966).

As charter flights became more readily available, Sanremo, Benidorm and the island of Majorca were sold to British holidaymakers, and by the mid sixties, package holidays were denting the appeal of British seaside resorts. Over the next thirty years, the trickle became a rush, and with the rise of regional airports and the near guarantee of sunshine, millions took holidays abroad, leaving towns like Blackpool, Scarborough and Cleethorpes to rust and decline. It was not a sudden or terminal collapse, but it was profound. Some seaside towns held up; others like Brighton reinvented themselves, while many looked back with bitter nostalgia on better days. Some were so beaten by change they became blighted and forgotten places pock-marking the coast. When Blackpool Mecca and Cleethorpes Pier were at their height as northern rare soul venues in the seventies, both resorts were already showing signs of disrepair. Twenty years on, coastal poverty had risen steeply and an analysis by the Office for National Statistics showed that once-thriving places were suffering. Skegness, home of the first Butlins holiday camp, had the highest level of deprivation, and Blackpool, whose Golden Mile still attracts more visitors a year than any other coastal town, had the second highest. For a place that was once the Gold Standard, and a city with a unique place in the story of northern soul, Blackpool was forced to introduce free school breakfasts for all its 12,000 primary school pupils, following fears that they were arriving for school too hungry to concentrate properly.

The problems were many and varied. Coastal towns buckled under the financial burden of repairing once grand buildings or Victorian piers ravaged by storms and fire. Many were left with venues that had no obvious use and no longer attracted TV stars or even cruise ship entertainers. Yet out of crisis came opportunity. Northern soul promoters were among the first to seize the possibilities. Many seaside towns were replete with obsolete dancehalls, many of which had sprung-wooden floors that suited the scene. Almost all of them had a ready supply of low-cost accommodation, either in the form of derelict holiday camps or rows of old-fashioned guesthouses. Venue owners and local councils, fearing the total collapse of their economies, welcomed the soul tribes, and unlike Greater Manchester of the sixties, with its ideological police force, many opened their doors to northern soul and smiled benignly on the weird rituals, obscure music and bulging eyes.

On Easter Sunday, 26 March 1967, at the height of public anxiety about bank holiday violence between Mods and rockers, a small cadre of Modernists queued outside the Twisted Wheel on the corner of Manchester's Whitworth Street. By all accounts it was a veritable fashion parade: smart mohair suits, braided blazers, see-through Italian raincoats and hooded parkas were all in evidence, alongside one or two Venetian striped school caps from northern preparatory schools. The group were waiting for a bus to take them to an event coyly described as 'A Coach Trip to Blackpool'; in fact it was a journey to the first ever northern soul all-dayer at the Twisted Wheel's coastal spin-off, a nightclub above a parade of shops near the Winter Gardens, in the appropriately named Coronation Street. From these modest beginnings, empires were built. Today, a phalanx of promoters fight tooth and nail to attract northern soul fans to coastal venues up and down the country. Arguably, the holiday resort weekender, which generally features two all-nighters and two all-dayers butted together, has become the new lifeblood for the scene, attracting people from across the age ranges.

When the Twisted Wheel bus drew up in Coronation Street most headed upstairs to the club, but a few others doubled back to Gary Wilde's cigarette kiosk in Victoria Street, in the shadow of the Tower, where the north's first dedicated rare soul dealer sold Capstan, Woodbine and Rizla papers alongside boxes of imported rare soul. Ian Levine, the DJ most synonymous with Blackpool, grew up witnessing the evolution of the seaside soul scene close up. 'The northern soul scene was very special,' he told *DJ History*. 'I've never been one to be told what to do. I was a soul rebel at fourteen.' That was in many respects an understatement. Even as a young teenager, Levine was a force of unbridled energy whose love of northern soul drove him to extremes. Educated at a strict all-boys' school on the Fylde coast, he found himself a couple of years below Stuart Bremner, a Twisted Wheel regular and top Blackpool Mod. At fifteen, Levine discovered one of the evergreen double-siders of the northern scene – Rose Batiste's 'Hit And Run'/'I Miss My Baby' (Revilot, 1966) – and hustled DJs at the Twisted Wheel to feature the Detroit classic; this at a time when most fifteen-year-olds would have stayed fearfully outside. His presence on the scene has been volatile, controversial and, for a time, even litigious. There was an acrimonious spat with journalist Dave Godin – no shrinking violet, either – and in an infamous war of words they threatened to sue each other. To this day Levine divides opinion. He is best described as a Rabelaisian character: extravagant, tempestuous, never restrained by humility, and always a fund of great anecdotes and soul knowledge. For a time, when I was working as a journalist in London, exiled from the north, I would catch up with him at his home in West London. We would spend nights reminiscing and testing each other with soul trivia, and I would listen to his stories of the bewildering lengths to which he went to unearth great soul music. I like him a lot but I have met many others on the scene who find him self-centred and sanctimonious. When he came out as a gay man on what is frequently a tough scene, he met pockets of homophobic abuse, which may have receded with time but in the mid seventies it was a stick to beat him with.

For all his many idiosyncrasies no one has ever doubted the powerful role that Ian Levine played in shaping northern soul. Ian Geoffrey Levine was from a wealthy family whose parents owned the Lemon Tree, a nightclub and casino in Blackpool. Unheard of at the time, they also owned property in Florida. This gave the young Levine advantages over his peers. He had more money to spend on records and travelled regularly to America, an almost unknown experience in a scene dominated by working-class kids from forgotten and deprived pockets of Britain. Levine's third advantage was one he shared with many other collectors: a voracious and at times obsessive desire to track down great unknown soul. Like the restless dealer Tim Brown of Todmorden, both announced that they wanted to own every soul record ever produced, a Himalayan task that even by the mid seventies meant securing tens of millions of records, many of which were ballads unsuited to dance floors.

On a family trip to America, Levine bought an entire warehouse of old records and shipped them home to work through forensically with his DJ partner, Colin Curtis, at Blackpool Mecca. They played their way through the haul and placed the vinyl into three piles: yes, no and maybe. The yes pile came to reshape northern soul. Among the records Levine had heard on his travels was one blistering and important sound, 'It Really Hurts Me Girl' by The Carstairs (Red Coach, 1973), a soul song of such earthy modernity it forced a change in dancing styles and brought about the shuffling modern northern era. It was not universally liked. According to Ian Levine, 'You had to be there at the time. It was unique and groundbreaking for the scene. The Carstairs was the first non-standard northern soul record to change a whole scene, and as such was historic. It was bloody rare, too. It took me six months to get a copy after hearing it on a Miami radio station in 1973.' Ian Dewhirst, who travelled to the Mecca on a weekly basis before heading on to DJ at all-nighters elsewhere, saw the record as part of a disruptive trend. 'It's extremely unlikely that any other DJ would have played a record like "Hung Up On Your Love" by The Montclairs [Paula Records, 1973] at the time. Crazy as it sounds,' he says, 'The Montclairs was even more challenging than The Carstairs. It was not an immediate hit. I can remember it clearing the floor the first few times Ian played it. Once people got used to the introduction and the song it caught on, but it wasn't an easy sell at the time. It was competing with traditional stompers. It was a bold record to play and just one of many that the Mecca used to play which probably wouldn't have worked elsewhere at the time.'

Not everyone was convinced by the Mecca's controversial policies. By breaking the link with classic sixties soul, some saw Levine, the Mecca and specifically the Carstairs record as akin to religious betrayal. It was northern soul's Clause 4 moment – a central plank of the scene's belief system had been kicked away. Civil war broke out, one of many skirmishes that have blighted the scene, pitting traditional sixties soul against what became known as 'modern northern'. Exaggerated claims were made, and accusations flew around like missiles. Many felt compelled to take sides; others saw it as not either/or but both, and embraced change, seeing it as a route to the next generation of obscure black music.

For Scottish soul fans, who travelled south to the top clubs, the Carstairs song had an arcane association. Carstairs was the name of Scotland's state psychiatric hospital – and the train to Wigan always ominously slowed down as it passed the hospital's intimidating walls. John Anderson was an exiled Scot whose dealership had started in his parents' council house in the South Side of Glasgow. His record warehouse, Soul Bowl, was now based in a clutch of farm buildings in King's Lynn, where racks of imported records from Detroit, Chicago and Memphis lined the walls. He thrived on some company from home, and when the drink flowed we often talked of the Carstairs List, northern soul collectors who John thought should be incarcerated. Among them was a guy from Bradford who only wanted to hear records on navy blue labels, a collector who prayed before he searched the racks, and a Japanese collector who, before he entered the record rooms at Soul Bowl, changed into a white jumpsuit, wore a face mask and carried his own disinfectant. John had diagnosed him as having obsessive-compulsive disorder: a condition that was rife among the collectors of northern soul.

Going to Blackpool Mecca felt different. The iconic metal tower gave it a status of its own. Many people made a weekend of it, arriving after work on Friday and booking into the cheapest B&Bs that stretched like racks of limp toast along Blackpool's red-brick side streets. Others came only for the Mecca and slept rough in cars and minibuses parked in an elevated car park next to the club. I frequently doubled up, going to Blackpool on

Saturday nights then travelling south to Wigan for the all-nighter at 2 a.m. The Mecca provided free coaches to and from major towns in Lancashire to attract customers, and the return coach to Wigan heaved with northern soul fans who had discovered this convenient transport solution. But it was not long before local drug squad officers also cottoned on, and the free bus was frequently shaken down before it left Blackpool.

Northern soul clubs had traditionally been in twilight areas, often tucked away in backstreets or in basements, but the Mecca was a highly professional operation, part of the nationwide Mecca Organisation made famous by Eric Morley, the entertainment impresario who founded the Miss World beauty contest and the television programme *Come Dancing*. Wearing a tie was compulsory for men, and the club was soon associated with the fashionable, sharp-suited and trend-setting element of the northern soul scene. It became the Harvard of the scene – the place where the major collectors and rival DJs congregated to hear the latest sounds – and in time it became an arbiter of taste and transformation.

The Mecca was a sprawling entertainment complex with ballrooms, restaurants, and cloakrooms bigger than some clubs. Alabaster palm trees were dotted around the main ballroom, the downstairs bar was called the Bali Hai (after the volcano in *South Pacific*), and fake tropical vegetation hung from the roofs. The rare soul area was at the top of the building, accessible by a bright orange escalator, in the Highland Room, which catered for the Mecca's biggest summer clientele, visiting Scottish holidaymakers. It was undoubtedly one of the most incongruous rare soul venues ever. Inside, the mood lurched from kitsch to killer soul. Ian Levine was the star attraction, but his collaborator, Colin Curtis, was an equally formidable talent. Soul writer Mark Rowland once said of Curtis that 'if he was black, gay, American and dead he would be the most revered DJ. If he'd moved to London he could have easily had the record industry position or national radio show his experience and knowledge warranted.'

The Mecca DJs pioneered some of the greatest rare soul discoveries in the history of northern soul but became associated with the most threatening quality of all: change. From the vantage point of today, the change was subtle and incremental, but at the time it seemed like a hurricane. Records that had strange disconcerting beginnings came in a wave; among them were Ronnie Walker's 'You've Got To Try Harder' (Event, 1974) with its space-age sound effects, The Commodores' 'The Zoo (The Human Zoo)' (Mowest, 1972) with its deliberately out-of-tune and avant-garde introduction, and 'I'm Your Pimp' by The Skullsnaps (GSF, 1973), a sinister dance groove with the ghetto refrain 'I'm your pimp, I wear my hat to the side and walk with a limp.' Two stunningly sparse records on the Creative Funk label by a New York collective fronted by vocalist Diane Jenkins also dominated the decks. 'I Need You' and 'Tow-A-Way Zone' (Creative Funk, 1975) were unsettling at first, but soon won over the doubters.

Feuding and in-fighting greeted the music like never before. It was as if the Mecca was at war with the most sacred traditions of northern soul and the conventional Motown dancer, but it stayed loyal to one northern soul rule: discovering obscurities. Oscar Perry and the Love Generators' 'I Got What You Need' (Peritone, 1975) was a tune of such instant coolness it gave the lie to those who argued that northern soul rarities were substandard; Lily Fields' 'Love Has So Many Meanings' (Sunburst, 1975), a late night café jazz song laced with modern disco, oozed quality. At the time, I wrote a feature for the soul fanzine *Talk of the North* which tried to make sense of the great northern schism: 'The Northern split was characterised by great personal ill feeling. Kev Roberts sacked from the Casino, Frank (Ian Dewhirst) censored for playing Boby Franklin's "The Ladies Choice" (Fee, 1973) and Bill Harris's "Uptown Saturday Night" (Warner Brothers, 1974), both of which were subsequently banned, and personal attacks on Mecca DJ Ian Levine. But out of this labyrinth came some of the greatest ever Northern sounds – Mel Britt, Lou Edwards, Kenny Smith et al. It was a period in which a great deal happened. The Mecca began playing new releases (a return to the policy of the Twisted Wheel), a funk all-nighter opened at Sobers in Manchester and Soul Bowl's John Anderson established himself as the main discoverer of rare soul, which guaranteed a flow of rare and "funkier" sounds, including East Coast Connection's "Summer In The Parks" (New Directions, 1974), Herbie Thompson and Black Nasty's "Cut Your Motor Off" (Big Hit, 1974) and The Del-Reys Incorporated "Destination Unknown" (Tampete, 1973).'

The Mecca and Wigan grew apart. People who once attended both began to choose, and the scene was irrevocably split, not between funk and stomp as the myth claims, but between those who thrived on change and those who resisted it. For those who disliked the Mecca's new music policy, a bigger change lay in wait. In February 1975, Ian Levine went on another trip to the States, this time to New York. This was not just one of his now famous expeditions to source obscure records; it was a trip that would not only change his life but crank up his notoriety to new levels. Levine had befriended a man called Herb Rooney and his wife, Brenda Reid, who were the lead singers with the group The Exciters (probably best known at the time for their Mod hit 'Tell Him' (United Artists, 1962) and 'Do-Wha-Diddy' (United Artists, 1963), a UK cover version hit for Manfred Mann). On the strength of their most successful northern soul record 'Blowing Up My Mind' (RCA, 1969), Levine had talked the group into making cover versions of two classic northern soul sounds – 'Love You Baby' by Eddie Parker (Ashford, 1967) and 'You're Gonna Make Me Love You' by Sandi Sheldon (OKeh, 1967). But he also imagined a third song, one of his own compositions, which he played ploddingly to Herb Rooney on a studio piano at a meeting in Manhattan. They agreed to record the song, which was called 'Reaching For The Best' by The Exciters (20th Century, 1975) and an in-joke for the cognoscenti since the title had once been used as a fake record accredited to a singer called Bob Relf on a sales list circulated by the bootlegger and rare soul con man, Simon Soussan. Levine was the producer.

'Reaching For The Best' became a much loved but deeply controversial record on the scene, the first 'tailor-made' northern release. To say it divided opinion at Blackpool Mecca would be to significantly underestimate the furore it caused. Many resented the way the scene was being 'manipulated', feeling that it was taking the rare soul scene in the wrong direction, and others cringed at the way Levine proselytised about his own productions. Other releases followed and received a mixed reception. Quality among them were the soul ingénue Evelyn Thomas's 'Weak Spot' (20th Century, 1976), Barbara Pennington's 'Running In Another Direction' (Island, 1976), and my own personal favourite, James Wells's 'Baby I'm Still The Same Man' (Polydor, 1976), a shuddering big-voiced song which had it sneaked into Britain on an obscure Chicago label would have been greeted on the northern scene as an underground classic.

Stunned by the negative reaction, Levine fought back, arguing that the scene was in danger of becoming moribund, and in one infamous outburst pronounced the death of northern soul. It was a remark he later retracted but not before he had pursued a career elsewhere; first as a successful DJ at London's biggest gay nightclub, Heaven, where he became a pioneer of the hi energy sound, and subsequently as a producer of boy band Take That. Ian Levine would have become the most famous producer to emerge from the northern soul scene had it not been for a rival, Pete Waterman. A northern soul DJ at the Locarno in Coventry, Waterman also owned a rare soul shop called the Soul Hole, which sold bootleg copies of big sounds from the Torch. In the eighties, the Stock Aitken Waterman production machine cranked out international hits for Bananarama, Kylie Minogue, Jason Donovan and Rick Astley.

According to Ian Levine, events came to a head at a Sunday

all-dayer at the Ritz in Manchester's Whitworth Street, in a ballroom venue situated between the Twisted Wheel and the yet to be imagined Hacienda. Levine told the DJ History website: 'It all crystallised at the Ritz. Neil Rushton was running these all-dayers there. Everybody came. It was a huge success. 1,500 to 2,000 every Sunday. All the Blackpool crowd came because me and Colin played and all the Wigan crowd came because Richard Searling DJ'ed. At that time we were playing all this modern disco stuff that we were playing at the Mecca: Doctor Buzzard's Original Savannah Band, Tavares, "Car Wash", "Jaws" by Lalo Schifrin. And they were playing anything with a stomping beat. It was like two football crowds: Manchester City and Manchester United. It didn't work. All of these Wiganites with their singlets and baggy pants were shouting, "Fuck off! Get off! Play some stompers!"'

Levine claims that events then took a more militant turn. 'They went for me, and one of the Blackpool guys, Steve Naylor, stepped in . . . and got his glasses smashed. They started wearing these "Levine Must Go" badges. It was all getting quite nasty because they hated the change in the music from the stompers to the modern stuff. I'll go on record here and say, "We went too far."' At the height of the ructions, two vocal northern soul diehards – Pete King from Wolverhampton and Paul Shelvington aka Shelvo from Leicester – painted a twelve-foot banner with the provocative slogan 'Levine Must Go' daubed on it. They paraded through the tables of the Highland Room. While some sympathised with their plea, others felt it was hounding a man who, though controversial, had been a major pioneer on the scene. I confess to mixed emotions. I was not a great lover of the tailor-made disco-style sounds but I was passionate about the Mecca having the right to leave the sixties behind and pursue a more modern rare soul policy. These disputes drove a wedge between friends. DJ duo Ginger and Eddie from Todmorden had been one of the scene's most popular double acts, but a rumbling difference over music policy, which at its most crude could be described as Wigan versus Mecca, finally erupted. At an all-nighter in St Ives in Cambridgeshire, Eddie supposedly played the contemporary disco hit 'Car Wash' by Rose Royce (MCA, 1976), an energetic track produced by Motown mega-producer Norman Whitfield. The manager of the community centre which was hosting the all-nighter walked up to the decks and told Eddie that if he did not stop playing 'Car Wash' he would be sacked. Ginger has always denied that he induced the manager to take action, but a split was inevitable. 'We had a fantastic run – a tremendous camaraderie,' Ginger said in his book *On the Right Track*, but the teenage friends saw less of each other and the split certainly soured their rising reputations.

Looking at it today, the Mecca wars were arcane, concerning records that the vast majority of young people in the UK didn't know even existed. But that was part of the secret strength of northern soul: even its civil wars were underground. Ian Levine moved to London, and Heaven, and while his annual trips to the USA continued, they were no longer driven by the pursuit of rare soul in old warehouses. One of his new shrines was the Saint, an influential dance music venue in Manhattan. Levine's tireless obsession with new music had not receded. 'I remember that I spent four weeks at a time, something like six times a year at the Saint. I kept going over to New York just for the Saint. I knew everything and every record that was played there. I studied them. That's why I made Heaven so special during that period because the Saint was my blueprint for Heaven. Up to eight o'clock in the morning was the stomping fabulous hi energy beat. The Saint was about beautiful music, like the northern soul thing before it, the swirling strings and sophistication.'

It took the intervention of an unassuming woman and a new wave of all-nighters to cohere the warring factions of northern soul. The Talk of the North all-nighters were originally held on a rusting Victorian pier in Cleethorpes that jutted out of the mouth of the Humber estuary on the north-eastern shores of Lincolnshire, far from the established epicentre of northern soul. It would be difficult to conjure up a more potent image of the decaying English seaside holiday resort than Cleethorpes. Serving the trawler towns of Hull and Grimsby, and a forgotten stretch of eastern England that stretches from Lincoln through the Fens to Northamptonshire, it was never the most fashionable place in England and had none of Manchester's surly self-confidence. The Cleethorpes Pier Talk of the North all-nighters started on 7 February 1975 and were the brainchild of Mary Chapman and her husband Colin, a couple who stood out as eccentric in an otherwise youth-dominated scene. Mary had started out selling costume jewellery on a market stall in Boston in Lincolnshire, eventually setting up her own record stall, which began to sell new soul releases and illegal pressings distributed by the Nottingham indie, Selectadisc. Having fallen in love with soul music and sensing there was an untapped market among the old Mods and soul rebels of Lincolnshire, she branched out from the market stall and hosted a rare soul night at the Magnet Tavern in Boston. As Les Cokell had done in his home village of Settle, the Chapmans held memorable New Year soul parties at her home in Walcot, an old Roman-era village near Sleaford. It was an open house for rare soul lovers. Mary Chapman was a likeable motherly figure who had the demeanour of a village schoolteacher; her affable approach to rare soul was in marked contrast to the warring machismo and unbridled egotism of Wigan and Blackpool. She was quieter, more modest and, for many, a welcome refuge from bickering and backstabbing.

Mary Chapman had seen the impact that Wigan Casino all-nighters had had in the north-west and was keen to find a local equivalent that could revive Lincolnshire and Humberside. Her weekend trips to the coast took her to many fading and crumbling venues – to Mablethorpe, to Ingoldmells, the home of the first ever Butlins holiday camp, and to Skegness in the south, then north to Scarborough and Bridlington, the resorts that traditionally served Yorkshire's mill towns. The Chapmans drove up and down a stretch of coastline that was all but forgotten by successive London governments. Mablethorpe had been devastated by a massive flood in 1953, within an hour all but destroyed. Attempts to rebuild its once charming seaside economy were thwarted by the infamous Beeching cuts in 1963, which closed down small and uneconomic railway lines. This disastrous policy isolated many small coastal and rural towns and rendered them even more inaccessible. Eventually the Chapmans' journey took them to Cleethorpes and to the town's iconic Victorian pier, which dated back to 1873 when it was built by the old Manchester, Sheffield and Lincolnshire railway company to attract tourists to the area.

The Pier was desolate and in disrepair, but picturesque. On a good day, you could see across the Humber to Spurn Point, the sand banks that jutted out from the East Riding of Yorkshire. Admittedly good days were few and far between, and when the mist settled, it brought a cold grey curtain down on the coast. Although it appeared to be an inauspicious start, the idea of running rare soul all-nighters on Cleethorpes Pier proved to be a masterstroke. The creaking old jetty had atmosphere by the spade-load, and an old ballroom inside the pierhead had been home to wrestlers, magicians and seaside comics. The corroding metal stilts, the uneven wooden walkways, and the lashing cold waves of the Humber estuary created a strange sense of movement on the pier, one that people claimed responded to the relentless passion of northern soul. Holidaymakers described Cleethorpes Pier as if it was moving in unison with the sea. Some felt that its curious movement was unsafe and it should be declared a no-go area. But those who travelled from South Yorkshire and Lincolnshire to dance claimed that the undulating movement of the pier gave it a special atmosphere. With hundreds dancing to Cleethorpes classics like Black Nasty's 'Cut Your Motor Off' (Big Hit, 1976), Kim Tolliver's 'I Don't Know What Foot To Dance On' (Castro

Records, 1975) and Rosey Jones's 'Have Love Will Travel' (Today, 1973), the pier lurched with the weight and determination of the crowd. Ian Dewhirst, who frequently worked there, told DJ historian Bill Brewster that it 'has to be one of the greatest venues ever as far as mystique goes', and DJ Jonathan Woodcliffe, skirting perilously close to northern soul cliché, remembers a trip to Cleethorpes: 'It was a freezing winter's night. The snow was being blown in almost horizontally from the North Sea. All I can remember is the door opening in the distance, a mountain of steam coming out and the smell of Brut and talcum powder . . .'

Mary Chapman had secured the support of the best-known faces on the Lincolnshire soul scene, including an influential DJ called Rick Todd who, until Cleethorpes opened, had been running Grimsby's top northern soul club, the Hawaiian Eye, a former rockers' café on the seafront that was invaded by Mods in 1967 and had been colonised by Lincolnshire's soul fraternity ever since. To begin with, Chapman was convinced that only locals would turn up, but they came from far and wide. Every fortnight, Cleethorpes attracted crowds of over 1,000; the dance floor would be packed with 700 dancers and a further 300 would be listening from the café and the side rooms. What really set Cleethorpes apart was not its scale but its unique personality: it was the contender, never the champion; it was friendly and rarely mired by disputes; and it had a hidden quality that marked it out from the attention-seeking Wigan Casino. Some big DJs played there, but in the main it drew on the second string of northern soul DJs, among them Ian 'Pep' Pereira from the Catacombs, Ginger Taylor, Poke, John Manship, John Vincent, Rick Scott, Chris Dalton, Dave Appleyard and Graham Coates, many drawn from the vicinity of Boston and Lincolnshire. Egos were left at the door and the music was king. Mary Chapman, an unlikely impresario, pointed forward to successful clubs yet to come. 'It was the most varied ever attempt on the northern scene up to that time. It led the way with a reputation for activating more unknown rarities as well as countless currently in-demand releases,' she claimed. 'The DJs were brave in the face of criticism and the dancers, often oblivious to the price tag on any given record, the most adventurous and skilful.' The underlying message was that Cleethorpes rose above the internecine wars that had split Wigan and Blackpool Mecca and drew on soul music from across the decades, irrespective of status or price. They even helped out with Ian Levine's tailor-made soul bandwagon and invited the Chicago Roadshow – LJ Johnson, Evelyn Thomas and Barbara Pennington – to perform Levine's latest releases at a New Year gathering. It was brave diplomacy, and a gesture that attracted respect and followers in equal measure. Cleethorpes Pier provided competition for Wigan, sometimes attracting bigger crowds and necessitating an overspill venue at the Winter Gardens. Journalist Dave Godin, exasperated by Wigan's betrayals and his fights with Blackpool Mecca, rallied to the Cleethorpes cause, warming to its modesty and authenticity. Its reputation swelled with the freezing waves.

December 1976 proved to be an epic moment in the history of British youth culture. The infamous Anarchy in the UK tour – featuring the Sex Pistols, The Damned, The Clash and New York's Johnny Thunders and the Heartbreakers – was limping through the north of England, like a bedraggled carnival, pursued by hacks of every description. The tour had been chaotic. One by one, venues had cancelled, with sixteen out of nineteen shows biting the dust. Local councils had been bullied into pulling the plugs on the shows after the Sex Pistols' incoherent performance on Bill Grundy's *Today* show, during which they were goaded into swearing for the cameras and acting like surly ne'er-do-wells. It was contrived theatre but no less historic for that. In his autobiography *No Irish, No Blacks, No Dogs*, John Lydon describes a tour teetering on the brink of bankruptcy and bad faith. The Clash travelled on a separate coach and relationships between the bands were tense. Johnny Thunders and his entourage of New York garage punks were heavily into heroin and looked on with a resigned contempt at the mad antics of the Sex Pistols. Lydon claims it all began harmoniously enough, but as venues cancelled and the press refused to back off, personal feuds erupted: 'Then The Damned decided they were the greatest thing since sliced bread. Egos made it fall apart.' Compared to the schism that had split northern soul, the wholesale fighting that marred the Anarchy tour was more like a shattered mirror – splintered and jagged relationships that became impossible to reconcile.

Blithely unaware that they were being worked like puppets, the tabloid press screamed with disapproval and gave the Pistols publicity beyond their wildest fantasies. Vilification was heaped on their spiky heads by politicians, newspapers and local authorities. What was not said was that the Sex Pistols were in some respects an art school band whose shows the previous year had rarely ventured beyond the London college circuit – St Martin's School of Art, Ravensbourne College and Chelsea School of Art. It was from the creative laboratory of fashion and conceptual art that their quixotic svengali Malcolm McLaren and fashion visionary Vivienne Westwood launched their early career. With all hell released on local councillors, Cleethorpes boldly stood up to the storm and refused to cancel the planned gig. It was one of only a handful of shows that survived the controversy. The noisy pseudo-anarchic circus rolled into town, but the Sex Pistols played to substantially smaller crowds than the underground all-nighters, which were now attracting well over 1,000 people to the seaside venue. Punk had become the latest moral panic across the UK and the wank stain of music papers like the *NME*, which had always ignored the underground northern scene in favour of new rock.

When I joined the paper as a black-music writer years later, I took great delight in reminding them that they had totally missed the UK's one authentic underground scene. Michigan-born garage rocker Iggy Pop got it right. He had grown up largely unaware of the underground soul labels that fuelled rare northern soul, and was contemptuous of the manipulation that drove punk. 'Punk rock,' he said, 'is a word used by dilettantes and heartless manipulators about music that takes up the energies, the bodies, the hearts, the souls, the time and the minds of young men who give everything they have to it.'

Although punk and northern soul sat uncomfortably side by side in Cleethorpes, Britain's two greatest subcultures had much in common. Both were underground and frequently misunderstood. Northern soul had grown up organically across a period of ten years since the height of the first-generation Mods and was a subculture that was more authentically the product of young people themselves, often hiding from authority, dodging the drug squad and attending self-managed clubs that were only sparsely advertised. Punk was largely contrived and skilfully managed in part by McLaren, driven by his genuine love of New York garage bands and an opportunistic interest in anarchism and the Situationist movement. Cleethorpes marked another milestone. A hastily produced *Anarchy in the UK* magazine, featuring punk rock's official scary feline Soo Catwoman on the cover, had been manufactured back at McLaren and Westwood's Seditionaries boutique on London's King's Road and carried by train to Cleethorpes. It kick-started the torn iconography and ransom note-style lettering pioneered by artist Jamie Reid and was celebrated as the first punk fanzine.

In 1975, a year before punk broke, I was hanging about at the front of the stage at Wigan when I was apprehended by the Leeds DJ and record dealer Pat Brady. He was on the verge of setting up one of the first northern soul fanzines and reasoned that I was at university and a big mouth so would be an ideal contributor to *Talk of the North*. It was my first ever commission and my first tentative step on a writing career that took me to the weekly soul paper *Black Echoes*, then the *NME*, and finally to a management career at Channel 4. There, I was able to return the favour. Pat Brady's daughter had graduated from Cambridge and joined my team at Channel 4, where she told me of an infancy surrounded by rare records. As a four-year-old, according to family myth, she had gleefully jumped on the settee, shattering a record worth £3,000.

Fanzines flourished on the northern scene. Up to 400 have been published since the mid seventies, some obsessive in their detail, others raging at the moon. Dave McCadden's fanzine *Soul Galore* was a brave attempt to cross northern soul and comedy. McCadden eventually joined the alternative stand-up comedy circuit under the stage name Dave Purdy, before dying prematurely of a brain tumour. Dave Rimmer's fanzine *Soulful Kinda Music*, Derek Pearson's *Shades of Soul*, Mark Bicknell's *Soul Underground* and Howard Earnshaw's *Soul Up North* all lasted the pace, while some followed the spirit of punk and burned brightly then self-destructed. Pete Lawson's short-lived polemical fanzine *The Gospel According to Dave Godin* was a brilliant mixture of uncompromising soul attitude with acidic commentary on DJs and venues, wrapped up in an intense love of the purest values of the scene. It lasted four issues before Pete Lawson's untimely death. The fanzine movement ultimately gave way to online forums and blogs, but not before the football team Wigan Athletic had dramatically risen and fallen back down the football league. The supporters' fanzine and web forum, nodding to the fame that the Casino had brought the town, took the name 'This Northern Soul: No fans, No history, No money, No worries.'

In December 1976, Cleethorpes became the unlikely centre of British youth culture, with a corroding pier that shook with the collective weight of northern soul dancers and a place on the itinerary of punk rock's most iconic tour. Such was the number of soul fans flocking to Cleethorpes, mostly through word of mouth, that promoters Mary and Colin Chapman were forced to open an overspill venue beneath the three domes of the Winter Gardens, where rare soul DJs crowded together onstage in front of alabaster pillars and beneath elegant old cornices. It was on this low-level stage that the Sex Pistols played to a half empty room and raged at the glass chandeliers. According to Winter Gardens manager Jim Johnson, a few windows were broken and the Sex Pistols 'whipped the audience into a frenzy'. How many historians of youth culture would like to be transported back to that eventful week, when the sounds were strictly underground, drugs deals were done on the Lincolnshire coast, and soul substantially outnumbered punk? But the Sex Pistols took the headlines and northern soul hid knowingly from sight.

The mid seventies was the high-water mark of seaside soul and a low ebb for the local economies of coastal Britain. Package holidays had gone mainstream, leaving deserted guesthouses to rely on a struggling clientele of elderly residents, the DHSS register, the homeless, single-parent families, immigrants and casual drifters. Multiple-occupancy housing had put new pressure on social services, and once grand houses were converted into makeshift bedsits and plywood hovels. Lidos, art deco buildings and splendid ballrooms that had enjoyed nationwide status in an earlier era crumbled, fell into disuse or were demolished. All-nighters began at Morecambe Pier and for a time they filled a void in the north-west. After the closure of Wigan Casino, Morecambe attracted hardcore dancers, including two athletic showmen from the east of Scotland: Willie Mercer and Stuart Spence. They helped me out with a feature on all-nighters, leaving the dance floor and agreeing to dance in a darkened alleyway for the camera, in what was a stunning display of urban dance.

When an amusement arcade caught fire, Morecambe's Central Pier was destroyed, leaving a charred and derelict mess. Fire and storms destroyed several vulnerable wooden piers across the UK, including iconic Victorian landmarks such as Eastbourne and Brighton. Ironically it was not the fire that brought Morecambe all-nighters to an end but events closer to the northern scene. In 1983, a major scooter rally besieged Morecambe, and the city council claimed that damage to the pier was unacceptable and that further northern soul events would have to be cancelled. Typically the town blamed outsiders, but one of the north's most notorious scooter clubs, the Morecambe Trojans, were local boys and had a legacy dating back to the late sixties. They had shifted away from their Modernist roots and were by the early eighties a gang of brigands, travelling on the back of stripped-back Lambrettas, inspired by punk and Oi! as much as stomping northern soul. The Morecambe all-nighter survived, moving briefly to the Dome, a tacky space-age building better known as a home for the goth Sun Festival, but it too was razed to the ground, by which time Morecambe's northern soul all-nighters had decamped to a third venue, the Carlton Inn, where time ran out.

For years, it seemed that only northern soul promoters cared about the coastal towns. Buoyed by the cheap accommodation, the potential of old under-used ballrooms, and the crises of identity that faced once famous holidays camps like Butlins and Pontins, they became the new attractions. Even the grubby ring of caravan parks that hung around Britain like a stain on an old cast-iron bath became an option for soul clubs, encouraging promoters to go beyond all-nighters and all-dayers to a new vogue: weekenders.

Prestatyn, Rhyl, Colwyn Bay, Llandudno and resorts along the North Wales coastline have always had a strong rare soul culture. Within striking distance of Wigan, and close to the conurbations of Liverpool and Manchester, they are geographically well positioned and regularly feature in promoters' hit lists. The regular Prestatyn soul weekenders attract over 3,000 customers. The North Wales coastline stages events that sweep over the entire Mod legacy, from northern soul, Motown, ska, R&B and 2 Tone, while rooms dedicated to modern soul, soulful house and rare groove reach out to different tastes and generations. It is one of several coastlines ideal for the dramatic scooter runs of the traditional bank holiday weekends. Perhaps the most successful seaside soul venue of all was the magisterial Southport Soul Weekender, which announced in May 2015 that it was closing down after twenty-nine years. Southport was a beacon of seaside soul and across time had built on its northern soul legacy and morphed into a festival by the coast. Nicknamed 'Ibiza without the weather', it launched in 1987 at a caravan park in Berwick-upon-Tweed, before moving to Blackpool for three editions, then Morecambe for one, before finally finding its longest home at Pontins holiday campsite in Southport. The driving force behind Southport was former northern soul fan Alex Lowes who spent his teenage years in Bolton and became a regular at VaVas, Wigan Casino and Blackpool Mecca, where Levine's progressive 'New York dance music' policy made a lasting impression. When he relocated back to his native Newcastle, Lowes worked as a council planning officer and began to imagine that the area could host a major event. 'It was a mad idea,' he told the magazine *Blues & Soul*, 'but, like the madman, I said yes.' So, in October 1987, in a windswept caravan park near Berwick-upon-Tweed, the Upnorth Weekender was born. Northern soul DJs such as Colin Curtis and Richard Searling, and others from the nearby Scottish scene such as Billy Davidson and Bob Jeffries, were joined by live acts from the rare soul scene, like the masterful Detroit vocalist Ronnie McNeir and Chicago's modern soul legend, Keni Burke. It became a roaring success. Subsequent events were held in northern coastal towns like Fleetwood and Morecambe, before a permanent home was found at Pontins holiday camp in Ainsdale near Southport. The Southport Weekender took place twice yearly at its height until the event moved south, relocating to a bigger site at a former Butlins holiday camp in Minehead, Somerset. Two significant musical events gave Southport new wind. Acid house and the second 'Summer of Love' made dance music raves and festivals *de rigueur*, and the arrival in the UK of the soulful

Chicago house sound built a bridgehead to new forms of underground dance.

By the mid 1990s, Southport had become synonymous not with northern soul but with the soulful side of house music and with the cult of the DJ. According to Alex Lowes, 'we started putting on real big-name DJs like Roger Sanchez, Masters at Work, Bob Jones and Trevor Nelson, who were all playing quality black music right across the board'. It was in the twilight hours, when the big DJs were packing up, that Southport introduced a new phenomenon to seaside soul. Mobs of strung-out dancers would improvise 'illegal parties' in and around their living quarters, using tape machines or small DJ decks slung together using power from the holiday chalets. The chalet party was born. It grew to become a feature of all the great seaside soul venues, including Prestatyn, a revivified Cleethorpes and the Scottish Soul Weekenders which recently shifted across the border to the Cumbrian seaside town of Silloth, where row upon row of caravans are rented out by the faithful from Manchester, Edinburgh and the north, and then turned into sandstorm raves.

Invading the seaside venues had another unforeseen impact on underground soul. At the rough end of the market, it was a low-rent culture where time had stood still: tatty caravan parks, down-at-heel coastal resorts, and hotels that invoked the catastrophe of *Fawlty Towers*. But soul events pushed further up-market, too. Events began to appear on the calendar that were aimed at older and more well-off rare soul fans. These offered an illusion of grandeur, and the word 'connoisseur' entered the vocabulary, somehow equating obscure ghetto soul music with fine wines and refined tastes. It was a far cry from a handful of chalkies in the toilets at Wigan. Blackpool's Hilton Hotel became the centre point for the Luxury Soul Weekenders, where five-star hotel accommodation at the Hilton, the Savoy and the Imperial, and well-maintained ballrooms, became part of the northern soul offering.

The lure of the seaside continues to the present day. Two of Wigan Casino's original DJs, Richard Searling and Kev Roberts, recently became collaborators in another seaside extravaganza, the Blackpool International Soul Festival at the Winter Gardens, which features big names from the vintage soul scene – Betty Lavette, Bobby Hutton and Gerri Granger. Traditional northern soul occupies the Empress Ballroom, and with a further nod to upward mobility, the connoisseur DJs occupy the Theatre Bar.

The mega-weekender came to dominate the scene in the nineties and helped to replenish the roots of the sixties rare soul scene, but it also brought with it a series of promoter wars that particularly blighted events in Whitby, Bridlington and Scarborough. All sorts of dirty tricks came into play: spoiler events, threats to DJs, bogus bomb scares and the settling of old scores. Yet other events thrived on goodwill and reputation. Ady Croasdell, the face of the 100 Club all-nighter in London and the brains behind the Kent label, a specialist reissue label based on sixties soul music, was hunting around for a venue that could host bigger crowds than he could attract to the packed and over-subscribed 100 Club. A graduate in International Relations from the University of London, Ady had moved to the capital from his native Market Harborough, where he was an early entrant into the northern soul scene. His first memory of the scene was 'going to a function at a solitary disused railway station about half a mile from the hamlet of Kelmarsh in north Northamptonshire', but it was at a regular all-nighter at the Lantern in Market Harborough that he became besotted with sixties soul. Croasdell masterminded the Return to Cleethorpes, a series of annual weekenders at the Winter Gardens and the Beachcomber Holiday Park on North Sea Lane. Hundreds of curious newcomers joined those immersing themselves in memories of the days when Cleethorpes Pier moved to the music and fans could get close to their heroes.

But as quickly as new coastal venues were discovered – or old ones rediscovered – the relentless march of history wiped them out. Demolitions came thick and fast. The 99 Club in Scarborough was forced to find new premises in a rundown hotel after the original venue – the Corner Complex on North Bay, formerly a children's entertainment complex dating back to the holiday heydays of the twenties – was demolished by the local council. Likewise, Blackpool Mecca, Morecambe Pier and, finally, the Winter Gardens in Cleethorpes all faced the same humiliating fate. Like the Torch and Wigan Casino before them, ruthless economics, with no interest in youth culture, triumphed. Plans to bulldoze the building and erect a music college on the site of the Highland Room sealed the Mecca's fate. At the time, the *Guardian* writer John Robb wrote: 'Architecturally it's hardly a tearjerker – the building was an ugly brutalist piece of sixties concrete. But the Highland Room was itself a key conduit of a vital youth culture. DJ Ian Levine put a funkier twist on his soul cuts, and went on to become one of the top pop producers in the UK.'

In 2007, North East Lincolnshire Council announced that the Winter Gardens in Cleethorpes were to be knocked down, ending an eighty-year legacy that dated back to the Edwardian era, when the building, originally known as the Olympia, was built by an amputee railway worker who invested his compensation money after an accident at work. Plans were unveiled for a £3.5 million luxury housing development and the Winter Gardens were doomed. In June 2013, six years after demolition, the site was still empty and being used as a car park. Its future remains uncertain. Morecambe's demise was even more poignant. The Central Pier closed in Easter 1986 after decking collapsed at the seaward end, and then a fire on 4 February 1987 damaged the amusement arcade at the shoreward end. Another fire destroyed the Old Ballroom on Easter Sunday 1991, leaving Morecambe's greatest landmark a pitiful sight. The owners were instructed by the local council to either upgrade or demolish but they chose to hedge their bets and sell the crumbling structure. In January

1990, repair work began, but it was too little, too late. An independent report condemned the area as unsafe and the pier, which had once hosted a hugely successful northern soul all-nighter, was demolished in March 1992. Locals complained that without the pier Morecambe looked undressed and had been stripped of dignity. It had lost its role as a watchful eye over the waters, too; in February 2004, twenty-three Chinese cockle pickers died in the freezing waters of Morecambe Bay, trapped by rising tides at Warton Sands. The global economy, the unpredictable coastal waters and an exploitative Chinese gangmaster had led them to their bleak deaths.

The DJ decks at Soul Not Dole, a regional soul club at Armthorpe Pit Club, Doncaster. Courtesy of Dean Roach and Terry Wright, Soul Not Dole, Doncaster.

7
SOUL NOT DOLE
1974–1990

The human race has only one really effective weapon, and that is laughter.

Mark Twain

'Fuck me. It's Mick McGahey.' The Mighty Bub's inimitable Yorkshire voice roared across the Casino car park. I was rushing into the fire exit of an old cinema to shelter from a torrential downpour and wait for the drenched crowd to die down. David Buttle, aka the Mighty Bub, was one of the gigantic personalities of the northern soul scene, a man huge in bulk and personality. He used jokes to befriend people, to entertain them and sometimes to bring them back to earth with a bump. The night we first met, he was wearing a Mod blazer trimmed in red braiding, tightly buttoned at the front and straining against his enormous girth. Public school blazers were common on the northern scene, but for a fleeting moment I thought he was in fancy dress as he looked uncannily like schoolboy glutton Billy Bunter. But his deep Barnsley accent left no one in any doubt about his working-class credentials. From that night on, I often heard the Mighty Bub's voice booming through scratchy microphones at soul venues across south Yorkshire, or his cackling laugh punctuating stories of his travels.

Bub was a soul fan and a coal miner, and at the time Mick McGahey was the Scottish vice-president of the National Union of Mineworkers (NUM) and a Marxist radical who spoke with a guttural Scottish accent, often featured in unflattering sound bites in the nightly news. My accent was nothing like Mick McGahey's but it was Scottish and close enough for the joke to work. Whenever our paths crossed at Wigan, Cleethorpes or in the motorway service stations that had mushroomed like blood clots along the arteries of the M62, Bub would hail me as 'Mick' or 'Brother McGahey'. It was always a friendly greeting, and sometimes backed up with a hefty backslap. Bub inhabited a larger-than-life world. He was a natural comedian with a big-hearted approach to life and a man who was difficult to dislike. His force of nature brought him to the forefront of the northern soul scene: he was a stomper at heart.

It was many years later that I came to fully understand Bub's joke. At the time, I thought it was based on Mick McGahey's high profile in the media; he was a firebrand leader of the miners' strike which ultimately brought down Edward Heath's Tory government. I had no idea that Bub knew him personally. He had met him at the Barnsley Miners' Forum. Nor did I know he had heard him speak at shop stewards' meetings. What many who came across Bub's salvo of jokes and formidable personality on the northern soul scene did not know was that he was just as big a character in the pits of South Yorkshire.

Like many of his generation in Barnsley, Dave Buttle had left school early and had been in the 'Plasticine class', one of the less gifted schoolkids who were destined to go down the pit. His first job was with the National Coal Board (NCB) at Dodworth Pit in South Yorkshire, where he arrived at a time of intense industrial strife and a generational dispute over pit closures. It's easily forgotten now, but Wigan Casino had opened against the backdrop of a state of national emergency and the three-day week. Although the all-nighters had closed down due to power cuts, many smaller northern clubs had cancelled, shifted their night or soldiered on with specially rigged generators.

The story of pit closures parallels the high points of northern soul. When the Twisted Wheel was at its Modernist height between 1965 and 1970, the National Coal Board closed down over 250 collieries. One pit closed almost every week for five years. In South Wales alone, 135 pits had closed, and the year before the Golden Torch was forced to close its doors, the 1972 miners' strike plunged Britain into darkness. A Doncaster miner, Freddie Matthews from Hatfield Main Colliery, was crushed to death under the wheels of a scab lorry outside Keadby Power Station in Lincolnshire. Matthews' death was viewed as a martyrdom of sorts and helped secure the image of the Yorkshire miner as the vanguard of Britain's most militant trades union.

Although Bub had yet to graduate to the big all-nighters, he was a regular at the Portcullis in Barnsley, his life already revolving around the twin pillars of Barnsley's teenage culture – the northern soul scene and the NUM. The strike of 1972 was a baptism of fire for Bub and it bound him to the union for ever.

David Buttle's gregarious personality set him apart but it was his bulk that made him unique. Even in his young days he tipped the scales at nearly twenty stone. His bed at home was propped up on house bricks and he once ruined a sofa at his friend Derek Greenhof's flat simply by sitting on it. Bub struggled with his weight throughout his life, and after an asthma attack underground he was stretchered from the coal face of Dodworth Colliery and sent home on sick leave. Rather than accept redundancy due to ill health, he returned to the pit, this time to a job that kept him above ground. Although he tried to lose weight throughout his early teens, medically regulated diets failed, and rather than give in to depression, he turned his weight into a joke. His red record box was emblazoned with the words 'Fat is Fun', and he frequently joked that his box was his lunch; he was known to drink a crate of Pils lager during his DJ sets.

Bub would always steal the show. He had the self-deprecating habit of playing northern soul records that celebrated fatness, such as Chubby Checker, Fats Domino and especially the hectic Chicago dance record 'The Fat Man/Working At The Go-Go' by Butch Baker (St Lawrence, 1966). The words were intended to reflect back on himself – 'Fat man is at the go-go and he's stealing the show.' He was an out-and-out populist who believed that the DJ was first and foremost an entertainer. Unlike almost every other northern soul DJ, he spoke at length between records, introducing them not with arcane label details but with jokes, drug innuendi and barbed insults aimed at the famous faces of the scene. He often played tricks on the dance floor, flicking the house lights on and pretending that a drugs raid was in progress. His favourite records were northern stompers or brassy upbeat instrumentals like The Mylestones and Little Leroy's cackling laugh-a-thon 'The Joker' (Andre, 1967) and Ace Cannon's 'Sea Cruise' (Hi, 1967), a northern soul anthem that reminds one of the Benny Hill theme tune more than ghetto soul. In his local community, Bub became synonymous with unabashed entertainment and became a DJ by force of personality rather than the power of his record collection (small in number and patchy in quality). He often defied the unwritten rules of the scene by borrowing big records from his long-suffering friends. He lent heavily on Derek Greenhof, and for over two decades they performed together at the 'Tracky', the Yorkshire Traction

Sports and Social Club. Northern soul collector Malc Burton followed their many escapades and describes them charmingly as 'the Two Ronnies of the northern scene'. It was personality rather than rare records that allowed Bub to move further up the jealously guarded ladder of the scene. He periodically appeared at Cleethorpes Pier, Samantha's in Sheffield, and at one of Yorkshire's most revered all-nighters, Clifton Hall in Rotherham. Although his records were borrowed from mates, his style was unique and broke with the sometimes po-faced seriousness of the scene. Unannounced, he would sometimes break into the zigger-zagger terracing chant borrowed from football hooliganism, and lead northern dancers in a surreal culture clash of pure soul music and working-class mayhem. It would not be too big a leap to claim that David Buttle was a stand-up comedian let down by history. He came too late in life to benefit from the old-fashioned social club circuit, parodied on Granada television as *The Wheeltappers and Shunters Social Club*, but he came too early in life to become an alternative stand-up comedian. He was too crude for television and too abrasively working-class for the fringe theatre of the university-educated new wave. Bub was more like Les Dawson, or Peter Kay today, rudely northern and unashamedly working-class. (I remember him telling a crowded dance floor at a midweek night in Barnsley that a local factory worker had been sacked for his beliefs – 'he believed you could wank in the staff canteen'.) Whereas most DJs ended their set with either a big high-price sound or one of the familiar ending tunes from Wigan's '3 before 8', Bub always ended with 'Michael (The Lover)' by The C.O.D.'s (Kellmac, 1967) in honour of Michael 'Mick' Cook, a soul boy from a pit village near Doncaster. Bub, Mick Cook and ten others had been travelling back from an all-nighter in Cleethorpes when their minivan crashed and veered off the road. Bub survived with extensive injuries to his arms, but Mick Cook died in the accident.

Bub's weight, which he never managed to control, was not

helped by alcohol and the drinking games he played with fellow Barnsley miners. They spray-painted a pit helmet gold and presented it as a trophy in drinking contests, and in a nod to the Tour de France, gave a yellow jersey to the lad who drunk the most. Even when he was DJing, Bub would instruct the bar staff to go up and down the optics until all his money was spent. According to Derek Greenhof, he was prone to overindulgence in everything: food, drink and laughter. His size allowed him access to legal diet drugs from his GP, and armed with prescriptions and medical letters he often taunted the drug squad with what Greenhof calls 'a degree of impunity'. Bub had one other memorable characteristic – a pathological hatred for Margaret Thatcher. Like many miners, he believed that she was destroying communities in the interests of profit, and whenever her name came up in conversations Bub would say, 'Thatcher – she hates northern soul, you know'. Margaret Thatcher became prime minister in May 1979, towards the end of Wigan Casino's reign, and advocated a free-market society curbed of union power. There is not a single shred of evidence that she even knew northern soul existed, but for Bub and many of his kind she personified the enemy of working-class people and the scourge of the north. In 1987, Bub was DJing at the Winding Wheel, a northern soul club in Chesterfield. Further down the bill was Karl 'Chalky' White, a mad-keen northern soul collector who has since become one of the scene's great archivists. Chalky recorded the night on an old cassette tape, and it is one of the few extant examples of Bub's unique approach to northern soul, a mixture of stand-up comedy, clowning at the decks and ferocious attacks on Thatcher.

In the late eighties, when South Yorkshire was still reeling in the aftermath of the bitter miners' strike of 1984–85, two industrial relations experts drew up a list of people they wanted to interview about the strike and its impact on the mining communities of South Yorkshire. In their book *Coal, Crisis and Conflict* (Manchester University Press, 1989), Professors Jonathan and Ruth Winterton of the University of Bradford listed among their interviewees a venerable group of contributors including the Right Honourable Gerald Kaufman MP (Gorton), the Right Honourable Tony Benn MP (Chesterfield) and David Buttle aka the Mighty Bub (Barnsley). To many people who associated Bub with mad japes on the northern scene, it was a preposterous juxtaposition, mentioning the fat-boy joker in the same breath as eminent left-wing intellectuals such as Tony Benn. But for the academics and those who had followed the strike close-up, it made perfect sense. Bub was a committed NUM member and had been a prominent picketer in the notorious days of Arthur Scargill's flying pickets.

Buttle was a complex character: outwardly loud and blokey yet inwardly troubled by his weight, unlucky in love yet devoted to his mother Elsie, keen to get free drinks from behind the bar yet always an informed socialist. More than anything in his life, he was proud to be entrusted to lead pickets as a Barnsley miner. Former Yorkshire miner Ian Winter remembers being on the picket line with Bub at Dodworth Colliery in 1983. A local dispute had broken out over a workplace fight, and miners were demanding the reinstatement of George Marsh, who had been sacked for hitting an overman. Although most NUM members accepted that assault was a sackable offence, there was a deep feeling that disciplinarian management had been overbearing and provocative. A series of sporadic disputes and stoppages had broken out over the summer when Bub was in Scarborough DJing at Rudie's nightclub. On his return to work in September 1983, the festering argument about despotic management had erupted into a full-blown strike. Bub was asked to lead one of the pickets and was positioned at the gates of Dodworth with a group of younger men, including Winter, who remembers a car drawing up and demanding access. It was a pit manager claiming that as a member of the construction workers' union UCATT he was not officially on dispute and not bound by the picket. 'I don't give a fuck about UCATT,' Bub told him. 'Even the pit's cat is not getting in today, never mind fucking UCATT. So turn round and go home.' Ian Winter claims he had never seen anyone so fearless in the face of authority and from that day on came to realise that Dave Buttle was something more than a joker.

For the sizeable cadre of pit workers on the northern soul scene, the great strike was seismic and character-building. The men were defending a way of life that was maliciously under threat. Grimethorpe miner John Davies had come to northern soul in a now familiar way, through a local Mod with connections to the big all-nighter clubs. 'Even at junior discos there was a guy who went to the Wheel, Cats and later the Torch – he was the man! His name was Ken Hancock,' Davies remembers. 'And through our suedehead days we all looked up to him. I was fourteen and already collecting, sometimes DJing at our local youth club at Willowgarth High School.' He remembers the day he got his first skinhead haircut with four other lads from Grimethorpe and went to show off his new look to his mother who was working in a local shop. Fearing that he had joined a weird new cult, she burst into tears, and of course she was right – he had. John Davies's introduction to the northern scene followed familiar rites of passage, but his village was unique. Grimethorpe was at the forefront of embattled change. With a population of around 10,000, it was officially the most industrialised village in England and famous for a different genre of music, the world-renowned Grimethorpe Colliery Brass Band, who featured in the film *Brassed Off*. Nicknamed 'Grimey', the village's coking plant rose triumphantly next to the M1 motorway but the place had coal-mining practices that hinted back to the Victorian era. According to Davies, who talked to me fresh from a northern soul weekender at Bridlington Spa, 'industrial relations in the mining industry varied from pit to pit. Some had very militant unions and bad management, and some got on very well. Having said that, we were never far away from a rag-up, sometimes for silly things, and sometimes it was well deserved. I have had weeks with only two shifts' wages to draw and I've been on strike for a nurses' dispute. But usually we went on strike for our own – at another pit.' Caught in the cold winds of the strike and with no money to fall back on, John Davies looks back on the dispute as a lost opportunity. 'The big strike was the last vestige of socialism as I have always known it,' he told me. 'From fighting with the police to giving your baby boy a wooden train set with a piece of track missing, compliments of the people of Poland, which hurt.' He remembers 'drinking coffee you could stand your spoon up in, compliments of the people of Nicaragua' and says ruefully, 'I think it turned us into individuals in the respect that we were together but you had to look after your families first. The first shoots of an I'm-all-right-Jack attitude crept in. The free enterprise system swept all before it and left us literally on reservations.' David Parry, a Coalfields Community campaigner, describes those 'reservations' with alarming candour: 'The fabric of the housing has deteriorated and many villages in the former coalfields have become like inner city sink estates except they are in semi-rural isolation.'

Unlike punk, which was more openly anti-authoritarian, the northern soul scene has often been written about as if it 'floated free' from the politics of the day, but the reverse was true. The northern soul scene was rooted in the industrial towns and cities of Britain, which across the arch of time faced unprecedented waves of deindustrialisation. The statistics shame the era: 6.8 million people were working in manufacturing when Margaret Thatcher came to power; that number is only two million today. During the sixties and seventies, cotton mills in Lancashire closed at a rate of one a week, sweeping a wave of unemployment through major northern soul towns like Bolton and Oldham. The jute mills of Dundee, a Scottish northern soul stronghold, disappeared almost overnight. Ravenscraig, a giant steel plant which employed 12,000 workers in Motherwell, near the modern soul club the Kilt in Newmains, is now the biggest brownfield site in Europe. In 1982, when the Stafford all-nighter opened, there were 170 working coal mines in Britain; by 2009 there were only four remaining, and the organisers at Stafford felt it necessary to offer reductions to northern soul fans carrying unemployment cards. The old Bankhall Mine in Burnley, which had hosted one of the north-west's best all-dayers, had closed, and although the miners' welfare club carried on valiantly, eventually it gave up the ghost. In the streets where John Davies grew up, forty-four per cent of ex-miners were still out of work many years after Grimethorpe Colliery had closed. To this day, a seam of soulfulness connects back to the great strike, and memories of a lost past cling like nicotine to the walls of some venues. By 1982, a new generation of northern soul DJs were pushing the boundaries. Guy Hennigan and Stoke-born collector Mark 'Butch' Dobson had found an old miners' welfare club near the M1 in Nottinghamshire. The now derelict Annesley miners' welfare is a footnote in the story of northern soul, but it was an important landmark for Nottingham miners who had not followed the Yorkshire and Scottish miners onto the picket line, holding out for a national strike ballot. As emotions escalated, the Nottingham miners were pilloried as scabs and their reputation was permanently sullied.

Terry Wright, Dean Roach and Steve Wagstaffe run the Doncaster-based soul club Soul Not Dole, which meets at Armthorpe Pit Club near Markham Main Colliery, the last mine to return to work at the culmination of the 1984–85 miners' strike. The memories are raw and there is no sign they will fade in this lifetime.

By 1985, I had travelled extensively across America while working for the NME and style magazine *The Face*, reporting on the sounds of inner city America – techno in Detroit, house music in Chicago and the percussive sounds of go-go in Washington DC. Although none of them related directly to northern soul, there was a connection; they were all dance music undergrounds predicated on small and under-capitalised record labels, and largely destined for commercial failure. In 1989, Glasgow's triumphant nomination as European City of Culture brought me home to Scotland, principally to work in television. The old industrial heart of Glasgow – the so-called second city of the Empire – was being refurbished. Grimy sandstone buildings, polluted with decades of soot, were being sandblasted to reveal their architectural splendour, and the black stains of industry were disappearing from the facades of the north's greatest buildings in Bolton, Leeds and Bradford, too. The term 'post-industrial' came into common usage, and Glasgow led the charge. The city's club scene was thriving and a small basement venue that was destined to become the most important dance music destination in the west of Scotland had opened. The Sub Club felt familiar – cool DJs, a low ceiling, basement soul and an underground reputation for drugs – and it was where the major DJs from black America came to play: Jazzy Jeff from Philadelphia, Lil Louis from Chicago and my friend, the irrepressible Derrick May from Detroit.

A few people on the hard core northern scene teased me that I had 'betrayed' the scene, forsaking the on-the-fours beat and walking out on my greatest lover – sixties soul. It was partly true, but not in a lasting sense; there was always something that dragged me back – like love, like crack cocaine, like one for the road. Suddenly and spectacularly it came. One day in *Black Echoes* I noticed a small advert for a new club, the Ruff Cut Soul Club. Located in a forgotten part of Scotland, on the A71 road through North Lanarkshire, the venue was Allanton miners' welfare, an isolated old social club near Shotts, a town of less than 10,000 residents in the midst of a failing coal- and iron-mining community. It was run by Jim O'Hara, a soul fan whose connections to the mining community were peerless; his grandfather, his father and his brother were all miners, most having worked underground at Kingshill No. 1, the mine that dominated the Shotts and Allanton area. Jim's family still lived opposite the social club.

At 2.30 a.m. I left Glasgow with a car-load of friends and headed for Allanton, through pitch-black streets of converted miners' cottages. Heavy curtains had given way to Venetian blinds, and the old rattling windows had been replaced with double-glazed window units. We turned into a dusty off-road car park, and before I'd even got out of the car, I saw Gaz Kellett in the headlights, looking like a dervish from another world enacting some tribal rain dance. Our friendship dated back to the first few weeks at Wigan, and we had stayed in touch sporadically across the years. It was clear that Gaz, despite his job as a bank manager, had not yet 'settled down' and his pleasantly deranged love of soul had brought him north, where he was dressed inexplicably in a terrorist balaclava. Jim O'Hara told me I had missed even more bizarre behaviour earlier. Another member of the Preston Cybermen had found a Hoover in the club's cleaning cupboard and had to be restrained as he started to hoover the dance floor and surrounding areas. We walked past the caretaker's cottage next to the hall and were barely over the threshold when other faces came into view: Guy Hennigan from Skipton was poring over labels as if they were hieroglyphs; Pete Lawson, wired as a fuse box, was preaching the gospel to a crowded room; and Keb Darge, back home in Scotland and boundlessly brilliant on the dance floor, was acting as if it was the biggest Hogmanay party in history.

They came from across Scotland and on coach trips up from Derby, Stafford and Preston – for the first time in the history of northern soul Scotland had an all-nighter that could compete with the north of England. Unlike the commercially minded promoters who were stretching the sinews of the scene elsewhere, Jim was not in it for the money, nor even the glory, he just wanted a place he could listen to great unchampioned records. The dance floor was sprung wood – an essential component of a great northern soul club – but the badminton court marked out in white lines hinted at the school gymnasium or perhaps Grandmaster Flash's tribute to cocaine. The bungalows opposite looked on in polite disbelief, the local drunks were mesmerised as they passed by, and the record bar and a makeshift series of trestle tables, aching with rare soul from the deepest ghettos of America, did brisk business until dawn. It was the kind of place the Mighty Bub would have relished. A mining community for miles around and the thumping sound of rare soul inside. His words flashed into my mind again – 'Fuck me. It's Mick McGahey' – the words he had first said to me in the storming rain outside Wigan Casino. Now remembered fifteen years later, they felt eerily prescient. McGahey had been born in nearby Shotts, but by the time the coal seams at Allanton had been opened up for mining in 1964, he had already taken up work at Gateside Colliery in Cambuslang, and was working his way up the steep ladder of militancy within the NUM. Allanton miners' welfare was one of the great all-nighters. It broke with one of the most damaging and debilitating habits of northern soul by 'banning' factionalism. Grudges and musical bifurcation were left at the door. Allanton had garnered a reputation for being hospitable, for being welcoming to any of the warring factions of northern soul, and, like an old Scottish Hogmanay party, the emphasis was on openness, good fun and forgetting the past. Although I was an infrequent visitor, it is a place I remain inordinately proud of, proof that finally Scotland had made a lasting impact on northern soul. Many had tried. There were great nights at Clouds in Edinburgh, Glenrothes had hosted clubs at the YMCA, the Exit Centre and the Crown Hotel, both promoted by the brothers Steve and Alan Walls, and for a brief spell one of Scotland's stand-out rare soul DJs, DJ Colin Law, tired of travelling hundreds of miles weekly down to the north of England, started an all-nighter at Bilston Glen in Midlothian. It, too, was a landmark of the Scottish mining industry and the site of one of the UK's biggest super-pits, which closed in 1989. Similarly Scotland's short-lived Shrine Soul Club, run by Michael Higgins and Gary Russell, was held in Whitburn, a small West Lothian mining town once dominated by the Polkemmet Colliery, which shut down as a result of underground flooding during the miners' strike.

Allanton was grassroots and back to basics. Jim O'Hara had taken to hanging up torn bin liners as makeshift blackout curtains to stop the summer glare streaming through the windows. He had struck a deal with the local council and a friendly caretaker's wife that he could get the keys to the building in the afternoon of the all-nighters to prepare the place. Tea urns in the ramshackle bar, trestle tables laid out for the collectors' zone, his mates working the doors, and a cardboard box for the takings. During the bleaker winter months, portable Calor gas heaters were lined around the dance floor to bring a modicum of warmth, but on the worst nights you could see cold air blowing from the mouths of dancers. Many of the DJs were not DJs at all, but rare soul collectors committed to giving great undiscovered soul music a platform. Few of them were trying to build a reputation or a career. Colin Law, Acky Buchan, Mark Linton and Andy Dennison, all from the Scottish rare soul fraternity, worked the decks and, according to Jim O'Hara, 'this mixture of respected collectors and DJs from both north and south created an incredible interest and buzz and attracted more and more people to travel as the months and years went on. The people that attended Allanton all seemed to be the same in terms of open-mindedness, attitude, enthusiasm . . .' Michael Higgins from the Shrine Club, a hardened northern soul traveller, and now a lecturer in Journalism at the University of Strathclyde, believes that fortune was on Allanton's side. 'I think part of it was to do with the timing. Most of the regulars had been around all-nighters for a good number of years by the time Allanton had come along, and a good few of them had even been away and come back. It felt like something of an Indian summer. A number of the big venues were in the process of closing, and Allanton arrived like an unexpected bonus. Everyone was also slightly older, and maybe a little more relaxed.' Fraser Dunn, another Glasgow collector, agrees: 'It was a purple patch in the scheme of things on the soul scene.' Northern soul diehard Chuddy, from Bradford, called it a 'journey to enlightenment', in part recognising the physical journey he undertook from England to Scotland but, more importantly, the journey to a new vision of the scene – one in which the fractious and at times nasty bickering of the past was laid firmly to rest.

At the time, Haydn Bye was working as a chef in Girvan, Ayrshire. He had to leave Allanton early to drive to work to fry up hotel breakfasts. He saw a difference in the attitude of the DJs. 'These guys had no airs and graces. They showed the music was bigger than them. You had every corner of the soul scene played without pigeon-holing – shuffling to an underplayed two-step one minute, then you had a banger erupting the dance floor the next. Some of the DJs shouted their enthusiasm – "What a fucking beauty this is" and "If you don't dance to this you are dead".' Allanton broke records that many had never heard, but unusually for a northern soul club it also brokered an amnesty with rarity, allowing DJs and collectors to play unknown records that were not always super-expensive. Joan Livesey, who DJs as 'Jumping Joan' and is one of a small handful of women who regularly operate the decks, claims that 'it was the right mix of absolutely everything – the music, the place, the people and, looking back on it now, the sheer madness of it all. A line-up so good it didn't need mere mortals from England but they let them have a go, anyway.' Lenny Harkins, a DJ at Glasgow's late lamented Caledonian Soul Club, run by Martin Gavin and held in a working men's club on the fringes of Glasgow's West End, remembers Allanton as 'a kaleidoscope of brilliant people, atmosphere and tunes'. Relatively new to the scene at the time, Lenny says, 'We didn't care. Oldie or newie, £5 or £500, if it was good it got played, if it was shite it got snapped.' Promoter and collector Alan Walls claims that Allanton at its height gave the scene a feeling of permanence again. 'There were good nights,' he admits, 'but they tended to feel like stop gaps to me. They came, blazed brightly for so many months, then fizzled out. By the time Allanton started, there was precious little to excite us down south. It felt as if the scene was dying on its arse and we feared we'd never again see a club that ticked all the right boxes. Then – *bang* – the roof fell in as this barnstormer of an all-nighter in the most unlikely of settings took off.'

The last hour at Allanton broke with tradition, too. The now clichéd '3 before 8' and the tired rituals of traditional northern all-nighters were abandoned, and an Edinburgh-based collector called James 'Jocko' O'Connor, one of the scene's likeable intellectuals, was given the privilege of bidding the night farewell. Jocko lived and breathed soul music. He had taken his nickname from the Philadelphia DJ Jocko Henderson, an R&B old-school legend who ruled the roost at Philadelphia's radio station WDAS, at the height of the civil rights era. O'Connor was an advocate of great soul and played much slower records than was normal at northern all-nighters, testing tolerance with searing beat ballads and deep masterpieces. Somehow it worked, and he became one of the reasons that Allanton gained respect south of the border. In February 1990, Jocko raised the bar on dedication and delivered a moving eulogy to Nelson Mandela, who at the time was incarcerated on Robben Island with his release pending. He played James Barnes and the Agents' 'Free At Last' (Golden Hit Productions, 1968), launching it with the immortal line: 'This one's for you, Nelson, if you're listening.'

Always good for a one liner, Jocko O'Connor claims that Allanton was an 'uprising of sorts'. He explains: 'It wasn't the first Scottish all-nighter to attract travellers or be known for playing top music, it was actually an evolution through Edinburgh's Clouds, the Walls brothers' Fife venues and some of the one-off

Edinburgh venues . . . However, where Allanton was different was that it was probably the number one all-nighter in the UK at that point. Previously our Scottish dos were supplementary to the main English nighters, but now Allanton was king of the castle, the Jacobite rebellion had one last uprising.' Like many of his friends, he had been a reluctant recruit to DJing. 'My personal experience of it was that it was the only place I truly loved DJing, like absolutely revelled in it. It was our time and place. Our Stafford. Our two fingers up to the rest of the scene, saying catch us if you can. And they couldn't. I was allowed to wear my heart on my sleeve. I felt honoured to DJ but also challenged and allowed to answer the challenge in my own way. It was often emotional, and afterwards I replayed it all for days. Nothing equalled that hour for me, and nothing will. I like to think I pushed barriers in style and genre, and buttons in making people think.' Among his many sounds were: The O'Jays 'I'll Never Forget You' (Imperial, 1969), The Fantastic Four 'I'm Gonna Live Up To What She Thinks' (Ric-Tic, 1966), The Magnetics 'I Have A Girl (Ra-Sel, release date unknown), Larry Laster 'That's Just What You Did' (Duo Virgo, 1967), Jack Montgomery 'Don't Turn Your Back On Me' (Barracuda, 1967), Jimmy Bo Horne 'I Just Can't Speak' (Dade, 1968) and Esther Phillips 'Just Say Goodbye' (Atlantic, 1966). It was, in the words of the true collector, 'soul and then some'.

Although his home village was reinventing northern soul, Mick McGahey was unaware. After retirement, he had been bedridden with severe emphysema, brought on by the curse of a life in the pits and years of heavy smoking. He contracted pneumoconiosis and died in 1999. It was only in his last days that the secret agents of MI5 lifted the surveillance on his affairs and he was allowed the dignity of a death in his own home, in what was a once proud working-class community. With mines, steel plants and their affiliated social clubs closing across the industrial north, nothing seemed permanent any more. Jim O'Hara, the driving force at Allanton, was made redundant on three successive occasions, while his family watched their world recede.

The intervening years had been unkind to the Mighty Bub, too. He remained loyal to the northern soul scene and continued to DJ throughout the eighties, appearing as a star act at Ady Croasdell's Cleethorpes weekenders. The seaside brine and chalet community suited his belly-laugh sense of humour, but behind the smiles, his life had become seriously affected by his ballooning weight. His public appearances became less frequent. He would often ring venues to find out about access and he grew increasingly worried about his health. Having taken redundancy when the great strike of 1984–85 ended, he opened an ill-fated American sportswear shop in Barnsley, a victim of the ideology that redundant miners should become entrepreneurs. After the loss of his job and the death of his beloved mother, Bub slumped into post-traumatic depression. His weight hit fifty stone, his alcohol consumption – legendary on the northern scene – now tipped into dependency, and eventually he was rushed into emergency care at Barnsley General Hospital with kidney failure. Doctors held out hope that a new synthetic drug called Xenical would help to reduce his weight, but it was not yet on the market and its only addition to his life was to provide a new fund of jokes about a superdrug that would keep people up dancing for weeks. One of his best friends, Derek Greenhof, was still loyally on call. Derek was by now working as a biomedical scientist in the hospital. 'I worked at Barnsley General so went to see him most afternoons,' he remembers. 'I took him odds and ends he requested – mostly chewing gum because renal failure leaves a metallic taste in the mouth. The ward staff warned me that his illness was probably terminal and I was eventually told of his death when I rang the ward prior to a visit.'

It was the sixth of November 1998. Bub was forty-five years

old. His death resonated across the northern scene and the mining communities of South Yorkshire. I was told over the phone while sitting in the gun-metal grey offices of Channel 4 where I was working as Head of Arts and Entertainment. I called the company's archives department and located a copy of a half-hour documentary about northern soul, which had been produced a few years earlier by an independent company in Manchester. I knew it featured a cameo performance by Bub, in which he hams it up for the cameras, and self-mockingly claims he's a stick-on to win the dance competition. He then exits right of frame in a trademark comedy walk. It was my last sighting of a gigantic northern soul character. I played the clip over and over again as a way of saying goodbye to a man who could make you cry with laughter and then finally, in his last hurrah, actually make you cry.

'He was a friend to everyone,' Derek Greenhof says. 'He could and would talk with everyone and anyone, he always remembered their names and interests, and he could talk about anything.' And that 'anything' meant politics, civil rights, geography and television comedy. He was a bright light who somehow I imagined would never fade. 'He could have been a stand-up comic,' Greenhof agrees. 'He would often fill a great deal of his DJ sets by telling jokes or funny stories – he always captivated everyone. He had a heart of gold and would do anything for anyone at all. We often worked for free at charity events, weddings, birthdays and so on. Bub loved the music but came into his own when he had an audience – the bigger, the better, the more he liked it. He delighted in having a full dance floor, he loved a good old-school stomper. The best word to describe him was that he was a showman.'

Bub's wake was held at the Falcon Centre at Barnsley College, which held 300 people. It was packed out, with many more queuing outside, unable to get into the building. The record they played after the funeral service was Timi Yuro's 'It'll Never Be Over For Me' (Liberty, 1969), which was played over and over until the building emptied. Timi Yuro, an Italian-American singer with the voice of an angel, had died a few years earlier with throat cancer. Since the seventies, her song – which owed more than a passing debt to Yuro's friend, jazz singer Dinah Washington – had become an anthem of departure on the scene. A Catholic burial in Barnsley cemetery culminated with a procession to the grave, delayed at the request of the funeral directors while the heavy casket was lowered uneasily into its final resting place. According to Derek Greenhof, 'I think that the entire South Yorkshire northern soul contingent was there, along with colleagues from the pits and some friends from all around the country.' The mourners then moved on to the Barnsley Catholic Club, the town's current northern soul venue, and commemorations went on until the early hours of Saturday morning. One final moment, which would have appealed to Bub no end, was that his father Butch Buttle, then well into his seventies and tutored in the ways of northern soul, took to the decks to end the night. Bub's father played the final set, featuring his son's favourite songs. He shouted out, 'I'm the original Butch', a humorous tribute to Mark 'Butch' Dobson, who throughout the eighties had emerged as the northern soul scene's most successful DJ. Father playing for son – it was a moving tribute to a lovable, committed and wholly remarkable man, and it was played out to a community that had refused to give in.

A few days later, at an all-nighter in London's 100 Club, I had a conversation at the record boxes with a group of rare soul collectors. News of Bub's death had reached London, a city he dismissed as 'just like Barnsley but with more wankers'. Even in death it was hard not to smile at his unfailing dedication to the deep north.

A mannequin leans against a traffic sign at the height of the 1968 Washington DC riots in the aftermath of the assassination of Martin Luther King Jr. Library of Congress

8
TICKET TO THE FREAK SHOW
1978–1986

When you're born you get a ticket to the freak show.
When you're born in America, you get a front-row seat.

George Carlin, comedian and social commentator

I already had a ticket but I was desperate for a front-row seat. Since my teenage days in Scotland, I had an overpowering desire to set foot on American soil, to discover every soul record that had ever been released and to walk across the Edmund Pettus Bridge that carries US Route 80 across the Alabama River. Black America was where real soul came from and it had shaped many of the decisions I took in life: where I studied, what I studied, where I worked, and what I focused on at work. No matter what challenges life threw at me, there was always an ulterior motive: getting to

America to rake around in record shops, thrift stores and flea markets. Translated into the language of northern soul, I would have done anything to get my hands on a dobber, a minter or a stone-cold classic.

America was a distant dream to most people in the heyday of northern soul, and only a few intrepid collectors had ever made the big trip. Travel was expensive, cheap flights had yet to be invented, and even Freddie Laker's doomed transatlantic trips were a few years away. Annual family holidays to Florida and Disneyland were for the very rich, and to my knowledge none of my immediate friends on the northern soul scene had ever set foot in America. Collectors at Wigan spoke of Martin Koppel, an English guy from Goole near Hull, who had emigrated to Toronto, where he ran a second-hand record store. He was within striking distance of Detroit and that set him apart from the rest. Another early traveller was Andy Simpson from Bradford, who had the cool audacity to write in his passport 'Employment – Record Collector'. But they were few and far between. Then, one Sunday morning on the windy promenade at Blackpool, I met the former Wigan DJ Kev Roberts, looking dangerously like Jimmy Page from Led Zeppelin, with long stringy hair blowing criminally in the wind. Kev was clutching a wooden box of singles like he would a baby. We had a brief conversation, one that would haunt me for months. He told me he was flying to America the next day, heading for Chicago and Detroit. Superficially I wished him well, but in truth it was like a dagger to the heart. Kev Roberts was younger than me, a precocious teenager when he joined the DJ team at Wigan, and now he was flying to Chicago to hunt for records. Although I did my very best to fake goodwill to all men, one rare record sprung nastily to mind – 'Jealousy' by Carlena Weaver (Audel, 1969). I made a silent vow that before the year was out I would fly to America, too – but not with Kev Roberts' hairstyle.

By day, I was living on Rochdale's notorious Ashfield Valley, a deprived council scheme which was so undesirable they gave keys to anyone willing to live there. I was working double shifts at Manchester's Piccadilly Station as a clerk in the control office and by night travelling to soul clubs across the north-west. The railways were unionised so you were paid triple time for bank holidays or double shifts, and I signed up for everything. The only hours that were sacrosanct were those that clashed with all-nighters. The cash rolled in – much of it diverted to buying rare records, but a growing stash was tucked away for America. Then, as if by magical providence, a letter arrived from the Scottish Education Authority in Edinburgh, informing me that I had won a major studentship to allow me to travel to any overseas university of my choice. I had read a feature in *Blues & Soul* magazine which congratulated Stevie Wonder for being awarded an honorary doctorate at Howard University, Washington DC. The list of the university's alumni was staggering – Carla Thomas, Donny Hathaway, Roberta Flack, The Clark Sisters – and they even had a department of Jazz Studies with Donald Byrd as a professor. I had barely reached the end of the feature before my heart was set on Howard, so I wrote letters to the dean, the head librarian and the student counsellors. A few weeks later, I received a nice letter advising me to visit the campus but informing me that Professor Donald Byrd was on sabbatical. He had just produced a record by a group of Howard University students known as The Blackbyrds, and their single, 'Walking In Rhythm' (Fantasy, 1975), was a break-out track for the burgeoning jazz-funk scene. The letter tipped the balance. I shopped around in a travel agent in Manchester and booked a Pan Am flight from London to Washington, still with nowhere to live. Fortunately my auntie came to the rescue. She was married to a Ukrainian whose brother, Pastor Stephen Shawel, was the Bishop in Washington DC and he had confirmed that I could stay on a bunk bed in the vestry of the Holy Family Ukrainian Catholic Church. The place stank of a pungent cocktail of mothballs and benediction smoke, and my first night's sleep was interrupted by the dramatic sound of police sirens, the whining signifier of urban crime and American life. It was a strange baptism. Next to me in the vestry was a glass jug of water, which I drank greedily from the spout, only to realise in the morning it was holy water intended for the font. Breakfast was modest. A communion plate of coarse bread and thin butter was handed round by a generous group of Ukrainians who had come for a meeting with the pastor. I watched as they rolled out a huge parchment across the table and pointed purposefully at the paper like architects from the noblest corners of Kiev. They spoke in hurried Ukrainian and the only word that made sense was the word 'shrine', which they shrieked in high-pitched voices, often and proudly. The word resonated with me. I was hoping to track down a copy of 'Hey Boy' by the DC Blossoms (Shrine, 1966), a record I'd first heard at Blackpool Mecca and hurriedly written down in my 'wants book', a small notebook I carried with me like a secular bible. I had not known until I arrived in Washington that the DC Blossoms were thousands of radiant plants that had been gifted to America by the Japanese as a symbol of peace and now lined the Potomac River. More importantly I had yet to grasp how significant the word 'shrine' was to my Ukrainian hosts; the parchment they had rolled out on the table was the grand architectural plan for a shrine to the Ukrainian faith, which they hoped to build when sufficient funds were raised. It was not for another twenty years that the Holy Shrine of the Holy Family would be completed, and it now stands resplendent on Washington's Catholic Row, a 130-foot-high structure topped with three golden domes and a bell tower – and a lasting monument to my selfishness. Not for the first time in America, my tunnel vision about rare soul music cast me as the fool.

Shrine Records is now the most famous record label in Washington DC's history and is commonly described as the rarest soul label ever. Among the twenty or so records released on the label, many are virtually impossible to track down. JD Bryant's 'I Won't Be Coming Back' (Shrine SR 108-1, 1966), Les

Chansonettes' 'Don't Let Him Hurt You' (Shrine SR 114-2, 1966) and The Prophets' 'If I Had (One Gold Piece)' (Shrine SR 116-2, 1966) are supremely valuable and easily reach prices of up to £5,000 and more at auction. The myth of Shrine Records has been eagerly cultivated over the last ten years and many on the northern soul scene have somewhat airbrushed the truth. Shrine was virtually unknown to the dancers and collectors of Wigan Casino and it was rarely on the lips of even the most initiated. Richard Searling had played Eddie Daye and the Four Bars' 'Guess Who Loves You' (Shrine SR 102-A, 1966) in the dying days of Wigan and Ian Levine at Blackpool Mecca had briefly played the DC Blossoms, a record that counterfeited the style of The Supremes. So when I woke up in the Ukrainian church and heard the word 'shrine' in a broken Eastern European accent it registered only because I had made tracking down a copy of the DC Blossoms my main objective. Back then, I had no way of knowing how legendary the Shrine label was to become in the years ahead, nor how much the price of those precious records would escalate.

Shrine took its name and its logo from the remembrance shrine to President John F Kennedy at Arlington Cemetery and was the brainchild of producer Eddie Singleton and his partner, Raynoma Gordy, the divorced wife of Motown magnate Berry Gordy. Driven by determination and a slice of revenge, Singleton and Gordy were eager to build Motown in the Capitol. It proved to be an over-ambitious and doomed project. Within two short years, Shrine had folded and its catalogue was lost to history, much of its stock destroyed in the riots that engulfed Washington DC in 1968, after the assassination of Martin Luther King Jr. Those riots were to recur in conversation throughout my stay in Washington and still traumatised the city over a decade later, leaving many people with an irrational fear of the downtown area.

My first full day in Washington was spent moving my luggage to a kind Ukrainian family who had agreed to take me in as a lodger. They lived north on Georgia Avenue in Silver Spring, Maryland, just across the state line from Washington DC. My new home was near Silver Spring's Metro station on the Red Line, only a few stops north of Howard University. Across from the Metro station was a small line of convenience stores, one of which had a small rack of records. Covering my tracks by buying that morning's *Washington Post*, I approached the rack self-consciously. It was not great pickings but not entirely disappointing, either; there was a stack of records on the local Juldane label out of Silver Spring which included Stanley Woodruff and the 'US' Trio's 'What Took You So Long' (Juldane, 1976) – a big sound at Cleethorpes and the Mecca – and an instrumental by Sons of Nature, 'Ride The Vibe' (Juldane, 1974). Neither was especially rare – barely enough to buy me a meal at Howard Johnson's, let alone fund the trip – but it felt good just to hold them, the first northern soul records I found in America, with many better finds yet to come.

I registered as a visiting student at Howard University, close to the old Howard Theatre, a Chitlin' Circuit stop-off where all the great soul acts had played. Although much of the surrounding area, including the decrepit old theatre, was like a ghost town, the university was much wealthier than I had imagined and attracted students from America's black bourgeoisie. I was taken aback by just how wealthy some of my fellow students were; I had been reared to think of the black experience as a 'ghetto culture', but this was the African-American middle class, the sons and daughters of orthodontists, real estate agents and morticians. The university had an organisation called the Beta Chapter, founded in 1907, which laid claim to be the first black fraternity and once boasted soul singer Donny Hathaway among its membership. I briefly thought about trying to join but my skin pigmentation was on the light side.

On my second day, while hanging around the music department reading For Sale notices, I fell into conversation with a visiting woodwind tutor, Dr Bowie. I later discovered he had been a significant figure on the Washington DC soul scene and was named on the credits of several northern soul records, including The Carltons' 'Ooo Baby' (Argo, 1964), The Ascots' 'Another Day' (Mir-A-Don, 1965) and Leroy Taylor's 'Linda' (Brunswick, 1967), the last of which had first come to prominence in the pioneering days of the Torch all-nighters. But what made him seem special to me was a filthy hardcore instrumental that had become a classic at Wigan all-nighters – Roscoe and Friends' 'Broadway Sissy' (TEC, 1965). The record was based on a ghetto dance craze called 'the Sissy', and was a flamboyant funk stepper that began in the gay clubs of New Orleans, before being picked up by other black musicians, including on Rufus Thomas's 'Sophisticated Sissy' (Stax, 1967) and The Meters' 'Cissy Strut' (Josie, 1969). Roscoe Bowie was pleasantly surprised that I'd heard of him but made it clear that his R&B years were in the past and he was now a serious jazz musician. He would always greet me warmly around the campus, shouting out to passing students, 'Hey, Stuart! Tell these guys I'm big at Wigtown.' He never managed to get Wigan's name right but the intention was there. It was through Roscoe Bowie's generosity that I learned a humble lesson about the ethics of being a rare soul collector. I told him I was keen to interview anyone from the old Washington soul scene to write articles for soul fanzines back home, but I confess my ulterior motive was to track down obscure sounds. Roscoe recommended several people, including the legendary Charlie Hampton, a sturdy old bandleader who had performed at the Howard Theatre with Walter Jackson, Jerry Butler and Patti LaBelle. Charlie had now retired from live music and was working as a music therapist at the Clifton T Perkins Maximum Security State Hospital in Jessup, Maryland. With no up-to-date home phone number, I was only able to make contact by circling the mental hospital and hoping he would emerge from its chilling gates. We eventually met and he put me in touch with a one-time music fixer known only as 'Sir Clarence'.

Clarence worked at a photographic store on Georgia Avenue. He was a painfully thin guy who was wasting away with the early stages of stomach cancer and whose connections with the music scene were now long gone. Kind beyond belief, he invited me to his home to talk music and share a drink. So I shopped cheaply at a corner liquor store and carried a tray of cheap beer through deserted streets to his decaying wooden-frame home on 14th and Kennedy. He had been an amateur promotions man, who was in it for love not money, and we talked for hours, mostly about his life, the studio sessions he had witnessed, and the groups he remembered promoting around local radio stations. They included a teenage family group called The Fawns ('Girl In Trouble', TEC, 1968) and many of the Shrine artists. Everything he talked about – the weather, the state of his house or the traffic on Georgia Avenue – led back to the past, as if he had very little to say about the present and no real hopes for the future. As he spoke, it became clear that he was consumed by loneliness and on the point of crying; at one point, he told me that I was the first white person who had ever set foot in his home. Eventually he shambled through to a back room and brought out an old suitcase, which he claimed contained every record that had ever been recorded in Washington DC. His stories were riveting, and although the discs were not all in great condition they acted as an aide-memoire as he piled them up into a teetering tower and talked about what they meant to him. He kindly agreed to sell me some of the pile but only on condition that he had more than one copy. We agreed $2 a record, which was more generous than the street rate, and in all I handed him a $20 bill. Among the hoard were two Shrine releases by sixties soul singers Ray Pollard and Jimmy Armstrong, whom I'd never seen or heard of at the time, and another local indie release by Betty Wilson and the 4 Bars 'I'm Yours' (Dayco, 1969), but of much more interest to a northern soul diehard of the mid seventies was Sam Moultrie's 'I'll Always Love You' (Warren, 1970) and William Cummings' 'Make My

Love A Hurting Thing' (Bang Bang, 1969). Clarence gave me no more than six records, which I have kept ever since and cherish as a lasting symbol of a fleeting friendship. I left his house half drunk and with pangs of guilt, unsure of how to get home and uncertain of the deeper moralities of record hunting. Sir Clarence had sold me records with no way of knowing their value on the northern soul scene, a value that has increased exponentially with time. What remains difficult to reconcile is that his small bundle of memories are now valued at well over £5,000, and rising. I had taken them knowing they would be cared for but it was a scant defence; they were bought from a man whose whole life had been undervalued. The pangs return every time I hear stories of black musicians who no longer own a copy of one of their own records while they are bought and sold in the UK for thousands of pounds. Those pangs have not faded with time nor were they confined to me. In a blistering exchange of letters between rare soul dealers Tim Brown and Pete Lawson, the two rivals argued about the best ways of rewarding artists who had fallen on hard times: to launch a support fund or to try to secure them new deals. The dispute – one among many between the two – identified several northern soul artists who were living in poverty, including Detroit vocalist Melvin Davis, a contemporary of Darrell Banks, who was buried in a pauper's grave.

Weeks later, I visited a housing project in South East Washington, where I had tracked down one of the city's greatest singers, Clifton Dyson, a giant of a man who sang so sweetly you would think he had a tongue laced with honey. It proved to be a disheartening day. His nephew was with us. He had recently returned from service duty in the Marine Corps and was an aspiring rap artist. Throughout the afternoon, neighbourhood kids would drop by the apartment to listen to the nephew launching into derivative hip-hop routines. It was clear that none of the neighbourhood kids had any idea who Clifton Dyson actually was, or that he had recorded songs that would stop you in your tracks. Nor did they know that his song 'Five Minutes' – credited to a local Washington group The Differences (Mon'ca, 1971) – was a must-have record on the northern collectors' scene. He was simply an old uncle who merged into the anonymity of his settee as if his brand of soul was obsolete.

Collecting had become my heroin. After a few days in Washington DC I had perfected a modus operandi that has served me well over many years in America. Written down on paper, it sounds like the machinations of a serial killer but here goes . . . Locate a general hardware store and buy a small box of cheap razors or a thin medical scalpel. Go to a newsagents and buy a large-format magazine and a small pack of light brown labels, always ensuring you get quarters, nickels and dimes in the change. Then head for the Greyhound terminal or Amtrak station to collect timetables for cities within two hours' reach of DC. New York is too far, but Baltimore, Philadelphia and, at a push, Wilmington, Delaware, are within striking distance. Next, locate a sizeable post office, preferably the one on Wisconsin Avenue near Friendship Heights Metro station, where the phone booths are located at the exit. Try to reach the post office at lunchtime when the counters are busy and staff are distracted. Casually begin to make bogus calls in the booths and appear to be consulting local phone directories. Lift the Yellow Pages directory out of its unit and place it flat on the surface. Using the razor or scalpel slice the pages at 'P' for Phonograph and 'T' for Thrift Stores. Slide the cut pages surreptitiously into the large-format magazine. Replace the handset and walk slowly out to the street. Do not over-act. No shouting down the phone or slamming the receiver. Act natural, be forgettable and, if approached, be courteous. Find a small café and check through the pages, circling those that carry inventory of old or deleted records. Then go to the nearest thrift store. Do not rush to the discounted records. Wander around the store first and locate the area that sells luggage and old suitcases. Identify a sturdy suitcase or weekend case small enough to carry as hand luggage on the plane home, ignoring satchels or backpacks which damage discs in transit. Using the labels purchased earlier, write clearly 'For educational purposes – no value'. If you are ever stopped at the airport, try to appear educated and never mention words like 'rare', 'one-off', 'big northern sound' or, worse still, 'it's worth a fucking fortune and a guy I know in Skelmersdale wants it badly'.

Work patiently through the records. There will inevitably be dross in abundance: ranch-loads of country and western, an orphan copy of 'Harper Valley PTA' and junk by groups like The Beatles, Bob Dylan and Bruce Springsteen. Leave them to fester in peace. Don't be lazy and clutch-search. A find might be hidden where you least expect it, so be methodical and inspect them all. America is a racist society, and soul is regularly lumped together with stuff that sounds black – gospel, R&B, reggae, jazz and hip-hop. Search them all and under no circumstances tire. In a boardwalk junk shop in Coney Island, I nearly gave up wading though racks of detritus and what is now lamely called 'vintage goods', only to discover a small seam of gold, a run of records on the Date record label including six mint copies of Johnny Moore's 'Walk Like A Man' (Date, 1967). It was a salient lesson well known to Yorkshire collectors – where there's muck, there's money.

In the seventies, most northern soul collectors who had made the trip to America were of the naive belief that they were unique until they came shoulder to shoulder with desperadoes hunting for rockabilly, doo-wop and garage rock. Far from being first, the author Marybeth Hamilton, in her fascinating book *In Search of the Blues* (Basic Books, 2007), charts a hundred-year history of collectors and black-music pioneers scouring the backwoods of America, visiting brutal prisons, outdoor chain gangs and hidden rural villages, searching for blues performers and for early recordings, some on the mythical OKeh label. Hamilton tells the story of record fanatic James McKune who unearthed his greatest treasure, a scratched copy of a primitive 1929 recording of

Charley Patton's 'Some These Days I'll Be Gone' on the brittle and easily broken 78rpm format. McKune became a founding member of the so-called Blues Mafia, a group of extreme record collectors who redefined attitudes to the blues in modern America. He lived and died in a single room in Brooklyn's Williamsburg YMCA on Marcy Avenue, his collection so small, so rare and so highly selective it was kept in a case below his single bed. Northern soul was not the unique leader I had imagined; it was part of a long legacy of trying to collect and catalogue the very best of the African-American heritage from jazz, to blues, and on to soul.

A week into my stay in Washington DC and by then shielding a pile of nearly one hundred records, I met a woman who was to change the direction of my life. Dr Lorraine Brown was a professor of English at George Mason University in Fairfax, Virginia, a passionate liberal with a deep interest in the civil rights movement. At the time, she was embarking on a unique project to catalogue the so-called Negro Units of the Great Depression, groups of black actors, writers and musicians who were given apprenticeships by the government. The controversial project had attracted members of the Communist Party of the USA and later fell foul of McCarthyism, the anti-liberal witch hunts of the post-war era. Fearing that the records might be too politically sensitive, the Library of Congress had stored them off-site in an aeroplane hangar near Baltimore. We were driving in her magnificent vintage early sixties Buick, from our meeting point at the Smithsonian out to her university for a more formal conversation. Lorraine's first real words to me were: 'Is it ever morally right to break into premises you don't own?' My mind flashed back to Andy Wilson and his research; he had interviewed many northern soul crooks who had 'screwed' chemists. I haltingly told her that under certain circumstances it was permissible to break into chemists to secure stimulants if your motive was to stay awake to enjoy the riches of African-American culture. She smiled and said, 'Good answer. I need you to help me break into a building near Baltimore.' We had only driven ten miles into the suburbs and I knew that I had met someone special. She not only became my tutor but a figure of almost motherly support who ensured that my stay in Washington became ever more rewarding.

Lorraine Brown had pulled off a master stroke. She had been at a dinner party where she met a librarian from the Library of Congress who told her about the archives that had been stashed in the hangar. She had then written to President Gerald Ford, deliberately timing her letter to land in the Oval Office in the fading months of his presidency, and before the next president, Jimmy Carter, took office. There was no reply, which was precisely what she had planned. Her letter ended with the words: 'If I do not hear from you, I will assume you are in agreement that the valuable assets should be moved to George Mason University on permanent loan, rather than be lost to the people of America.' She had then hired two U-Haul trucks and with a gang of other students we broke into the Baltimore hangar and took crates of historic records back to the university. The next day, armed with a crowbar, I prised open a wooden crate and found an undiscovered manuscript by the playwright Arthur Miller called 'They Too Arise'. Miller had been unemployed during the Depression and had joined the Federal Theatre Project, and his script had almost been lost to history. It was my most precious find on American soil, bigger than the mint copy of Herbert Hunter's 'I Was Born To Love Her' (Spar, 1966) that I found in a police charity yard sale in Wilmington, Delaware.

A fellow student working on the Federal Theatre Project told me that the Library of Congress required every publisher to lodge two new copies of books with the library and that this requirement had been extended to records. My mind went into overdrive and I imagined that somewhere on those august shelves were copies of the most desirable northern soul records of the era: 'Job Opening' by the Del-Larks (Queen City, 1967), Eddie Parker's 'I'm Gone' (Aware, 1966) or even a great record that Richard Searling was playing at the Clifton Hall all-nighter in Rotherham, John and the Weirdest's 'Can't Get Over These Memories' (Tie Records, release date unknown). Driven by a mixture of greed and naivety, I made enquiries at the Library of Congress. The desk librarian looked blank and sent me to the civil rights holdings of the Smithsonian Museum on Jefferson Drive, probably the most unusual place I have ever crate-hunted. Although there were some great books, the small manila box of records was deeply underwhelming. Many of them were textbook civil rights records – Sam Cooke's 'A Change Is Gonna Come', The Staple Singers' 'A Long Walk To DC' and various versions of the Reverend Martin Luther King's most famous sermon, 'I Have A Dream'. Only one record stood out, an elusive northern soul song by the otherwise obscure Dickie Wonder called 'Nobody Knows' (Sound of Soul, 1969), which was featured on an old Black Panther Party album called *Free Angela*, a fundraiser for the jailed Black Power activist Angela Davis. Most songs on the album were sung by a phenomenally undervalued soul singer Larry Saunders, the Prophet of Soul who was better known for his blistering modern northern song 'On The Real Side' (Turbo, 1974), which had been massive at Blackpool Mecca and Cleethorpes Pier. I looked around furtively. There was ample time to slide it into a magazine and down into my bag, but conscience kicked in. Stealing from a civil rights library was about as ethical as nicking a ten-dollar note from Rosa Parks' purse. So, instead I asked at the desk who had donated the record. After a few minutes of consultation, I was told it had been sourced from an African-American bookshop in the Adams Morgan neighbourhood. After two or three wrong turnings, I managed to track down the store, which was tucked away in a basement beneath a towering brownstone apartment block. It mostly sold children's books, Afro posters and glass bongs. I paced around the shop trying to look like Malcolm X's long-lost Scottish cousin until I noticed there in a dim back corner a thin rack of albums. Three mint copies of *Free Angela*. I took the albums to the counter, gratefully accepted a ten per cent discount from a natural soul sister and bundled the liberated vinyl like a hostage out into the piercing sunlight – my integrity and wallet intact.

Collecting is a risky business. I have searched in crime-infested ghetto backstreets and unfriendly rural stores in the Deep South but unlike other northern soul collectors I have never been challenged at gunpoint or robbed of my savings. The biggest risk I have ever faced was duplicitous bootlegs. Illegal releases have been a running sore through northern soul since the days of the Twisted Wheel and have grown in deceptiveness ever since. It all took an acrimonious turn in the late summer of 1964 with the release of a Motown hit called 'My Guy' by Mary Wells. The song had already topped the Billboard 100 in America and was a summer hit for Mods across the UK, reaching number 5 in the pop charts in June 1967. But a drama was unfolding behind the scenes at Motown. Raynoma Gordy, the estranged wife of Motown owner Berry Gordy, was now living in New York. She had made the reckless decision to bootleg 5,000 copies of 'My Guy' to sell directly to record stores on the East Coast, to reclaim money she believed she was due. Most were sold in the USA, but some inevitably trickled into the UK where they were treated with a mixture of scorn and reverence: illegal and yet closer to the heart of Motown than most readily available records. The FBI were informed of the bootlegging by Motown's management in Detroit and arrested Raynoma Gordy. The humiliating night she spent in a jail cell provoked a retaliation and lit the fuse that became Shrine Records. Through his lawyers, Berry Gordy offered to drop the charges, but only if his wife signed a 'general release from Motown and all of its entities' in what became a staging post in their bitter divorce. It was with the proceeds from her divorce that Raynoma Gordy and her new partner, the producer Eddie Singleton, set up Shrine Records in Washington DC.

The arrest of Geoffrey Collins proved to be another landmark.

Bootlegging gripped the domestic UK industry, too, and EMI led a national campaign to control independent pressing plants who, feeling starved of commissions from the majors, often took on illegal or unlicensed work. Collins was a market trader in London, who became known as the 'Bootleg King' and was accused of counterfeiting a Jimi Hendrix album, *Live Experience 1967–68*, using tapes from the BBC archives. Collins had used a Leicester-based pressing plant called Industrial Commercial Plastics, which was also the favoured pressing plant of adventurous northern soul bootlegger, Jeff King. Using the bogus Soul Sounds label, King had exploited the demand for rare records from the Twisted Wheel days, including Leon Haywood's 'Baby Reconsider' (Fat Fish, 1967). As the net tightened on the Leicester pressing plant, King faded from the northern soul scene, pursued by false rumours. It was said he had been arrested and put in jail, but the laws against bootlegging were simply not strict enough. Collins was eventually fined a meagre £20, the maximum permissible for breach of the toothless Dramatic and Music Performers Protection Act of 1971, and industry magazine *Billboard* claimed that 'this insignificant deterrent has proved to be the greatest problem facing the record industry in its fight against what now amounts to a 2.5 million-dollar bootleg industry'. With King's disappearance, the baton of counterfeit soul was passed to Selectadisc, a shop owned by former miner Brian Selby from Hucknall in Nottinghamshire. Selby's big break came when the recording industry abandoned the recommended retail price policy and opportunities to sell deleted, discounted and cheaply imported records rose. Selectadisc, based in Nottingham's Arkwright Street, became a magnet for Mods across the English Midlands and a wonderland for young people discovering rock and pop music. John Heathcote from Derby, who was known as Hector and more often by his rhyming name 'Hecta from Selecta', worked in Selectadisc's distribution arm. He remembers that the job frequently put him in contact with the scene's many questionable characters and that one day he was confronted by two men who he claims 'looked like they'd been up for days. It turned out they had robbed a chemist up north and wanted to swap gear for tunes. They produced a bag of about 250 pills and asked for an equivalent amount of records.' Selectadisc drifted away from northern soul soon after Wigan closed and supported the post-punk independent music scene, selling records by The Fall, Buzzcocks and the Human League. But for those far from Nottingham, the shop was synonymous with the twilight trade of suspiciously pressed vinyl. There was even a brief flirtation with legal issues on the short-lived Black Magic label, including the effluent 'Papa Oom Mow Mow' by The Sharonettes (Black Magic, 1975), a crass but catchy stomper produced by the notorious bootlegger Simon Soussan.

Soussan is a mystery and a miscreant who arrived on the northern soul scene in Leeds in the early seventies. He lived in a small flat in the city's Holbeck area, but from those anonymous beginnings he grew to become one the scene's most gifted collectors and most notorious bootleggers. It is not entirely clear where he came from, nor why he chose to settle in Leeds. A serial con man with an ability to charm and deceive, Michel 'Simon' Soussan had even changed his name when he arrived in Britain, supposedly concerned that Michel sounded too girly. The most likely explanation is that he was a French-Moroccan and possibly a Sephardic Jew who had been granted a French passport under the terms of the Crémieux Decree, which gave French citizenship to North African-born Jews. Soussan relished the con more than anything else in life and left a trail of unfulfilled promises, clever deceptions and exaggerated misrepresentation wherever he went. His life took him on a tangled journey from Casablanca to Paris and then to Leeds where he first heard northern soul, and that became the gateway to Wigan Casino. After that he lived briefly in Mexico, then in Los Angeles, and ultimately in bankruptcy. Ian Dewhirst knew him better than most. He spent six months living with Soussan in California and has said with studied understatement, 'The guy's a human chameleon. He was an incredible talent whether you liked him or not, and certainly his nose for northern soul was just incredible. Many times I've seen him in warehouses or garages . . . and he'd suddenly pull a record out, study it and say, "This is the one, baby boy. I can smell it," and he'd be right. He had an encyclopaedic knowledge of arrangers, producers, writers and publishers, and no matter how old-looking or straight the label was, he'd often see something that most people would have missed at the time.'

Soussan was universally loathed on the northern soul scene, but his notoriety brought dark fame, and even today collectors are fascinated by his exploits. He is the scene's greatest anti-hero, the Scarlet Pimpernel of rare soul. I first came across Soussan's name via bogus record lists mailed to me at my home in Rochdale, but his name permeated like a toxic smell in the record bar at Wigan Casino where he had been supplying Wigan's DJs with a string of often great rare records. Most were then immediately counterfeited and the market flooded with cheap bootlegs (often via Selectadisc in Nottingham). One infamous night at Blackpool Mecca, Soussan arrived in the company of Wigan's Richard Searling, and a crowd jostled around him, many demanding repayment for records that had never been honoured, others taking him to task for bootlegging big records. In the ensuing chaos, DJ Ian Dewhirst was attacked with a pint glass and his face seriously injured. Soussan escaped down the escalator and returned to America to perfect ever more grandiose scams.

Sometime in late 1975, on the edge of the dance floor at Wigan, I had a conversation with Dave Greet, a soul collector from Reading. Dave had always approached life with a benign smile and neither of us took life too seriously. Pointing back to the record bar, he said to me as if in confidence, 'Some of the guys are suspicious of Bob Wilson.' I told him I shared the suspicion and I couldn't believe that Wilson had won two caps for Scotland. It was a joke of its time. Back then, Bob Wilson was Arsenal's

Chesterfield-born goalkeeper and had controversially made it into the Scotland football team. Wilson shared his name with a virtuoso pianist from Detroit, a respected instrumentalist who was nicknamed 'the White Ramsay Lewis'. Back in 1965, the Detroit Bob Wilson had fronted a driving keyboard-led dance release called 'All Turned On', credited to Bob Wilson and the San Remo Quartet (Ric-Tic, 1965). It was a northern soul classic with a pedigree dating back to the Twisted Wheel and had been regularly played at the Torch. In 1974, nearly ten years later, Soussan sent an acetate to Wigan which became an instant success. It was a storming instrumental, first known by a cover-up name as 'The Detroit Sound', but became universally known as 'Strings A GoGo' by the Bob Wilson Sounds (Soul Galore, bootleg, 1974). Bootlegs of 'Strings A GoGo' flooded the UK soul market. Jerry Hipkiss, a collector and DJ from the south-west of England, remembers the record arriving newly pressed at an all-dayer at Whitchurch, where 'they shifted box-loads'. It became one of the fastest-selling releases in the history of northern soul and is still a deeply loved instrumental. On their arrival, via the shelves of Selectadisc, it was noted that the record credited Soussan as the composer – a travesty and the mother of all frauds. Soussan was not a music composer and nor was Bob Wilson still part of the Detroit soul scene. He had moved south to Nashville where he was working as a session musician with the Sound Stage Seven label. But the scam took a new twist when the bootleg was exposed by intrepid detective-collectors as a complete fabrication; it was revealed that the track was not by Wilson at all, nor from Detroit. It was an obscure instrumental called 'Double Cookin'' by The Checkerboard Squares (Villa, 1969). Working from his base in California, Soussan had nearly pulled off the perfect crime, making cash from a bootleg and registering it as his own composition in the hope of generating copyright income as the writer and producer. The real rights owner was Herb Campbell, a DJ at Sly Stone's San Francisco radio station KSOL, but Villa

Records had run out of cash, folded and were no longer active as a company. When the garrulous Soussan came along to prey on their failed back catalogue, the company was already mired in failure and escalating debt. Neither Bob Wilson, nor more importantly The Checkerboard Squares, made a penny from one of the northern soul scene's most successful instrumentals, and not for the first time Soussan pocketed the profits.

It should come as no great surprise that Soussan also featured in the story of northern soul's most expensive record, the world-famous 'Do I Love You' by Frank Wilson (Soul, 1965), which in May 2009 reached the staggering figure of £25,000, at auction. By 1976, Soussan had secured a green card, settled in Hollywood, and was trying to break into the film and music industry. He would arrive unannounced at record company offices, hustle into industry parties, and insinuate his way onto the sets of popular television shows. One of his regular hangouts was Center Studios on Hollywood's Las Palmas Avenue, where the syndicated dance music show *Soul Train* was recorded. By the time he was working in Hollywood, Leeds Central had been airbrushed from history and he was living in Beverly Hills with a new wife. His connections with Wigan were changing, too. Soussan saw an opportunity to leave bootlegging behind and make legitimate records for the emerging disco market. Two northern soul DJs, Ian Dewhirst from Leeds Central and Neil Rushton who had made a mark on the scene running rare soul events at Dudley Zoo, had both flown to Los Angeles to hunt down rare records. Over a series of conversations led by the irrepressible Soussan, the three of them concocted a plan to make a disco medley of northern soul records aimed at the US market. But Dewhirst rightly reckoned the source music would be too obscure for the mainstream and encouraged Soussan to think again and make Motown hits the basis of the idea. The idea was not entirely bogus and in fact became the foundation of the disco hit 'Uptown Festival' by Shalamar. Soussan sold the idea to *Soul Train* impresario Don

Cornelius who provided Jody Watley and Jeffrey Daniel, dancers from the popular TV show, to front the band. At the time, the show's booking agent, Dick Griffey, was simultaneously building one of black music's major dance labels, Solar Records. Although Griffey claimed credit for the group's name, and subsequently much of the earned income, it was Soussan who had christened them Shalamar, a name derived from an old northern soul classic, 'Stop And Take A Look At Yourself' by The Shalimars (Verve, 1966). The record was a hit, and Soussan used its success to build a short-lived reputation as a disco producer, but none of them made money from the Shalamar deal. Ian Dewhirst said many years later, 'He was a small-time hustler who got out-hustled by much bigger, more respectable hustlers.'

Backstage on the set of *Soul Train*, Soussan met a Motown employee called Tom DePierro, a dance promotion executive who at the time represented Thelma Houston and Jerry Butler. DePierro was handsome, bearded and openly gay, but more importantly to Soussan he had access to Motown's west coast archives and allowed Soussan access to rare Motown records, including Frank Wilson's 'Do I Love You (Indeed I Do)' (Soul, 1965) and The Andantes' '(Like A) Nightmare' (VIP, 1964). When DePierro turned his back, Soussan supposedly disappeared, stealing the discs which were never returned to Motown and never would be. DePierro's life then took a tragic turn. He contracted AIDS and tried vainly to convince the recording industry to put sexual 'warning stickers' on disco records as the pandemic spread. After years of struggling to pay medical bills, DePierro died prematurely in January 1986, aged only thirty-five. His death provoked an alternative version of the story which claims that, desperate for money, DePierro actually sold the records to Soussan.

Soussan knew that the Frank Wilson record was obscure and could tell that it had the ideal pounding Motown beat for the northern scene. But even he didn't know how rare the record actually was. In the mid sixties and for reasons buried in history, Frank Wilson agreed with Motown's Berry Gordy that he should abandon a solo career as a singer and focus only on producing. The release of 'Do I Love You (Indeed I Do)' was cancelled and only a small number of pre-release copies sneaked out, most of which disappeared or were destroyed as radio stations moved to tape. So when Soussan arrived at his home in Beverly Hills he had in his hands one of only two surviving copies of the record. His first instinct was to resort to type; rather than return the record to Motown and negotiate a legitimate reissue, he bootlegged 'Do I Love You' under a false name and false label. When it arrived at Wigan in 1977 it came as a white acetate credited to Eddie Foster, a little-known west coast soul singer, whose record 'I Never Knew' (In, 1967) was an evergreen northern soul classic. Soussan had already counterfeited the record in bulk and had shipped thousands of copies to the UK, once again flooding the market.

Years later, when Soussan sold his personal record collection and finally parted company with northern soul to move on to the burgeoning Latino dance market, the original record resurfaced. A convoluted chain of ownership brought it into the hands of top UK collectors. Separately another copy was discovered in Detroit and, for a brief spell, both copies were housed incongruously in Todmorden, West Yorkshire, at Tim Brown's Anglo-American Records. Over time, originals of Frank Wilson were owned by several northern DJs, Jonathan Woodcliffe, Kev Roberts and the Scottish rare soul DJ Kenny Burrell, who in 2009 announced he would be selling his copy in a public auction to be overseen by master dealer John Manship. The record eventually went to an undisclosed private dealer for £25,742, a staggering price for a record readily available via download, CD or even on a legal vinyl issue latterly reissued by UK Motown.

Myth has continued to thread round the Frank Wilson record; it became the very last record to be played at Wigan Casino and one of the very few northern soul records that is acceptable to play on a reissue. Frank Wilson's 'Do I Love You' is a song which I have always had mixed feelings about, loving its mystique but tiring of its overexposure. At the time of the auction, the National Galleries of Scotland had secured the £50 million it needed to prevent Titian's sixteenth-century masterpiece *Diana and Actaeon* being sold at auction. Fearing that Kenny Burrell's copy of Frank Wilson would also leave Scotland, I wrote a tongue-in-cheek feature for the *Sunday Times* arguing that northern soul was as worthy of public investment as high art: 'Comparing a soul record to a masterpiece by Titian will seem ludicrous to the uninitiated. But leave aside the mores, prejudices and snob value that separate high art and popular culture, and the strange world of northern soul bears very deep similarities with art. Both are driven by collectors who are fixated by rarity, authenticity and the provenance of their collections. So far, both have also resisted the pressure of recession and the value of collections has either increased or held strong. Words like rare, original and limited edition exist in both communities. Respected dealers existed in both worlds and auctions are a familiar mode of transaction. Art and soul share a culture where fakes, bootlegs and shady attempts to replicate the look of original works are not uncommon.'

In the very month that Frank Wilson's super-rare record was being bootlegged in Los Angeles, I was 2,000 miles away in Birmingham, Alabama, on a grant-aided mission to interview an old black actor called Curtis Smith, one of the few surviving members of the Federal Theatre Project. I had arrived by Greyhound coach from Washington DC after a long, uncomfortable and arse-pounding journey. My accommodation was on the low-rent edge of the city in a highway motel. Despite nylon bed sheets and serial-killer cigarette burns on the bedside table, it had the virtues of a dirt-cheap taxi company, whose offices were next to the motel. I had already slit three pages from the local *Yellow Pages* in a phone booth at the Greyhound station, and had bought a pocket map to help me navigate my target areas. Birmingham had become my latest obsession, not only because of the role it had played in the history of the civil rights movement, but because it was home to some of soul's greatest music and one of my favourite soul singers of the era, the legendary Sam Dees. A sophisticated balladeer, he was every bit as good as official greats like Bobby Womack and Al Green. Birmingham was a sudden and short-lived adventure. I had taken a copy of an old photograph with me. It is a dramatic black-and-white photograph taken hurriedly by Press Association photographer Bill Hudson as Birmingham descended into chaos. It shows a teenager, Walter Gadsden, then a Parker High School student, being attacked by rampant police dogs. Behind the teenager and the dogs, on the corner of 16th and 6th Avenue, is an otherwise insignificant pit-stop diner called the Jockey Boy Restaurant, a black-owned café located across from the 16th Street Baptist Church, which had been bombed by the Ku Klux Klan. The racist attack had killed four children and the photograph captures the full apartheid shame of the Deep South.

Since the day I first saw the photograph in a book at Hull University Library, I had developed a strange longing to visit the Jockey Boy Restaurant. So I took a cab to the intersection and went in through the corner door. After a cursory glance at the menu, I ordered a heart-clogging breakfast of pancakes with maple syrup and bacon, and decided that the Jockey Boy would be my base as I hunted record shops across Birmingham. Coincidentally events had brought the past dramatically to life. A local Ku Klux Klan activist, Robert Chambliss, then aged seventy-three, was standing trial in Birmingham's Jefferson County Courthouse charged with four counts of murder relating to the 1963 church bombing. Suddenly the city was pulled back into its dark past of bomb plots, racism and segregation.

The song that had taken me to Birmingham was nothing to do with civil rights. It was a storming love duet called 'Let Me Be Your Full Time Groover' by Bill Brandon and Lorraine Johnson

(Moonsong, 1973), a pounding soul duet that had been played at Wigan Casino. With some clever detective work I had managed to locate the offices of Moonsong Records in an unremarkable low-rise brick building on US Highway 78, near a row of auto-repair shops. It was located within the premises of the *Birmingham Times*, a local African-American paper owned by Jesse Lewis, the first black man to control a Coca-Cola franchise in America. The name was familiar. Jesse Lewis had been credited as a producer of 'Full Time Groover' and his name recurred on other records by Sam Dees. But far from being a musical overlord, he was a controversial local businessman who had part-funded studio time and so was guaranteed a vanity credit. Everyone was out of town. I called at Lewis's offices only to find he was in Atlanta. I peered through the locked windows of Moonsong and saw nothing but strewn mail, some of it tantalisingly addressed to Clinton Moon, the label owner. He, too, was out of town. The building was locked and disused. I subsequently discovered that Sam Dees was gone, too. He had left Birmingham after the success of his classic debut album *The Show Must Go On* (Atlantic, 1975), tired of Jesse Lewis's overweening presence, and then moved to New York. Their dispute was not only musical. Dees, like many of his generation, was astounded that Lewis and his newspapers supported the segregationist Governor George Wallace as a presidential candidate. Dees was quietly political and had released *The Show Must Go On*, one of the best soul LPs ever, full of layered love songs and social commentary such as 'Child Of The Streets', 'Just Out Of My Reach' and the haunting single, 'Signed Miss Heroin'. It was an album I could recite almost word for word, and I was keen to meet him, but he too was out of town. I would not run into him for another ten years when he flew into Glasgow to appear on a Channel 4 show, *Halfway to Paradise*, recorded in a converted flea-pit cinema in Glasgow's East End. Sam Dees sang alone at a grand piano – spine-chilling. The camera crew, many of whom had worked on the underfunded independent film *Gregory's Girl* and were hardened cynics, gathered on the studio floor and gave him a spontaneous standing ovation.

So, everyone was out of town. Bill Brandon and Lorraine Johnson had been lured to New York to pursue a brief career in the disco scene and Candi Staton, another substantial Birmingham talent, had been swept away with the success of her 1976 hit 'Young Hearts Run Free'. The only person I managed to lay eyes on was a local schoolteacher called Rozetta Johnson, who at the time was a much loved music teacher at Birmingham's Ramsay High School but was better known on the northern soul scene as the emotive singer who fronted 'Chained And Bound' (Clintone, 1971), a big all-nighter record at the Torch. I approached her in the car park of her high school and told her I was the proud owner of her record. She shook my hand gracefully and drove off.

Back at my motel, I ticked off the failures. Not a single lead had turned up anything of value. The interview with the old actor had been monosyllabic and a deep disappointment, Sam Dees had gone, and Moonsong was closed. With the clock ticking down on a mid-afternoon Greyhound bus back to Washington DC, I headed to Bruno's supermarket to stock up for the long haul home. Near the supermarket was a record and tape store, which for two days I had mistaken for an optician's. It was called IBrights and was within walking distance of the Jockey Boy diner. Set at an angle at the far end of an off-road mall, the inauspicious shopfront opened up to a set of stairs to a room cancerous with smoke. The assistant was an overweight white woman, whose hair was nicotine blonde. She waved a Kool cigarette in the air like an orchestral baton, and neither her painted lips nor her shrieking southern voice gave me confidence that this was anything more than another dead end. The room was stacked with 8-track cartridge tapes and scruffy beer crates with party goods and bunting. The second-hand records were stashed further back in an L-shaped corridor crammed with *Guns & Ammo* magazines, true crime books and horror memorabilia. I searched uninterrupted for nearly an hour, trying not to listen in to a conversation between customers that set civil rights back by decades. What had begun as a grey and overcast day suddenly erupted into burning sunshine. Each new box revealed another and another find, almost all of them on southern regional labels; many I knew were safe bets, others downright risks. The shop was selling deleted stock which had been salvaged from a shop in Hoover, Alabama, and in the box racks was a seam of great rare soul: Don Varner 'Tearstained Face' (Quinvy, release date unknown), Bessie Jones 'No More Tears' (Abet, 1968), Eddie Billups 'Shake Off That Dream' (Seventy Seven, 1973), Anne Sexton 'You've Been Gone Too Long' (Impel, 1972) and a Sam Dees rarity, 'Lonely For You Baby' (SSS International, 1968), a record that I had not even heard at the time. I tucked it away with almost childlike excitement. There was even a scuffed copy of Candi Staton's local record 'Now I've Got The Upper Hand' (Unity, 1967), which I took into sanctuary to save it from further damage. In all, I paid $35 for my haul, and armed with records of proven brilliance I made to leave. The woman with the Kool cigarette had taken the money with neither a blink nor even the vaguest hint of eye contact. Her thickly mascaraed eyes were a blank canvas, and she spoke through me to a regular about a parking dispute outside, then, without glancing at me, she swished her cigarette at another rack of records hidden under a window frame. They were clearly marked 'Country and Western' and were separated from the rest of the stock by a tape rack and a tangled stack of old car radios. It was there, in the segregated South, in a tightly packed wall of discs, some of them splattered with grey paint, that I finally found it. For some reason, unfathomable and beyond geographical logic, there was a copy of The DC Blossoms' 'Hey Boy' (Shrine, 1966), the record that I had torn nails and broken sweat to find in its native city.

For northern soul collectors there is nothing more visceral than 'a find'. A sudden surge more emotional than meeting an old friend, more powerful than an away goal, and more satisfying than sex itself. I stared in wonder at the light blue label and the iconic burning Shrine logo. I checked for vinyl cracks and deep scratches, but whatever its wandering history, the disc was virtually pristine and had survived its orphan years with no damage. The paint that had splashed over it like semen on a truck driver's T-shirt had stained the sleeve, but the record itself was flawless. It was a moment of sheer unadulterated joy. I had an uncontrollable urge to snatch the Kool cigarette from the woman's hands, kiss her peachy lips, rip off her velour pants and make urgent love to her over the cash register. But sense prevailed. I calmly gave her another dollar bill and waited obediently for my fifty cents change. As she handed me the loose coins, her lips curled into a chubby smile, and she gave me the most generous grin I'd seen in three days in Alabama. It had the look of post-coital ecstasy – the look of true love.

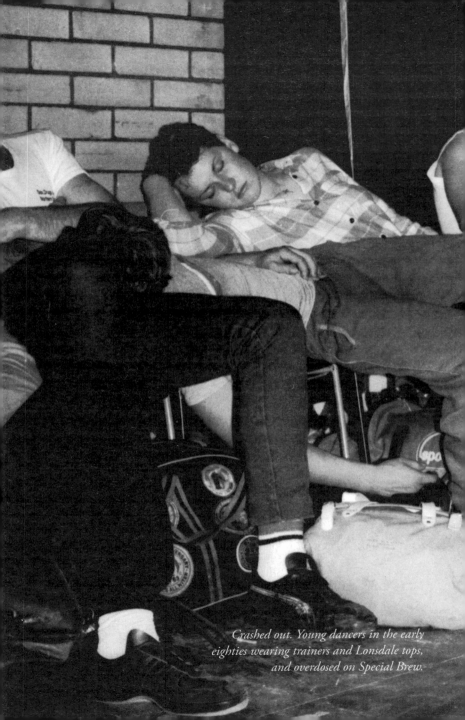

Crashed out. Young dancers in the early eighties wearing trainers and Lonsdale tops, and overdosed on Special Brew.

9
THE NEW MODEL ARMY
1980–1985

Rage, rage against the dying of the light.
Wild men who caught and sang the sun in flight,
And learn, too late, they grieved it on its way,
Do not go gentle into that good night.

Dylan Thomas

The good nights were rarely gentle. We were on the second train, the carriage was alive with anticipation, the gabbing was now gibbering, and fear of entrapment was taking hold. It was late on Saturday night. Drivers, signalmen and station staff were desperate to clock off before the pubs shut, but it was never going to happen. A serious signal failure and electrical outages had halted trains in and out of Stafford Station, but rather than accept the sage advice of the guard and stay put, I followed the crowd. A door burst open, feet crashed to the stony ground and bodies scuttled up the banking. More doors opened behind us. A girl with her dress hauled up and tucked into her knickers like a primary school gym class jumped from the train, and about twenty more soul fans urged each other up the slope to Stafford. Shoes perfectly groomed for dancing but not for steep railway banks were slip-sliding away. Liberated by the climb, and wheezing with laughter, one girl started singing Robert Knight's 'Love On A Mountain Top' (Monument, 1973). Her voice was shrill, northern and unrestrained, and although she didn't know many of the words, the hook line was enough – 'making love on a mountain top'. I can picture her now, her lanky frame half lit by the streetlamp above, her hands raised in triumph, and her bag sliding back down the slope towards me as if it had a life of its own.

So this was Stafford. Fuelled by pharmaceuticals and with hope in my heart, I reached the top of the wet banking and then followed a route that led through hedges and a section of ruined stone walls to Eccleshall Road on the B5013. Like the tunnels in *The Great Escape* – Tom, Dick and Harry – we had seriously underestimated how close we were to our target. Rather than disembarking in the backstreets of Stafford, we were stranded near an industrial estate on the sodden banks of the River Sow. Almost everyone was wearing flat leather soles or, for the first time on the northern scene, old-school trainers. One by one, screams pierced through the darkness as we trudged through muddy tractor ridges that seemed to stretch ahead for miles, indistinguishable in the dark from clumps of slimy cowshit. We were confronting our own version of Ypres – a smell so gassily pungent it would have suffocated any battle-fit soldier. It was a sharp, caustic chemical smell that lingered in my nose for days, clinging like sweat.

For the next twenty minutes, a gang of around ten of us sat on a steep bank that led down to unwelcoming country lanes, scraping our shoes clean: polishing the rims with hankies, digging excrement out of the soles with broken twigs, and cursing the bovine nation. It was at the height of our disgust and disorientation that 'Dandy Dave' Curtis from Stalybridge, in professorial tones, told us that we were not far from Hopton Heath, a key battlefield in the English Civil War. Dave was a mine of information, and in what must rate as one of my favourite crack-up stories of all time, he began to recite the great battle sites of the English Civil War: Cropredy Bridge, Marston Moor, Hopton Heath . . . He recited them with neither care nor concern for our mental health. Dave had not chosen his audience well. Pumped up on amphetamine sulphate – 'the beggar's cocaine' – we were stranded in a rural lane and desperate to get to Stafford. We walked, hitched and hustled for taxis, until an hour later the bedraggled army reached the dance floor, in twos and fours, sliding not on talcum powder but on cowshit from the battlefields of the English Civil War.

It was a metaphor that had more than passing relevance. The history of the northern soul scene can be told as a series of civil wars. There was the original war that forced jazz and blues from beatnik coffee shops as self-confident Mods triumphed. There was a more nuanced and subtle war of attrition that edged R&B off the agenda to be displaced triumphantly by sixties soul. There was the infamous and at times bitter war between the Mecca (modern soul) and Wigan (oldies). There were brief regional skirmishes with the southern legions of jazz-funk and various wars between promoters that pitched venues unhappily against each other. But it was Stafford that took the role of the New Model Army and became the vanguard of change on the scene.

DJ and collector Dave Thorley, the driving force of Stafford, once said, 'When Stafford started it was northern soul's last stand.' He was right. There was much at stake, and many of those who had left the scene with the closure of Wigan were proclaiming the death of northern soul. For a few perilous years, the survival of Britain's greatest youth subculture hung in the balance. By 1982, a glint of sunlight came through the grey clouds and the northern soul scene witnessed a minor revolution. Wigan had closed. The ugly commercialism it had unlocked had moved on. Most London-based record companies had given up trying to unearth hits from the northern scene and the television crews that had rushed to Wigan had moved to the next passing fad. With an audible sigh of relief, northern soul returned to the underground, and a new all-nighter opened at the Top of the World Club in Stafford's Newport Road. In time, it picked up the pioneering baton of clubs like the Twisted Wheel and the Torch in Tunstall by shaping a policy that was right for the times and rewrote the script for soul clubs to come. Stafford was for those who stayed. For those who refused to give up and for those who were young enough to be discovering the scene for the first time round. Those who left had their reasons, too. The great exodus of the early eighties was driven by many factors: people grew up and grew old, abandoning the gear and the all-nighters for a more settled family life; some faced up to the realities of their careers. In some professions, like teaching, the police and social work, there was understandable concern that a culture of drug-taking and all-nighters would be compromising. DJ and promoter Rob Wigley had taken a job on the railways in an era where he felt pressure to give ground to his career. He describes an era of 'longer shift patterns, regular weekend work, stringent and random drug and alcohol testing'. Some even left for other subcultures. For those who got turned on by wearing their granny's net curtains and stuffed seagulls on their heads, New Romanticism had arrived. Jazz-funk and modern variations of soul, especially soulful house, took others away. Some emigrated abroad to Australia and Canada in search of a new life, but one of the biggest exoduses for some of us was the move to London, drawn by the magnetic power of the capital and the narcotic appeal of the creative industries: fashion, the media, music and advertising.

Between April 1982 and February 1986, Stafford's Top of the World became the saviour of the scene and one of the greatest northern all-nighters ever. It was never the biggest nor the most famous club but many argue that Stafford was the best. Like Wigan Casino, the Top of the World was an old-fashioned ballroom whose reputation was transformed by northern soul. The venue opened in 1965 with what the local newspaper, the *Stoke Sentinel*, described as 'lavish fittings and carpeting', a multi-coloured lighting system and a revolving bandstand. It was owned by an anachronistic old entrepreneur, Eddie Fenton, a man of his era whose pencil-thin moustache and bushy eyebrows gave him the demeanour of a retired fighter pilot. Fenton was a stickler for protocol. He installed a barber in the club to shave men's sideburns to regulation army length; those who did not conform were refused entry. Fenton made national news in 1966 at the height of the Mod scene, when a seventeen-year-old office worker from Stafford, Krysia Stanejko, was refused admission because she was wearing a trouser suit styled by the leading boutique of the swinging sixties, Biba. Fenton could not concede that women might want to wear trousers to a nightclub and stuck to his ancient ways, swatting criticism away until the inevitable day when change caught up with him. The Top of the World was eventually subsumed into the expanding Mecca entertainment chain and came under the control of the more forward-thinking Tony Marshall. Within days of starting his new regime, Marshall had ripped up the rule book and, according to an excited news report, allowed teenagers to enter the premises wearing 'polo-neck sweaters, trouser suits, shoulder-length hair – and young women were allowed to display a modest amount of midriff'.

In the late seventies, discontent was growing at Wigan Casino. I remember a long conversation with a lad known as 'Guy from Skipton', his eyes popping with religious zeal, part chemical and part ideological, as he raged about the direction the scene was taking. Like myself, he was a committed collector, who had been motivated to listen to soul by his older sister and then by the music we had heard at local youth clubs. For me it was Letham

Community Centre; for Guy it was the Otley Street Youth Club in Skipton on the fringes of the Yorkshire Dales. We shared a loathing for tailor-made sounds and the malign influence of master bootleggers like Simon Soussan, who was by now flooding the scene with bogus records and deceptive pop. Guy raged like a prophet about the DJs at Wigan, who he dismissed as a 'shower of fucking wankers', a description that held a kernel of truth. What he really meant was that Wigan's commercialism, its indiscriminate play list and nostalgic oldies policy ran the risk of ruining northern soul. In the dying days of Wigan, Guy trapped me near the stage. He was raving: 'What the fuck are we going to do? We've got to fucking do something.' Guy harboured a righteous anger for years to come; within a few years he would shoot to fame at Top of the World in Stafford as Guy Hennigan, one half of a DJ duo known as the Sixties Mafia. The other consigliore was a fellow Scot, Keb Darge, one of the northern scene's greatest ever dancers and a whirlwind of a man who had a tempestuous talent for unearthing obscure records. By now based in London, Keb was a rare beast on the northern soul circuit – a top dancer and a man passionate enough to want to DJ. Shirley Wishart, who went to secondary school with him in Elgin, describes him as a quiet boy in his younger days. 'He was a bit different then,' she told me. 'Very boyish-looking – a bit like a young Bruce Lee – and quite shy, but always an individual.' Martial arts had helped to bring Keb's self-confidence to the fore, and while many around him were deferential to the top DJs, he had the courage to challenge their authority and bring them down to earth.

Work took me away from the jihad and I sidestepped Keb and Guy's holy war. My writing career was taking off and I had been lured like a snake-tongued traitor to the London media where I greedily sucked on the tit of pop culture. Keb was working nightshift in a butcher's warehouse, scything his way through horse meat, and would dish out advice whenever we met. 'Make sure you don't wank yourself to death listening to The Smiths,' he told me when I joined *NME*. Then, one night at a 100 Club all-nighter it was a more straightforward 'fuck off and write about Bono'. As fellow Scots, Keb and I shared a deep love of 'put-down' culture, in which the word 'cunt' has many rich meanings, none of them to do with the vagina. We had grown up in Scotland surrounded by bald cunts, speccy cunts and fat cunts.

Guy Hennigan and Keb Darge first bonded at an all-nighter in Peterborough. 'We sat in the record bar room plotting a revolution in the soul scene,' Keb claims. 'He had a fire in his belly that I was attracted to.' By force of personality and self-belief, they embarked on a campaign to 'save northern soul', and for a period of at least five years it was the nearest to a jihadist movement that the rare soul scene had ever witnessed. Together they went on to defy the presumption that all the best sounds had been found and with a veritable 'New Model Army' of collectors they dug furiously, discovering even more obscure music from the high-point of the sixties, sounds which became the next generation of northern classics. The term 'sixties newies' – meaning soul music from the sixties that had not previously been played on the scene – entered the vocabulary of northern soul. Guy was a bus convenor who had run buses to big all-nighters for years while Keb was a tape man who recorded and then circulated tapes to others on the scene. Through those simple skills, they had reached into the grassroots of the scene and quickly built a crusading group of followers. By guaranteeing promoters that they could bring a crowd, their reputations grew and grew. According to Ady Croasdell, the driving force behind the 100 Club all-nighters in London, the Sixties Mafia DJs were not stuck in the past, either. They were reacting against oldies or the 'nostalgia' records that had taken a grip of the scene. Ady claims that 'DJs Keb Darge and Guy Hennigan in particular were fed up with the staleness of constantly played oldies and reckoned there were still a lot of records hardly known by the public, let alone collectors, that could turn the scene on its head.' Their desire to rebuild a soul caliphate founded on rare sixties soul touched a nerve. We stayed in touch over the years at clubs from Glenrothes to Gloucester, but the Sixties Mafia were hyper-committed and always on duty, while I was an interested onlooker, fascinated by sixties soul but also gripped by new and emergent forms of black American music: modern soul, Chicago house and hip-hop. Our tastes were diverging, but they remained devout and wedded to an irreducible Quran: northern soul was not a passing fad, it was the electricity that lit our lives.

Stafford raged against the dying of the light. The wave of pessimism that had gripped the scene after Wigan closed was brushed aside. Stafford broke sounds that became anthems in the north: Sam Fletcher's 'I'd Think It Over' (Tollie, 1964), The Groovettes' 'Think It Over Baby' (Reness, 1968) and Jackie Day's 'Naughty Boy' (Phelectron, release date unknown), a blistering dance record with classic Motown characteristics, including a fierce saxophone break which is delivered by Jackie's husband, Big Jay McNeely. Gradually there was a gear-shift of sorts, and slower, more pleading songs were played: Donald Jenkins and the Delighters' 'Somebody Help Me' (Cortland, 1963) and a rousing beat-ballad from Hollywood by Cal Green and the Specials, 'I'll Give You Just A Little More Time' (Filmtown, 1967). Indicative of the new sound was a slow-paced remorse song from the early sixties by Big Frank and the Essences, 'I Won't Let Her See Me Cry' (Blue Rock, 1965), a B-side that had lain unknown for over two decades.

Big Frank turned out to be obscurity writ large. Franklin Delano Murphy shared the same Christian names as President Roosevelt but was a balladeer who had styled his big-band soul style on Frank Sinatra and Tom Jones. In August of 1983, when Guy Hennigan played the song on heavy rotation, Big Frank was working as a narcotics parole officer in New York, where State Governor Nelson Rockefeller had introduced draconian laws for the possession of heroin, cocaine and cannabis. Fearless and determined, Hennigan had changed the game. Unlike many of his era who were wedded to the past and believed that true northern soul was the frantic stomper of the Wigan years, he began to schedule songs that were slower but always with big and pronounced beats. At times, soul teetered on the brink of sounding like Carnegie Hall as big voices boomed out tear-jerking love songs. Among them were Romance Watson's 'Where Does That Leave Me' (Coral, 1965) and Tommy Navarro's 'I Cried My Life Away' (DeJac, 1964), songs that would have been seen as pedestrian in the fiery inferno of the Torch. Against the odds, the new sounds worked and Stafford became the club that tore up history. Mark 'Butch' Dobson, then primarily a collector but later to become the scene's most famous DJ, claimed that breaking with the past was what defined the era. 'That was one of the things I liked about Stafford. They didn't give a fuck about what was before,' he argued. 'It was about what was happening now. The crowd had some dignity.' Part of their dignity was not being hung up about the past.

Stafford had another role to play – it became the northern scene's great healer. It bridged the false dichotomy between sixties and modern soul by playing both in the same venue. Stafford resisted the temptation to rerun the ancient battles that drove Wigan and Blackpool Mecca into bitter rivalry. Much of the credit for that foresight must go to Dave Thorley, a knowledgeable and forward-thinking collector from Gloucestershire who had been a DJ at the highly underrated Yate all-nighters in the seventies, and was a featured DJ at all-dayers at the Ritz in Manchester. His collection of new and independent modern soul from the urban ghettos of America was counterweight to the big anthemic sounds of the sixties and featured relatively unknown artists from inner city independent labels such as Washington DC's Ronnie Dyson, Detroit's Oliver Cheatham and Philadelphia's 'Loveman' Ronnie Stokes.

Dave Molloy had a theory and it was a good one. We met up one Sunday in Wigan to retrace our steps, and for a disorientated hour or two he led me through strange streets. Like a Vietnam vet returning to a battlefield, I was taken from the mainline stations to a doorway on the corner of King Street, where I had once been trapped and body-searched by the drug squad. All that remained were shades of dismal brown paint and old Victorian struts that supported the roof of Wigan Wallgate. Then, through an unfamiliar landscape, he took me to the spot where the Casino had once stood. It was now an anonymous shopping mall. A few yards from Top Man, Dave paced out ten exaggerated steps, like a football referee marking out the defensive wall. Then he stopped, looked around and, much more carefully, like an archaeologist mapping out ancient Egypt, he estimated that we were standing at the front of the stage where Wigan Casino had once stood. This was the area of the old ballroom that the late Fran Franklin, a mixed-race girl from Muirhouse in Edinburgh, called 'Scots Corner'. It was where I had first met Keb Darge from Elgin, the Dumfries Boys, Tommy Cockburn from Falkirk. Where I first came into contact with the eccentric Gaz Kellett, a stick-thin boy with a chewing tongue and a cartoon mind, and Caesar and Mary Evison and Julie Pender. All the names flood back when I think of those few square yards of wooden floor.

Dave offered to buy me a coffee at the Casino café in the food court above the escalators. It was a kitsch little place, decorated with poor-quality memorabilia and unseemly tat, and neither of us had the heart for it. We talked for hours, lost in music, wandering back over forty years of northern soul: the places, the DJs, the sounds, the scandals. We talked at length about what brought him to the scene. He had grown up in an Irish immigrant family from County Mayo who had settled in Farnworth near Bolton, home to two very English heroes, comedienne Hylda Baker and footballer Alan Ball. Dave had been introduced to northern soul by his older brother Jim, a Bolton Mod who became a teenager as sixties soul blasted the western hemisphere. When Jim brought a girl home, it was Dave's job to switch the lights on and off to create the impression that their Bolton council house was a disco. He vividly remembers helping his brother to seduce local Mod girls to the sound of Chuck Woods's 'Seven Days Is Too Long' (Roulette, 1967) as the front-room bulb flicked into action. Dave was reared on some of the great sounds of the early years, and among his play list as he dutifully switched the lights on and off were Tony Clarke's 'Landslide' (Chess, 1965), a Golden Torch classic with the greatest intro of any northern soul record, and the more genteel 'Rescue Me' by Fontella Bass (Checker, 1965), a song that has been covered, but never bettered, by a long list of female singers including Diana Ross, Cher and Pat Benatar.

The Molloy brothers had bought their first soul records at Edwin P Lees, an electrical shop on Bolton's Newport Street which stocked lightbulbs, extension cables and bedside lamps. Upstairs was a rack of chart records and a small box of imports. Dave's love of browsing and collecting was born. He was not alone. Bolton was crackling with the sound of sixties soul. Troggs on Peel Street in Farnworth was one of the wildest and most exciting local clubs in the north-west. He began to make friends – Judith, whose dad owned the butcher's on Mather Street, had been a regular at the Twisted Wheel; her boyfriend Richard Searling was a student and was also buying great sounds. Searling was destined to become one of the northern soul scene's greatest ever DJs, and with Dave his trusted confidant the pair drove millions of miles in search of northern soul.

We were sitting in an olde worlde pub in Wigan, only a few hundred yards from the Casino, when I asked Dave to describe the most influential moment in the history of northern soul. Was it the forced closure of the Twisted Wheel by Manchester's drug squad? The opening of Wigan? The wars with Blackpool Mecca that split the scene so acrimoniously, or the arrival of Stafford? To this day, he has a remarkable photographic memory and a treasure trove of memorabilia that stretches across the history of the scene, including one striking picture of a girl wearing a necklace of red and brown amphetamine capsules. Dave described going to a St Patrick's Day all-dayer at Manchester Tiffany's, by then a decaying nightclub in the city's Oxford Street. It was March 1982. Wigan was dead, the Torch was ancient history, and the scene was on its knees. The venue was only half full, the atmosphere was sullenly quiet, and less than 250 diehards had turned up. Halfway through the day, he was approached by Manchester-based collectors Dave Withers and Rod Shard, and invited into a small room behind the stage. A few others followed them to gather round a small portable cassette tape recorder. Rod pressed a button and played a previously unheard tape of sixties sounds. It was dynamite. Dave Molloy describes the feelings as 'pure electricity'; it was 'a moment of sheer disbelief'. On the tape were a series of unreleased tracks by high-end Motown artists, including the Four Tops, Gladys Knight, The Velvelettes and Marvin Gaye. No one was certain exactly who the artists were but through some ingenious detective work over the months ahead they began to identify the artists and titles. Dave Withers and Rod Shard had been sworn to secrecy and so could not reveal the source of the records, but it was less than twelve months before Motown celebrated its twenty-fifth anniversary. Plans were afoot to release previously unavailable tracks from the vaults, so the unissued tracks had probably leaked at a highly porous moment in the corporation's history. Whatever the circumstances, they were hot property in every sense of the term. Although there was no vinyl to see and not even acetates to handle, it proved to be one of the greatest finds in northern soul history. They were not simply rare. They had never been released, and as far as the northern soul scene was concerned they didn't even exist. The first and most natural instinct was to cut acetate copies and play them as cover-up songs, but that was taking a risk with copyright and breaking the promises they had made to their source. And the small coven of collectors who gathered around the cassette player faced another dilemma: the records were of such unforeseen brilliance, to leave them on a tape would cheat the dance floors of the northern soul scene. So strict legality was set aside, acetates won the day, and the music leaked onto the scene without the permission of Motown.

On 1 May 1982, at a Stafford all-nighter, Dave Molloy looked on as Dave Withers played one of the most exemplary and passionate sets in the history of northern soul. The illegal and unreleased Motown records were given their first public outing. He describes collectors being frozen in disbelief, dancers cheering music they had never heard, and a buzz bouncing round the walls. In keeping with northern soul protocol, all the tracks were 'covered up' and credited to a mix of either real or imagined rare soul singers. One track, which was in fact an unreleased track by Marvin Gaye called 'This Love Starved Heart Of Mine (It's Killing Me)' (unissued) was credited to Detroit vocalist JJ Barnes. Barnes was a Ric-Tic artist who had a vocal style similar to Marvin Gaye and frequently blamed Motown for forestalling his own career. The pick of his bunch was the heavily prophetic 'Lonely Lover', also by Marvin Gaye, an alternative version of a cherished song once recorded by Jimmy McFarland and a song that grew in resonance. Paradoxically Marvin Gaye was in the last throes of his own now tragic life. After a period of near abstinence from drugs while living in exile in Belgium, he had returned to America for his Sexual Healing concert tour where he became addicted to cocaine again. On Christmas Day 1983, Marvin gave his father, Marvin Gaye Snr, an unlicensed Smith & Wesson pistol, ostensibly to protect himself and the family home from intruders. By now paranoid and suicidal, soul music's greatest soloist was trapped inside a wooden-frame home at 2101 South Gramercy Place, in West Adams, Los Angeles, with a vengeful father and a mother ill with kidney failure. He was fatally shot by his own father on

1 April 1984 after a series of heated family arguments. The autopsy revealed that Marvin Gaye had been using cocaine and angel dust. After plea-bargaining, his father was given a six-year suspended sentence. Showing remorse at the trial, he told Judge Ronald George, 'If I could bring him back, I would. I was afraid of him. I thought I was going to get hurt.' But nothing could bring him back and Marvin Gaye was buried on 5 April 1984, at Forest Lawn Memorial Park, Glendale. The funeral was attended by over 10,000 people, including many of the Motown colleagues whose unreleased records were now causing such a stir at Stafford. Among the mourners were members of The Temptations, Gladys Knight and the Pips, The Marvelettes and The Velvelettes.

History was being played out on a strange stage. To maximise the impact of the unissued Motown tracks, Dave Withers and Rod Shard did not keep them possessively for themselves. They lent out acetate copies of several tracks to others, including former Wigan DJ Richard Searling. Searling was given two tracks by The Temptations: 'Tear From A Woman's Eye' from January 1964 (featuring Eddie Kendricks) and 'Angel Doll' written by Stevie Wonder and Clarence Paul. The Motown acetates, the quality of the recordings and the subterfuge around them, gave the tracks a heightened significance on the circuit, turning many of the scene's top collectors into sleuths. They had a veritable case-load of tracks to choose from, including 'Suspicion' by Motown's vocal harmony group The Originals, which was offered up to audiences as 'Baby Have Mercy On Me' by The Prophets. It is not entirely clear why that disguise was chosen except that the name was sufficiently vague and several groups with that name had emerged across the years, including a major northern oldie 'Fever' by The Prophets (Smash, 1967), a classic at the Twisted Wheel. The group's name then morphed into The Georgia Prophets, and causing further confusion an ultra-rare record on Washington DC's iconic label Shrine was also credited to The Prophets – 'If I Had (One Gold Piece)/ Huh Baby' (Shrine, 1966). Helped by the camouflaged name, many collectors believed it was a released record out there waiting to be found. Dave Withers chose to play one of the newly discovered Motown records twice on the same night – The Marvelettes' 'Sugar's Never Been As Sweet As You' (unissued), which across time was variously credited to Patty Gilson & Tonettes and another fake name, Little Lisa, a minor Motown artist who had left the company with no visible success. One reason that the track jumped off the decks and found instant success was the clever way it descants on the Four Tops' ultra-classic song 'I Can't Help Myself' (Motown, 1965), even tanta-lisingly using the hook line 'Sugar pie honey bunch' throughout.

I was told about these Motown singles via the rare soul grapevine and agreed to write about them in a feature in *Black Echoes* where I was freelancing, but with the proviso that I was circumspect about how they had come to Britain. In the early days of Stafford, my in-tray at *Echoes* groaned with new records for review. One day, I opened a package that had been sent from Fuquay-Varina, a small town in North Carolina. Inside was a so-what electro-funk 12-inch disc called 'Nasty Rock' by the Garrett Crew, which was heavy on synthesisers and vocoders and allegedly attracting attention on the German electronic scene. I was about to throw it into the office review bin when I noticed it had been padded with unusual ballast – three copies of a 7-inch record. The record was Glenda McLeod's 'No Stranger To Love' (HGEI, 1983). It had all the promise of obscurity and was ideal for the modern DJs at Stafford. I rang the record company in America, but they had already gone bust, and when I tracked down the producer he had turned his back on the record business and opened an amusement arcade. I kept one copy for my own collection and sent the others to DJs Ian Clark and Dave Thorley, knowing that it would get exposure on the two dominant all-nighters of the time, the 100 Club and Stafford. For a long while they were the only three copies that existed until repressings turned up, fuelled by the northern soul demand.

Unlike most northern DJs who spend more on vinyl than their wardrobe, Dave Thorley cut a smarter shape, preferring styled suits and neat shirts to the sweaty vest and Indian ink tattoos of the old-style northern scene. He also instituted another small but significant culture change at Stafford, encouraging well-known collectors to shape musical policy and help the club to unearth sounds that could define the era. Stafford turned long-time collectors into DJs, including from the first night Dave Withers. He was an articulate figure on the scene who had appeared in the now notorious Granada television documentary that at the height of Wigan Casino had opened the curtains on the underground northern scene, allowing prying eyes their first real glimpse of what was until then a word-of-mouth subculture. Frustrated with the lack of opportunities, Dave Withers moved to America where he eventually settled, living in an apartment that overlooked the intersection where Rodney King was murdered by the LAPD, the incident that triggered the riots of 1992. Withers is now a manager of one of the rare funk scene's top 'crate-digger' stores, Big City Records in Union City, New Jersey. Others followed, among them Peterborough's Jimmy Wensiora, Bradford's George Sharp, Ady Pountain, another Yate DJ who had helped push Stafford as a venue from the outset, and most dramatically of all, Guy Hennigan. Collectors also influenced behind the scenes, including Tim Ashibende and his friend Mark Dobson from Stoke, better known by his nickname 'Butch', who had one of the best rare soul collections in the world.

For those who came of age in the early eighties, Stafford was king. Rightly so, they came to resent older northern soul fans who yearned for the past and came to describe life after Wigan as 'the lost years or 'the wilderness years'. It was a view of rare soul history that Stafford utterly dismantled. The New Model Army dug deeper than any previous generation had done, finding records that were now twenty years old and in many cases supremely rare. One example among many is Blue Steam, a four-man harmony group from Durham, North Carolina. When they released 'I Want A Girl' (Catamount, 1975), it was not short of quality, featuring great old-school vocalists and instrumentation from Kool and the Gang's rhythm section. But the record stiffed due to poor distribution. It was only sold in a local milk bar and a ghetto barber's shop in downtown Durham until Dave Withers found a copy, played it at all-nighters and rescued it from anonymity.

As Stafford's reputation grew, its fortunes became interconnected with another club, one more famous for its role in the evolution of punk rock than northern soul and based at the famous address of 100 Oxford Street, London W1 – an oasis for those of us who had deserted the north to find work in London. Britain was changing. Since the seventies and the opening of Wigan Casino, the economic gap between the old northern industrial cities and the suburban south had widened to a gulf and the north–south divide had become an entrenched feature of British life. Between 1971 and 2011 – across the lifespan of northern soul, the south has racked up a thirty per cent cumulative growth lead over the economies of the north. Shane Meadows' *tour de force* drama *This Is England '90* followed the personal consequences of social decline and traced the decades that witnessed northern soul, Mod revivalism, punk, the rise of the rave scene and the battering impact of unemployment on the north. The final episode was shot on Sheffield's Gleadless Valley estate, which at the time was ranked within ten per cent of the most deprived areas of England, where a third of children lived in poverty. Paul Mason, a regular at Wigan Casino as a young man and now the economics editor of Channel 4 news, reviewed *This Is England '90* and composed a damning and near biblical indictment of social change: 'So as we laugh at the hapless youngsters of *TIE90*, and snicker at the analogue drabness of their world, let's remember. This is what it was like just before we got divided into the saved and the damned: when you could still riot without a balaclava, walk into a job centre with your head held high, and when a whole family could – if it had to – live on the earnings of a dinner lady.'

By the early eighties, when I returned north it was always nervously. Living in London and writing about new forms of soul music, I felt to some degree I had turned my back on the scene: snubbing my own family. On one trip north to Stafford, I was buying water from a garage on High Green when I felt a fist screwing into my back and a voice saying, 'Christ, I thought you were dead.' It was Pete Lawson, one of the scene's erratic livewires. We then walked the few hundred yards to the Top of the World as Pete berated me for writing about hip-hop, scolded me for not reviewing rare sounds any more, and launched into a swerving but brilliantly lucid analysis of amphetamine and its role within northern soul. He was convinced that a recent police campaign against northern soul all-nighters, Operation Crossbow, was having a detrimental impact on the quality of amphetamine. It had already forced the closure of clubs in Newton Aycliffe and stemmed the supply of illegal drugs elsewhere. According to Pete, it had a knock-on effect on Stafford. 'You can't get good gear now, Stuart,' he said ruefully. 'It's all shit student stuff now.' With those words, we parted as Pete met another passer-by, who he hugged like a child.

O

In the spring of 1993, northern soul was rocked by the murder of Pete Lawson. The news leaked out to his closest friends and family first, but the dramatic circumstances of his death meant the story was picked up by BBC Manchester's *North West Tonight* and ITV's *Granada Reports*, taking the story to viewers across the north-west of England. I was in London at the time and had just joined Channel 4 as a commissioning editor and was phoned by a friend from my days at Wigan. He was short on detail and unsure of the exact circumstances of Pete's death.

Pete was a larger-than-life figure who had had a colourful past.

However, he was also a victim of mental health problems, which were only known to some people on the scene and which at times gave him a deceptively threatening aura. A close friend, the late Frank Jackson, a major face in the rare soul scene in the Liverpool area, once said of Pete: 'He had evaded diagnosis over many years, had been tested for conditions like paranoid schizophrenia, but eventually later in his adult life he was diagnosed as suffering from a bipolar condition. Over the years he was diagnosed as everything from schizophrenic onwards, until they finally settled on manic depression and he learned to cope with his situation, which he didn't hide and would tell anyone about, but he would have pissed on your sympathy as he was a very self-possessed individual and took pride in himself. This was a hurdle he overcame on his own and you could take it or leave it as far as he was concerned.'

Peter Lawson was from Ormskirk, due north of Liverpool. His parents' red-brick council house was near Crosshall Brow, a road which led eastwards through Skelmersdale and Orrell down into Wigan. The two of us arrived on the scene almost simultaneously. We had both made a few awestruck visits to the Torch before its closure. Pete went there with a formidable Ormskirk crew, which included his older brother and a generation of local men obsessed with amphetamine and up-tempo soul. In the photographs that exist of Pete back then, he looks angelic with his page-boy blond hair and innocent smiles, almost a different person to the cropped-hair warrior he became in later life. By the time Wigan Casino opened, Pete had already attracted a degree of notoriety. In the days before a dedicated black-music media, he had taken out a small ad in the *NME*, advertising a list of super-rare records. I sent off for the list and began to deal with him directly. His letters were courteous, but his service was not; he had built up a cleverly deceptive trade in Emidiscs, the acetate pressings that duplicated rare records. It was a murky trade but hardly high-level bootlegging. Much of it was done in the full knowledge of both buyer and seller that the acetates provided were not on the original label. Pete had discovered a facility in Carnforth called High Bank, on the southern edges of the Lake District. It was owned by a technological oddball called Derrick Marsh, who Pete and another Ormskirk collector, Keith Bradley, had charmed into making duplicates of big northern soul records. The facility was officially known as Deroys Sound Studio and its business was mostly church organ music, Christian sermons and local folk groups. The studio's greatest claim to fame was a single by the Blackburn Rovers FC squad for the season 1972–73, called 'By Gum We'll Make It A Day' (DEROY, 1972). Pete's acetate scam attracted compliant rare soul DJs and the attention of a journalist at *Blues & Soul* magazine called Frank Elson, who threatened legal action against Lawson and Bradley. In one of his columns in the summer of 1974 he wrote: 'It seems that certain people, including very well-known DJs, have found a way of making money that makes the regular pressers look very soft indeed. These people are obtaining records from lists on approval, maybe as much as £40 worth, getting Emidiscs cut then sending the originals back saying they don't want them. Then, not only are they playing the Emis but they also have a few extras cut and sell them for £5. The crookedness here is twofold. Not only does the DJ get the latest sounds but he also makes a hell of a lot of money out of the ordinary soul fan [and] the fan who buys the cutting is getting a bad deal because these things are cut, not pressed, from acetate and they rapidly wear out so you're not getting much for your £5.'

My early doubts about Pete were exacerbated when I sent him a postal order for £7 for an original copy of an in-vogue record by Louise Lewis, Miss LL's 'Wee Oo I'll Let It Be You Babe' (Skyway, 1968). A week later, I discovered it had been bootlegged on a mass scale. When we eventually met in the record bar at Wigan, Pete sensed I felt cheated, but rather than just blank me, he reassured me that my original would grow in value and, if it didn't, in ten years' time he'd refund every penny. It did, and is now worth ten times what I paid for it. Within minutes of talking to him, a song by Robbie Lawson, 'Burning Sensation' (Kyser, 1967), was blaring over the Casino speakers. In a whispered confidence, he said, 'Don't tell anyone, but that's my dad.' Through the fug of gear, I nearly fell for it, but his face cracked into a smile and I just managed to avoid being reeled in. We laughed at his daft flight of invention and although we never became bosom buddies we shared similar obsessions and so happily co-existed.

Pete Lawson lived and died for northern soul. His passion for the music oozed from every pore, and his diatribes for or against records were the stuff of legend. There were many versions of the same guy: the massive risk-taker who used to dive across the bonnets of cars outside Wigan Casino – 'car-surfing' – as they drove past; the vulnerable Pete whose mother worried about his health across a lifetime, seeking inconsistent help from doctors, hospitals and well-meaning experts; the fearsomely intelligent Pete Lawson who could argue forensically about Tory policy and the ideological war against the north; the relentless Pete who would play every B-side imaginable, believing that the scene may have missed a classic; the autistic spectrum Pete who kept lists, letters and clippings as if they held the key to the riddles of the universe; the fuming polemicist who wrote scathing letters to fanzines denouncing DJs and promoters; the record shark who drove a hard bargain selling sounds; the generous Pete who frequently spent his last pound on friends; and the self-aware Pete who talked openly about mental illness in a cultural scene hardly prepared for the conversation. In all, he was a bundle of contradictions: partly truth and partly fiction. Many collectors have admitted that they wish they had kept the cardboard sleeves of records bought from Lawson. They were invariably covered in intense and sometimes surreal musical criticism, with scribbled comments on the record, its uniqueness and even the people who featured on it. Tony Smith from London did keep them. 'Not a day goes by where I don't find a record sleeve with some mammoth rant or sales spiel scrawled all over it in Pete's inimitable handwriting.'

Jim O'Hara, the driving force at the Allanton all-nighters, was someone Pete admired. He thought the back-to-basics all-nighter had rekindled the underground roots of northern soul. When Allanton closed, and sick of being made redundant three times, Jim moved briefly to Sicily where he worked in a series of holiday jobs. Pete wrote to him religiously, trying to attract him back to promote another northern club. He wanted it to be just like Allanton but nearer Ormskirk. According to Jim, who is now a business manager working with high-tech fabrics aimed at the military and high-risk industries, the letters were like jazz sketches, jumping from one subject to another and always driven by passionate ideas and zealous language. Although on the surface incoherent, there was, according to Jim, always an underlying logic to his letters. Dave Molloy has kept correspondence, too, in particular a blistering dispute between Pete and one of the northern soul scene's top record dealers, Tim Brown. The exchange of correspondence would baffle outsiders: Pete lacerates Tim for not going out to all-nighters enough, not taking amphetamine and hiding away in his business; Tim retaliates by criticising Pete's unrealistic fundamentalism that the true northern soul diehard should be blocked, up all night and wedded to rare sixties soul. In the extraordinary heat of the correspondence, Pete proposed that Tim donate fifty per cent of his earned income to a poverty fund for soul singers who had fallen on hard times. Pete agreed to do the same. He was on the dole at the time.

Frank Jackson, one of Pete's closest friends, described him as 'ferociously independent – the alternative was to wallow in his problems and that was never going to be him'. Jocko O'Connor, an Edinburgh-based collector and DJ at Allanton all-nighters, also befriended Pete at Stafford. 'I had my fall-outs with him over the years, but he was a very special person. No one should also forget Pete's influence on records in the eighties. His search for new stuff in the days of Stafford was relentless. I still miss him,' he said. 'What went on in his head was a diagnosed illness that Pete had to live with till his death. His anger was driven by his passion for northern soul, which was his life.'

Although it was never as pronounced as the industrial decline of the north, Stafford took place against a backdrop of escalating mental health problems in the UK, and the most vulnerable subgroup were young men like Pete Lawson. We were living through great memories but a horrendous epidemic. Major forms of depression were at an all-time high and over 250,000 people are now diagnosed as bipolar. The charity CALM estimates that two in five British men have contemplated suicide, now the most common cause of death in men under the age of thirty-five. With the benefit of hindsight, Pete showed some of the classic signs of bipolar disorder – talking rapidly, jumping from one idea to another, thoughts racing through his head, not needing or valuing sleep, and being argumentative and aggressive. But there was much more to him than a list of symptoms. Michael Higgins, now a university lecturer, was a teenager when he first met Pete at Stafford. He reflects on his kindness, his willingness to impart knowledge to younger soul fans, and his generosity. More a cultural mentor than a threat. Dave Molloy is convinced that Pete was 'much tougher on people who were established on the scene', including DJs, club promoters and journalists. He was in that respect the bipolar opposite of a bully, in that he would seek out people on the fringes of the scene and make them feel welcome.

Gis Southworth, a late arrival on to the northern scene who had been a Preston punk before finding his way to Stafford all-nighters, had befriended Pete, and along with another Preston face, Stuart Raith, was helping him with his fanzine. Gis was also planning his wedding and had already put Pete's name down on the invite list, despite fearing that he might criticise the 'Wedding March' as too slow and not rare enough. 'Jumping' Joan Livesey, a collector and DJ also from the Preston contingent, has talked openly about cherishing Doris Smith's 'No Good Guy' (Limelight, 1967) at a Keele all-nighter, the weekend before Pete was killed. He had given her the £40 she needed to buy the record. 'That record means more to me than anything – partly because Pete bought it for me – but partly because it reminds me so much of that weekend.'

According to Frank Jackson, in the days before Pete was murdered he had gone with him on a hectic round of drink, drugs and all-night soul. 'He had been living away from Ormskirk for a while and come back only relatively shortly before his death. He hadn't been very well, I think, and knew enough to get home, and though his old lady wouldn't let him move back he got a nice flat and got mentally strong again, much of which was down to his close relationship with his lifetime best mate, Mel, who stood absolutely no messing.' Ian 'Mel' Melia – a former soldier, an Ormskirk rare soul collector and probably Pete's closest friend – had been a steadying rock for Pete over many years. He spoke to me candidly about Pete's mental health record and then returned with great dignity the following day to say he would rather his memories remained private and off the record. They will. But they were also uniquely helpful in trying to make sense of one of northern soul's most complex characters.

Pete Lawson's death was cruel beyond description. Soon after settling back in his hometown, his life ended. Pete was murdered at a house on Thornfield Crescent in Little Hulton, Salford, in brutal circumstances. He had gone there to visit a one-time associate, Ian 'Macca' McMullan. No one knows what happened in the house, but those who heard the court testimony confirm the humiliating circumstances of his death. No one can convincingly explain a motive: perhaps an argument over records escalated into a frenzied attack, old scores were being settled, or Pete's argumentative personality may have been provocative? It remains conjecture. Frank Jackson, the last person from the northern soul scene to see Pete alive, remembers them parting at Burscough Bridge Station after a game of pool. He watched Pete disappear in what Jackson has described as 'a good state of mind'. When Pete failed to report home to his mother, she anxiously called round his northern soul pals to see where he was. Frank took a call from her but dismissed it, assuming that Pete would show up as he had done so often in the past. Then he describes the stark realisation that something had gone badly wrong: 'I felt the cold chill as the Granada reporter on the telly said the body of a man had been found in a flat in Little Hulton, followed within minutes by a call from Greater Manchester murder squad to come and interview me. It was a pretty gruelling session as they brought out his record box, jacket and the shoes his mum had bought him for his birthday for me to identify.'

Towards the end of his life, Pete was publishing a fanzine, *The Gospel According to Dave Godin*, in which he tried to evoke a true gospel of northern soul. It included a lengthy interview with the soul fan turned radical journalist, Dave Godin. Dave Molloy made the lucid point that, more than anything else in life, Pete craved respect and status on the scene, much more than he valued money or personal gain. Pete saw his chance to meet Dave Godin as a privilege, but the night he returned from interviewing Godin, by now a vegan more interested in foreign-language cinema than rare soul, he told Dave Molloy, 'He looks like a fucking tramp.' It was a typically honest assessment of someone Lawson adored.

Pete Lawson's requiem was as much a celebration of northern soul as a life lost. The coffin was carried by Frank Jackson, Dave Molloy and Ian Cunliffe, and supported by two originals from the Ormskirk crew, Mel and Little Mick. Dave Godin travelled from his home in Sheffield to read the eulogy. His sonorous words rose through the silence of the crowded parish church in Ormskirk like a Sermon from the Mount, as northern soul grieved one of its greatest characters. They played Pete's all-time favourite record, Jerry Williams' 'If You Ask Me (Because I Love You)'

(Calla, 1967), a title that he had devotedly tattooed across his chest. It was a song rich with irony. Jerry Williams was a supremely talented but psychologically complex writer-producer who had taken on the alter-ego 'Swamp Dogg', in part because he was uncomfortable with the demands of the music industry. 'I became Swamp Dogg in 1970 in order to have an alter-ego', he once said, 'someone to occupy the body while the search party was out looking for Jerry Williams, who was mentally missing in action.' The search party has yet to find the real Pete Lawson.

The author in London (circa 1981) wearing a Demob XLNT Harrington based on the original Mod jacket.

10
LONDON CALLING
1984–1990

I had neither kith nor kin in England, and was therefore as free as air – or as free as an income of eleven shillings and sixpence a day will permit a man to be. Under such circumstances, I naturally gravitated to London, that great cesspool into which all the loungers and idlers of the Empire are irresistibly drained.

A Study in Scarlet, Arthur Conan Doyle

My life had taken me to the beautiful south, or as Arthur Conan Doyle preferred to call it, 'that great cesspool into which all the loungers and idlers of the Empire are irresistibly drained'. It took me a while to settle in London, and maybe I never did, but the more my career shifted from northern soul fanzines to pop journalism, the more London became a necessary evil. It was a love–hate relationship from the outset. I thrived on the remarkable multicultural diversity and lived in black communities but in truth I was always an outsider. London was a different country and would become stranger as its power grew.

At the time I arrived in London, a young Scottish novelist called Martin Millar had written his cult novel, *Milk, Sulphate and Alby Starvation*, a precursor to Irvine Welsh's *Trainspotting* which I read voraciously. It spoke to me in volumes, telling the story of Alby Starvation, 'the first true British anti-hero of the giro generation'. Alby is a Scottish boy who discovers he is lactose intolerant and advocates that everyone should give up milk. For his troubles, he is pursued through dodgy nightclubs and backstreets by a hit man hired by the Milk Marketing Board. The book described things I'd never seen in print before: shit wraps of amphetamine, sulphate paranoia and wandering in lowlife streets through the night. The book is set in Brixton – then yet to be caught up in the property bubble – in a world of reggae bars, makeshift soul clubs and multiracial communities on the edge of erupting.

What is now largely forgotten about London in the eighties was that the single biggest migrant group had not come from overseas but from the rest of Britain, from the regions of the north and the Celtic nations. Two things drove them: necessity and wonder. London was a phenomenal magnet. It had a burgeoning economy and offered jobs when the north's manufacturing base was in steep decline, and it had been a hive of fashion, nightlife and creativity since the sixties – powerful attractions for the young.

Many thousands of Scots had moved south to London before me. In 1983, when Stafford was celebrating its first anniversary as the northern soul scene's top all-nighter, I was writing for *Black Echoes*. It was a year that was book-ended by two deaths that captured the transient experience of being in London in that era. The first came when the paths of two Scottish migrants crossed in

Oxford Street, and the day has stayed depressingly in my memory ever since. Stephen Sinclair was an emotionally detached punk from my hometown of Perth who was living a desperate life in north London, where he had graduated from solvents to heroin abuse. On 20 January 1983, he met an older and seemingly generous Scot who had grown up in a fishing village in the north-east of Scotland and had left home to join the Metropolitan Police but now worked in a Jobcentre in Kentish Town. Dennis Nilsen was a conscientious employee, a local activist in the trade union movement who had a reputation for helping the homeless. It was a manipulative conceit. By then, Nilsen had already murdered more than twelve people, many of them drifters. Scotland's diaspora was growing daily, and the streets around Euston and King's Cross in particular were crowded with vulnerable young people who had come to look for what was euphemistically called 'a better life'. For many, it was the polar opposite; London was a city that was increasingly tough on young people and in the years to come would be hostile to anyone with slender means. Nilsen fell into casual conversation with Stephen Sinclair, bought him a burger and invited him back to his grim attic flat at 23 Cranley Gardens. Lured by a man with an accent that spoke of home, Stephen was strangled with a ligature, a blue-and-white football scarf, the colours of his hometown team, Perth's St Johnstone FC.

O

Towards the end of the year, I was stuck for an hour on a London underground train near Victoria with Steve Caesar from Leeds. It was Saturday, 17 December 1983. That weekend, we had decided not to travel north to an all-nighter but to make our way to a pub called the Cornet in London's Lavender Hill, where the upstairs room had been colonised for a rare soul night. The name of the night had been borrowed from an old Twisted Wheel song by Shorty Long, 'Function At The Junction' (Soul, 1966).

The train refused to move and time ticked away. A whispered conversation – when the mobile phone was a thing of the future – along the carriage brought the garbled news that an IRA bomb had exploded at Harrods in Kensington, and that all underground trains in the vicinity were on shutdown. My thoughts were only of impatience. I was desperate to get to the club and, immersed as I was in modern soul and underground hip-hop, neither offered the amphetamine buzz of sixties soul. We arrived unfashionably late and were greeted by a bar full of exiles and hardened soul fans from the London area, many from the Mod revivalist scene and some with a pedigree that dated back to London's original purple-heart clubs. Until that night, I thought London was so fixated with passing fads and the next big thing it was a city marred by shallowness and could never match the authenticity of the north. But that night, and in the months that followed, I met Mark 'Binsy' Taylor from Willesden, Tony Smith from Islington and Ion Tsakalis, a financial planner from Brighton, all steeped in great soul music and all of whom regularly travelled together north to Stafford. It was through these three guys, who I have known periodically for several decades, that I realised that where soul was concerned, the prejudices I had built up about the north–south soul divide were wrong.

When I awoke late the next day, it was to numerous phone messages. I discovered that the bomb that had ripped through Harrods had killed my cousin Phil Geddes, a young journalist then working at the *Daily Express*. Like me, he was an exile from the north. He had been born in the northern soul hotspot of Barrow-in-Furness but our paths had diverged; he had gone to Oxford where he had immersed himself in the elite campus life and become editor of the student newspaper, *Cherwell*. Philip was at Harrods with his girlfriend. They had briefly split up to buy each other surprise Christmas presents. She had walked away to safety and he had walked in the direction of the bomb at Hans Crescent. He died instantly, indiscriminately, his body torn apart by the callous blasts of terrorism. Philip was a migrant in every respect, the great-grandson of Irish immigrants and the son of a Polish refugee. The next week, on my way to his funeral, I was trapped again in an underground bomb scare and missed my planned train north to Preston, arriving at the funeral with only minutes to spare. It was a day I learned a precious lesson about the intrusive power of the media. Cameras from Granada TV tracked our family everywhere we went, desperate for close-ups of the dead boy's mother, my auntie Norah, who was inconsolable and hanging on to my mother as if her life had been shattered. It had. She never fully recovered and died in a hospice on Walney Island, a seaside island at the foot of Cumbria where she had taken me as a child.

The images of my grieving auntie went around the world and triggered a bizarre set of circumstances. In some news reports, Philip was described as the son of a Polish tailor from Barrow-in-Furness, whose birth name was not Geddes, but Gedewicz. An old woman in Hamburg heard the name on the news in Germany and jumped to attention – that was her name, and surely the name of her long-lost brother who she presumed had been killed in the Holocaust? In a matter of a few emotionally fraught days, my uncle Michael, a Polish émigré who for the previous twenty years had been a gent's tailor in Barrow, lost his only son but was then reunited with his sister, who he thought had died in the extermination camps at Treblinka. It was a traumatic period which challenged every imaginable logic in life and in death.

O

The northern soul exiles in London had become a surrogate family. We congregated at Demob, an über-cool designer clothes shop on Soho's Beak Street, which had become a hub for the orphans of Wigan Casino. The shop provided a full range of northern soul delights, some of them even legal. Demob was the brainchild of designer and fashion entrepreneur Sue Brick, a lifetime devotee of northern soul, and her then husband Chris Brick, an acid-fried visionary who was a major figure in the South Wales contingent. At the time, the South Wales lot were a dominant presence in London's underground club culture. Chris Sullivan ran the Wag Club in Wardour Street and Steve Strange, another northern soul fan, was the host of the New Romantic Blitz club and the lead singer of pop band Visage. The club scene was in creative flux, and a significant strand of influence had come down from the north, where the cocktail of illegal drugs, hardened soul music and underground venues were the drivers of what was to become the warehouse party scene, and which in the second 'Summer of Love' became the illegal rave scene. For months, I spent my lunch hours at Demob picking up flyers and chatting by racks of clothing. The fashions were mainly influenced by northern soul's past: Harrington-style jackets bearing the logo 'XLNT' and wide work jeans that hinted back to baggy Spencers from the heyday of Wigan. It was where I plotted the weekend ahead, usually sharing thoughts with Lesley Walker, an ebullient girl from York who worked there, but who I had known for fifteen years. We had first met in her native York when I was a student, jumping the mail train to northern soul clubs like the Ebor Suite and Hypnotique, a great northern soul club set in the romantically named Lady Peckitt's Yard off Walmgate.

Our plans began to follow a pattern: a warehouse party, a new start-up venue, a trip to Stafford or a major northern anniversary all-nighter. Word of mouth was king. Sometimes it was the 100 Club, secret all-nighters run by the Demob crew or by Sean McLusky of the group JoBoxers and his friend Mark Wigan, a graphic artist whose name alone pointed to an obsession with the northern scene. We became regulars at the makeshift all-nighters at Battlebridge Road, squats behind King's Cross, or at all-night schlock horror screenings at the Scala Cinema, which had a soul club on the mezzanine floor. I was bounced into DJing now and again, and, fearful of empty floors, stuck to known classics or records of unambiguous brilliance. Northern soul classics such as Don Thomas's 'Come On Train', James Fountain's 'Seven Day Lover' (Peachtree, 1970) and Gil Scott-Heron's 'The Bottle' (Strata East, 1974) were modern sounds that reached out to almost every subset of dance music, from funk to warehouse boogie. The few times I agreed to DJ were mostly benefit nights, where there was a supportive crowd and no one really minded if you cued a record at the wrong speed. Mistakes were always greeted with ironic cheers. One night at Camden Palace, then a huge nightclub in north London, I supported a benefit for the hostage John McCarthy who had been kidnapped by Islamic jihad terrorists in Lebanon. John had studied with me at Hull University and lived a few doors down during his time as a student. The DJ console was hidden high in the gods of what was a cavernous dancehall, and with no support DJ I was reduced to the humiliating ritual of urinating into an empty pint glass behind the decks. Another night was a 'Red Rave Party' with British soul band Black Britain and my one-time flatmate Rhoda Dakar, lead singer of The Bodysnatchers, under the banner of Labour's Red Wedge movement. Steve Caesar and I spun northern rarities to a roomful of enthusiastic but baffled Marxists.

The best-known warehouse parties were at obscure venues run by Dirtbox, one of London's most innovative clubs, or in the dank railway arches of Battlebridge Road, north of King's Cross. Funk, soul, punk and northern soul were thrown together in a mess of musical forms, and the buzz of illegality made the nights compelling. It was not quite northern soul but it was a proxy for it. Some nights became a ritual reworking of the American Civil War as soul music went head to head with its bastard neighbour, rockabilly, the primitive fifties rock music – relentless and rare – that has since snared several northern soul fanatics into its trap, among them Keb Darge and Mark Linton. The First Lady of Dirtbox, Debbie Sim, once famously said, 'I like a broad age range, but girls make the club, definitely. They're real hardy, they dress outrageously, drink like men, and they're absolutely gorgeous. I don't like pussy girls who drink Evian and get early nights.' Dirtbox attracted several faces from the northern soul scene who were openly non-pussy, among them Amanda Sullivan and Sue Brick who were pioneers of what became known as vintage style.

Underground warehouse parties flourished long enough to influence rave but just as suddenly died away, and I had not fully comprehended at the time how dependent the scene was on the fluctuating London property market. Disused buildings, old warehouses and railway arches were soon bought up and gentrified, and venues became harder to find or more expensive to rent. Then, squats, cheap bedsits and eventually whole neighbourhoods like Brixton, Islington and Hackney surrendered to market forces. The underground London club scene – once predicated on cheap property – was always likely to be temporary, and the most belligerent black dance scenes like jungle and grime were eventually driven out of the centre of London to the fading periphery, or to no-go sink housing estates. Recently police were called to quell a riot at an illegal rave in Lambeth, a place once pock-marked with disused buildings and where underground soul clubs flourished beneath the arches of the Southern Rail network. The riot unfolded into a metaphor for London. It had erupted in the streets behind luxury apartments overlooking the Thames and the Houses of Parliament and in the shadows of Damien Hirst's new £25 million art gallery. It was the death spasm of a London now lost to underground dance music. My upbringing in Scotland and experiences on the northern scene soon curdled into a political resentment that grew with each general election. The south had made a Faustian pact with Thatcherism that had not only wreaked havoc on the industrial north but seemed to be at war with many of the things I had grown up to respect: trade unions, teachers and council house communities.

As a writer for *Black Echoes* and then the *NME*, I regularly travelled to America and was now on the mailing list of nearly every record company in London, but nothing they sent came with the same excitement as a find in America or a record from one of the northern scene's top dealers. I was still regularly in touch with John Anderson, the Scot who ran Soul Bowl and now managed a UK label called Grapevine with former Wigan DJ, Richard Searling. They were releasing great northern soul legally. One day, he told me, he had been visited at his rural barn by a small cadre of London DJs on what was then known as the rare groove scene, a subset of funk that had been pioneered by DJs like Barrie Sharp (Cat in the Hat), Trevor Shakes (Maunkberrys) and Derek B, whose pirate radio show, *Good Groove* on Kiss FM, was the leading show on the London soul scene. Two emergent DJs, Norman Jay and Paul 'Trouble' Anderson, had broken with playing the latest imports and were digging deeper into the soulful past, unearthing beats that were being sampled in the early years of the hip-hop scene. Norman Jay had been to Wigan several times and had taken the concept of rarity down south. He applied the northern soul concept to funk and boogie, using pirate radio stations and one-night clubs to drive the rare groove scene in London, featuring records by funk legends James Brown, Lyn Collins and Fred Wesley. Among their top sounds at the time were Fred Wesley and the JBs' anti-Nixon funk song 'You Can Have Watergate Just Gimme Me Some Bucks And I'll Be Straight' (People, 1973), The Jackson Sisters' 'I Believe In Miracles' (Prophesy, 1973) and Sweet Charles' 'Yes It's You' (People, 1974). I knew from memory that a treasure trove of records from the James Brown stable was lying unloved in a deleted record shop in Charlotte, North Carolina, so one weekend, using a bucket shop to secure the cheapest flight, I flew out to America, stayed at an airport hotel, scoured the shop and returned a day later with a case-load of rare groove, mostly on King, Brownstone and People Records. None were super-rare in the northern scene's obsessive sense of that word but their value was rising sharply, and I sold multiple copies to funk fans in London. As I swept through the shelves, taking records only in the best condition, there was northern booty, too – a pristine copy of an evergreen northern rarity, Cody Black's 'I'm Slowly Molding' (King, 1966), and a double of Willie Hatcher's 'Head Over Heels' (King, 1971). But like many before me and since, there was always one that got away. In a room full of King Records, out of Cincinnati, one title eluded me: Junior McCants' 'Try Me For Your New Love' (King, 1967), a massive tune at Stafford, which Pat Brady had unhelpfully 'covered up' as a song by Carl Carlton. His plot succeeded. For years I didn't even know what I was looking for, and when I got the information I needed, soul obscurity confounded me yet again. In the mid sixties, Junior McCants was working in an aluminium-manufacturing company making garbage cans. He suffered long periods of illness throughout his life, and in the summer of 1967 he died of cancer. As a mark of respect, King Records cancelled the release of his record. Only a few highly precious promo copies had leaked out, and as Stafford's reputation for unearthing rare sounds rose, I had yet to even touch a copy, let alone own it.

Back in London, I was living in a cramped second-floor flat at 55 Fermoy Road in an unimpressive street parallel to Harrow Road. For a brief period during the Stafford era, it was a street that was home to some of the rarest records in the capital. My old Wigan pal Steve Caesar lived in a flat opposite and we swapped records daily, even setting up a sign system to confirm we were both in. One day, I came back from work to see albums and 7-inch singles strewn all over the road. Caesar's flat had been burgled and the thieves had dropped most of their loot as they escaped north to the infamous Mozart estate. The thieves had got a few trinkets and cash but left a hoard of rare northern soul records behind them, including Caesar's cherished Baby Washington collection – Minnie Jones and the Minuettes'

'Shadow Of A Memory' (Sugar, release date unknown), Little Eddie Taylor's 'I Had A Good Time' (Peacock, 1967) and a box of Blackpool and Cleethorpes classics. The moral of the story is never break into a house unless you have a copy of John Manship's rare soul price guide in your swag bag.

New scenes were emerging at this time. Keb Darge was for ever shifting ground, sometimes playing super-rare modern records and pioneering what became known as the deep funk scene. Through his residency at Madame Jojo's, an old burlesque club in the heart of Soho, Keb's restlessness took him to rockabilly, garage rock and DJ residencies in Japan and the Philippines, where he turned activist and fought against local corruption in the wake of Typhoon Yolanda in 2013. In a fragmenting world of subcultures, collectors on the northern scene became aware of other rival scenes: the Carolina beach scene, which played softer nostalgia soul, and the Chicano low-rider scene, which was principally a culture that pimped up cars, and, closer to home, London's rare groove scene. But still the sound of the sixties exerted a special hold, and the headquarters of the soul fraternity in London became the monthly all-nighters hosted by the 6Ts Rhythm and Soul Society, at the 100 Club in Oxford Street. It was a club which became a movement and grew in reputation in the years to come.

The origins of what became the 100 Club all-nighters began back in August 1979, when Wigan Casino was still open, at a time when it would have been sacrilegious to think that one day its mighty crown would be stolen by a smaller venue in the heart of London. The 6Ts Rhythm and Soul Society's first venue was a function room at the Bedford Head pub in Covent Garden, and the DJ line-up that night featured the crème de la crème of the London sixties soul scene – Tony Rounce, Randy Cozens, Tony Ellis and Terry Davis. Rounce played the first record, reputedly Johnny Taylor's 'Just The One I've Been Looking For' (Stax, 1967). The choice spoke volumes. It was neither a particularly rare record nor for that matter a hectic dancer, and that clear dividing line separated the 6Ts scene in London from the more aggressive northern soul scene. Other records featured that night were Solomon Burke's 'Stupidity' (Atlantic, 1964) and Carolyn Crawford's 'Forget About Me' (Motown, 1963), both from the early sixties and looking back to the original Mod clubs of Soho. Randy Cozens was a first-generation Mod who had remained stubbornly faithful to the early Modernist movement and carried the baton of soul and R&B for decades after. When he died of cancer in the summer of 2003, he had already left a phenomenal legacy, driving sixties soul culture in London, and with Ady Croasdell, then a distracted student studying International Relations at University College, London, had launched the 100 Club. In an obituary published in the soul magazine *Manifesto*, Eddie Piller, a second-generation Mod, promoter and driving force of the acid-jazz scene, spoke passionately of Randy's influence: 'I've made no secret to anybody that Randy Cozens changed my life. He was a Mod of the old school, preaching a gospel of soul, soul and more soul.' In 1979, the pop newspaper *Sounds* published a Top 100 Mod Songs, compiled by Randy Cozens, and Piller describes it as being transformational for his generation. 'All that the new generation of Mods had to go on was The Who, The Jam and the Small Faces. We were so naive about the true Modernist path that it just hadn't occurred to us that there was anything else out there. Randy changed our assumptions and was the most genuine and down-to-earth person I'd ever met on the soul scene.' It was Randy Cozens that found the 6Ts crowd's next venue, the Starlight Rooms upstairs at the Railway Tavern in West Hampstead, a place that he rightly believed had a 'spirit' of its own. The pub stood next to the old Decca Records studio and was formerly the Klooks Kleek club, an R&B hangout that had been a formidable place in the 'swinging sixties' and, for some, London's rival to the Twisted Wheel. It was the place where 'Mod' acts such as Little Stevie Wonder,

Zoot Money, Rod Stewart, and The Graham Bond Organisation all performed. Cozens acted as the scene's unofficial mentor. 'Randy had little time for the politics or egos that so dog elements of the UK scene,' the DJ and collector Steve Guarnori said by way of testimony. 'He preferred instead to let music do the talking.'

Among the DJs who came to the fore in this period were Randy, Mick Smith, Pete Widdison and Ian Clark, a classy collector who also had immense professional skills as a graphic artist and in years to come would transform the amateur look of rare and northern soul club flyers. A line was drawn between what the London DJs considered to be great underplayed sixties material and the frantic and at times relentless pace of the classic northern stomper; another subtle distinction was being drawn that would lead to further disputes in the years ahead. There were those in the north who could never countenance any London club matching the passion and rarity of northern soul, and those in London who saw the north as belligerent and tribal, too keen on rarity over quality. They were both right and probably both wrong.

West Hampstead's Railway Tavern remained the headquarters of London's rare soul fraternity for fifteen months, and word spread well beyond the small gang of former Mods, northern exiles and soul obsessives. Magazines like *i-D* and *The Face* were in their infancy and busy minesweeping London for the slightest hint of a new youth trend. One particular West Hampstead record emerged out of the shadows of the past to become a major pop hit. Nina Simone's 'My Baby Just Cares For Me' (Bethlehem, 1958). A forgotten recording from the late fifties by one of black music's most talented and temperamental vocalists was hidden away on the album *Little Girl Blue/Jazz As Played In An Exclusive Side Street Club*. The song found its way to the decks at West Hampstead, and thirty years after it was recorded became one of the club classics of the decade, picked up at trendier Soho clubs like the Wag Club in Wardour Street and Le Beat Route on Greek Street, and then by art directors working on a commercial for Chanel N°5 perfume. The song's underground popularity forced a re-release and it stormed to number 4 on the UK's *NME* singles chart. Unimpressed by whether old soul went mainstream or not, the West Hampstead project rooted out more and more forgotten sixties stars, including Ray Charles, Etta James, Arthur Alexander and Baby Washington, and as the club's reputation grew, so did its connections with the specialist London recording scene. Three specific ventures were bringing the obscure to market, among them the blues reissue label Charly, the R&B label Ace, which employed Tony Rounce as a senior consultant, and finally the soul reissue label Kent, which employed Ady Croasdell as head of A&R and the creative Ian Clark as a freelance designer.

By 1980, the West Hampstead group were homeless and running one-off nights across London at Notre Dame in Leicester Square, the Horseshoe on Tottenham Court Road, the 101 Club in Clapham and then finally at the 100 Club. From the outset, the 100 Club brought a different attitude to rare soul – unrestricted fun – and its flyers were witty, self-mocking and often accompanied by cartoons. Ady Croasdell gave himself the fictitious nickname Harboro Horace, inspired by his hometown Market Harborough, while the elegant Ian 'Clarky' Clark brought graphical imagery from the fifties and sixties into the club's posters. The 100 Club has everything. You walk in through a street-level doorway beneath an iconic sign showing a blaring R&B trumpet, you go down a tight stairway, a half turn and you're past the ticket booth, and then down into a dungeon-like club propped up by industrial warehouse pillars. Opposite the stairs is the stage, to the left is the record bar, and next to that some infamously seedy toilets with stained sinks and poor plumbing. It was as if all the elements of the Twisted Wheel, Plebeians and the Catacombs had been mashed together and transported to Oxford Street. The 100 Club's reputation spread and rare soul fans came from far beyond the capital. One visit that will stay locked in my mind for ever was the arrival of the infamous Cybermen from Preston. The

Cybermen had come of age at Stafford and were the improvisational 'brain child' of Preston soul boy Gaz Kellett, a hyper-enthusiastic soul addict whose eyes bulged from his head like a frog with contact lenses. Gaz and the Cybermen broke the piety of northern soul with practical jokes, daft stunts and costumes that would have shamed a Butlins redcoat. Gaz wore metal saucepans on his head, danced at Stafford wearing a battered Prussian war helmet and at least once was seen entering a club wearing a colander. What the Cybermen brought back into vogue was the fun of travelling to big all-nighters, turning up at events hundreds of miles from Preston, in Scotland, on the North Wales coast and most spectacularly of all at the 100 Club. The Cybermen were a convoy that frequently followed the Sixties Mafia DJs, Guy Hennigan and Keb Darge, but as the eighties waned they increasingly followed the next generation's top rare soul DJ, Mark 'Butch' Dobson. In many respects their equivalent was to be found in a different era and in a very different musical context. They were northern soul's answer to the Merry Pranksters, Ken Kesey's band of lysergic troubadours who did so much to promote the hallucinogenic benefits of LSD and the rise of the hippie movement. The Cybermen took an equally flamboyant approach to stimulants and had the same off-piste view of the world. One of my greatest ever nights at the 100 Club was witnessing them down from the north and full of fervour, hope and speed. I had been in London for a few years, my career had taken a professional grip, and trips to the northern all-nighters were now sporadic. But the sight of Gaz Kellett in full flight soon ignited past passions. We had first met fifteen years ago on the floor at Wigan Casino and become instant friends; our rituals followed the same weekly pattern, seeking each other out on the dance floor, hugging, laughing and launching into diatribes about the big sound of the week. Gaz was like a meteor rushing through the hemispheres of rare soul, taking all before him. To see him in London was a thrill, a cure for the homesickness and cynicism that often plagued me. The glint of his ping-pong eyes and the pounding sound of Bobby Wisdom's 'Handwriting On The Wall' (Out A Site, release date unknown) told me that rare soul and insanity would never die. Scattered throughout the dark basement of the 100 Club were the rest of the Cybermen – Billy Mercer, Tony 'Stan' Stanhope, Gis Southworth, Stuart Raith – and various young speedheads who had followed in their trail. As I heard the surreal tale of their lengthy and indirect journey to the 100 Club and their incoherent plans for the return home to Preston, I was left jealously wanting to join them on their spaced-out way. Every subculture has its minstrels; for the counterculture it was the Merry Pranksters, for punk it was Siouxsie Sioux and the Bromley contingent, and for northern soul it was unquestionably the Preston Cybermen.

The 100 Club survived the experience and its reputation grew like wildfire. It was now on the radar of overseas tourists and was attracting soul fans from Germany, Japan and Scandinavia. More than any other venue, it built a commonwealth of rare soul, a global movement that simply grew and grew but perhaps the club's greatest single influence was the relationship that Ady Croasdell and Tony Rounce established with the specialist music industry. They worked for Ace and Kent Records, heritage labels which became the pre-eminent reissue record labels in the world and grew from the humble origins of a record stall run by vinyl junkie Ted Carroll. His red beard and balding head made him look more like a Franciscan monk than a record hound, but it was Carroll that gave Croasdell his first commission, when he casually asked him to compile a northern soul album from titles available to his nascent business. Ace Records was founded on what Carroll has described as 'the three Rs – reclamation, restoration and research', and much of the eighties was spent identifying and reclaiming the lost music of the past. Initially the focus was on old R&B labels from the post-war era, including rockabilly, rhythm and blues, and cajun; then Carroll secured the catalogue rights to the original Ace Records in Mississippi, Chess Records from Chicago and Modern Records of Los Angeles. Armed with a deep knowledge of sixties and northern soul, Ady Croasdell rose through the ranks at the company and released a slate of compilation albums drawn from the vaults of their American partners. With these two strands weaving seamlessly together, the 100 Club became an academy for the Kent label. Sounds were sourced by Croasdell and his team. Album covers were designed by Ian Clark, now a major DJ at both Stafford and the 100 Club, and fans from the northern scene chipped in with record information, sleeve notes and even modelling assignments. An early compilation featured Wigan Casino dance champion Steve Caesar dressed up as a schoolteacher in black cloak and mortar board.

Like the twilight rogues of Stafford, the hunt for great soul led Ady Croasdell to discover unissued records from the studio tapes left behind in dusty cupboards and in musicians' lofts. Unlike the bootleggers of the past, Croasdell was working with the consent of the rights-holders, but it was no less adventurous. Among the many titles brought to life by Kent were sounds that were frequently played first at the 100 Club, and then pressed on either special issue albums or on limited edition anniversary discs only available at the club's all-nighters. In the mid eighties, Croasdell and his Kent colleagues gained access to the vaults of two of New York's famed soul labels, Musicor and Wand Records. Out of the hundreds of tracks they discovered, many were versions of already known soul records but they periodically came across unissued tracks. A primary example was the music of Melba Moore, a glamorous actor-singer who was raised in Newark, New Jersey, where she was a contemporary of the late great Linda Jones. Moore became a successful Broadway actress, starring in the counter-cultural musical hit *Hair*, and recorded her debut record 'Don't Cry Sing Along With The Music' (Musicor, 1966). A frantic feel-good pop song, it should have charted but somehow didn't, and it ended up becoming a northern standard at the

Torch. As a successful acting and television career took over, Moore's old Musicor sessions lay dormant until Croasdell discovered a hidden gem, 'Magic Touch' (Musicor, 1966, unissued). Croasdell played 'Magic Touch' from a cut acetate at the 100 Club and the record caught fire. Unissued material was coming thick and fast. Not all were great. Some were pedestrian and under-produced, but among the unloved were a few decent records that capricious history had been unkind to. The legendary Wand label became a seam of great recordings, including Chuck Jackson's 'Millionaire' (Wand, 1966, unissued) and historic tracks by Maxine Brown with Otis Redding acting as her producer. They included 'Baby Cakes' and 'Slipping Through My Fingers', both recorded at the now legendary Muscle Shoals Studio in what became a hectic and unprecedented year for Maxine Brown. In October 1967, she was rushed into becoming Marvin Gaye's emergency replacement for Tammi Terrell, who had collapsed on stage with a brain tumour, and in December her most recent producer Otis Redding died in a plane crash.

It was on the west coast that Croasdell made one of his most famous discoveries, adding a final twist to the saga of 'Strings A GoGo', the instrumental which master bootlegger and notorious dissembler Simon Soussan had landed on the northern soul scene at Wigan Casino. Soussan had discovered an engaging high-tempo instrumental which had become a rare soul favourite thanks to the compliance of the Casino's top DJs. He had bootlegged the unknown instrumental as Bob Wilson Sounds' 'Strings A GoGo' (Soul Galore, 1972, bootleg) and tried to pass it off as his own recording. Sleuth-like collectors rumbled the con and exposed the track as a late sixties instrumental 'Double Cookin'' by The Checkerboard Squares (Villa, 1967). The Villa vaults, or what was left of the label's limited resources, were taken over by Fantasy Records, which in turn was sub-licensed to Ace/Kent and thus came within Croasdell's grasp. Alec Palao, a researcher with Ace Records, worked methodically through the tapes and an entirely unknown record surfaced, The Magicians' '(Just A Little) Faith And Understanding' (Villa, unissued). The opening bars were instantly recognisable to anyone who had visited a northern all-nighter; it was the long-lost vocal to what was still popularly known as 'Strings A GoGo'. Croasdell played it for days, bewildered by what the search had thrown up, and when he played it at the 100 Club there was a disbelieving charge to the DJ decks, many thinking it was a studio stunt rather than an original and unknown song.

By the millennium, there was a new and lasting schism within northern soul, the latest division in a series of civil wars: those who wanted to look back to the grand days of the past and saw northern as a revivalist and reunion scene, and those clubs that kept the torch burning and insisted on new discoveries and an upfront music policy. Each new era brought with it ever more demanding clubs. When Stafford closed, new venues like Andy Dyson's Lifeline Soul Club began a substantial journey, first at Sheridan's in Dewsbury and then took to the road. Lifeline attracted the best DJs and rarest records in the UK but struggled to secure a permanent and lasting venue, so with necessity as the mother of invention, the caravan moved on. Rather than capitulate, Lifeline pioneered another new direction for northern soul – the peripatetic all-nighter – and went to Retford in Nottingham, Colsterworth, a remote village in Lincolnshire, and the Sutherland Road Community Project in one of northern soul's heartlands, Longton in Stoke-on-Trent. It was Lifeline that also pioneered the 'co-pro', where two clubs collaborated in co-promotion to bring different clubs together (most successfully with the R&B Club POW WOW).

As the 100 Club thrived and the northern scene adapted to life after Stafford, numerous new clubs emerged in Rugby, Burnley and Prestwich. Many more cropped up to pay homage to the past. Many thousands of people who had drifted away from northern soul returned to swell the ranks of new faces who had discovered the music via the scooter scene and still more who had lasted the journey and never left. Most promoters agreed that one DJ had broken out from the pack to become the greatest DJ in the history of northern. Mark 'Butch' Dobson from Stoke was already a respected collector when he took to the decks. His collection was outstanding and included many of the ultra-rare records that even after two decades of travelling to America I could only drool over. Something else remarkable was happening. In the early nineties onwards, as rave culture spread like a virus through popular music, so-called super-DJs soared on the back of the acid house scene. Stoke became a centre of some significance. Sasha, a Welsh-born DJ whose real name was Alexander Coe, had a ground-breaking residency at Shelley's Laserdome in Longton, not far from where Butch had grown up. Their modus operandi could not have been more different. Sasha was lauded by the media. Butch remained unknown and underground. Sasha was frequently flown in a private jet or helicopter to appear at three clubs in one night. Butch drove to and from obscure venues in an unremarkable car. Sasha was paid a king's ransom to appear at mega-raves and eventually remixed tracks for Madonna and The Chemical Brothers, while Butch worked for cash in hand and was known largely to a rare soul cognoscenti. Sasha attracted front covers, fashion spreads and promotional posters; Butch was more comfortable in the shadowy world of record boxes and vinyl warehouses. Although their lives were played out side by side from a base in Stoke, they were a contrasting commentary on underground dance music: in the case of acid house, how quickly it went mainstream, and in the case of northern soul, how it is hard-wired to retreat into the shadows and resist attention. Butch's era as the leading DJ of northern soul defied the predictions made in the heyday of Wigan Casino, when doubters claimed that the great records had all been found and vinyl was on its last wobbly legs. One of Butch's biggest records, Patrinell Staten's 'Little Love Affair' (Sepia, 1969), was a shrieking crossover-song on a tiny soul label, produced defiantly in Seattle, the city that was on the cusp of giving birth to the Microsoft Corporation. Patrinell Staten and her group The Casanovas had no resources and could only afford to press 250 copies of the record. Without a promotions budget, it soon stiffed and faded into obscurity.

Butch's personality resists easy definition. He is quieter and more unassuming than most DJs but has a zealous streak that is born out of the northern scene's unforgiving fundamentalism. He once stormed across the floor at an all-nighter in Winsford Civic Hall, Cheshire, and hurled an acetate of a mega-rare Chicago tune, The Admirations' 'You Left Me' (Peaches, 1966), across the room, disgusted that it had been ripped off. At another all-nighter, he castigated a more traditional DJ for playing another brilliant but overexposed Chicago classic, Mel Britt's 'She'll Come Running Back' (Fip, 1969). Butch has the integrity and mindset of the collector that can tip into a borderline autistic obsession with what is right and what is not. Listening to Butch's guest spots at 100 Club all-nighters kept me on the right track throughout my years in London. On one memorable occasion, cheered on by the Preston Cybermen acting as his away-day hooligan gang, Butch raised the bar on what dancers expected of a rare soul DJ. He played a set so stunning in quality and so wrapped in rarity it would have stood the test at any great soul club past or future. It would have worked anywhere from the Wheel to Wigan Casino. You can't dance to integrity but you can tell when it's missing.

Behind the decks at Soul Tempo at the Showcase club all-nighter, Madrid, 2014.
© Brian Cannon

11
THE TWISTED WHEELS OF TECHNOLOGY

Technology is anything that wasn't around when you were born.

Alan Kay, computer scientist

When I was born, SodaStream was science fiction and pop-up toasters were the stuff of luxurious fantasy. As for television, the screens were still black and white and watching snooker was a mind-fuck. But there was compensation in the primitive things of life – playing records was an elegant ritual and the portable Dansette record player the height of technological sophistication. The newest models even had a stacking mechanism that allowed you to play six records in a row, although the fifth record invariably slipped and your copy of 'Baby Love' would scratch like hardcore hip-hop, a form of dance music yet to be invented. The stylus was not something you ever replaced nor was it a term you used much. Records were played by 'needles' and your mum always had hundreds of them in the kitchen cupboard, next to the roll of Sellotape and the Swan Vestas matches. It was an era when even the term 'new technology' had yet to be invented and the nearest thing to the digital revolution was the disappearing dot when the telly was switched off.

From the advent of the 45rpm disc, the technological needs of the northern soul scene were modest. Clubs came as they were, a dimmed room with a wooden floor was enough, and the VIP room was a corridor of urinals and broken sinks where DJs and top collectors hung out. Lighting systems were irrelevant, and as for lasers, they were what Goldfinger used to fry James Bond's testicles. As long as dancers could hear the music – loud and proud – there was no need for pyrotechnics or surround sound. Northern soul remained the same basic experience from the opening night of the Twisted Wheel to the triumphs of the 100 Club. Harold Wilson's 'white heat of technology' was largely ignored, you paid with a crumpled fiver at the door, and vinyl was totemic, defining the scene like conch shells in the Solomon Islands. As a young man living in Manchester in the seventies, I was coached in the spiritual value of vinyl. Dave Ferguson, a rare soul collector from Burnley, once told me to treat vinyl as if it were a child and that every broken record was a 'bereavement' which even the magic of super glue could not bring back to life. It was a wise lesson. Only a few years ago, I buried a smashed copy of Jerry Butler's 'Moody Woman' (Mercury, 1969) in a shallow grave in my back garden, as if it were a family pet. Until 2006, I had always believed that a broken record signalled the end of its life, until the twisted wheels of technology magically made music ethereal and eternal.

By the new millennium, northern soul should have been dead in the water, but spectacularly in the summer of 2006 the scene rose from its slumber like Lazarus on green and clears, and new digital technology triggered a resurgence. It was as if the moribund rare soul scene had had spark plugs fixed to its temples, and like a fading patient – dormant but not dead – it sprang to life, charged by the potential of the worldwide web. After years of living in an analogue world dominated by plastic discs, digital technology suddenly smiled on the arcane world of northern soul. Magically all the giant innovations of social and digital media had something to offer.

It was around the time of Lifeline's tenth anniversary that a young American immigrant of Bangladeshi origin called Jawed Karim turned his back on the University of Illinois to take up a job at the fledgling PayPal online currency company. Within a year, Karim and his co-workers had launched YouTube as a closed beta project, before launching it spectacularly to the world. The first ever YouTube video shows Karim at San Diego Zoo and is entitled 'Me at the Zoo'. It was uploaded on 23 April 2005, short, personal and with no great technical sophistication. It carefully gave out a message – 'you can do this, it's easy'. Within a matter of months, a Japanese northern soul fan called Takumao, who runs a Tokyo-based website for Japanese Mods called 'Too Darn Soulful', uploaded two of his own personal videos. The videos showed him dancing to victory in a dance contest at a weekender in Cleethorpes. They were primitive, home-made and poorly lit but they shone a light on new media, showing how ordinary people could share northern soul moments with friends and like-minded souls.

Within months of YouTube going mainstream, almost every significant northern soul title had been uploaded and commented on. As the potential grew, new niche channels emerged, finely honed to appeal to the scene's lust for obscurity. In May 2007, a young girl called Jemma Page uploaded a video version of the ultra-rare Frank Wilson single 'Do I Love You (Indeed I Do)' saying, 'I made this for my dad'. It is simple in the extreme, featuring the sound track and a rostra image of the single's original label. It has now been viewed over 880,000 times, more than many editions of the BBC's flagship current affairs programme

Panorama. Another upload of the same song by the former Mecca DJ Ian Levine features Frank Wilson improvising at a piano in his Los Angeles home. Levine's video has also been watched over 800,000 times and a further one hundred uploads of the song are also available. In total, Frank Wilson's uploads have been watched by nearly four million people, which on the basis of current viewing figures would make it more successful than the biggest shows on Channel 4 and BBC Two. The flurry of publicity that the Frank Wilson song attracts every time rare copies are auctioned has given it greater visibility than any other northern soul discovery. It may never reach the dizzy height of K-Pop anthems like 'Gangnam Style', which became the first YouTube video to surpass one billion views, but quality trumps quantity every time. Frank Wilson is great and truly rare.

From its meteoric appearance in the summer of 2005, YouTube went beyond trophy discs to northern soul's back catalogue of the unknown, the underplayed and the super-rare. Northern soul collector Gaynor Martin runs a modest YouTube stream which features a subtle yet emotionally demanding soul song, Coco and Ben's 'Good Feelin'' (Earthworld, 1979), short-circuiting the traditional relationship between the DJ and the crowd. In the early seventies, to hear the top rare sounds you had to follow Ian Pereira (Pep) to the Catacombs in Wolverhampton, Richard Searling to VaVas in Bolton or Barry Tasker to the Pendulum in Manchester. It was a DJ-led journey. The only other way of hearing top sounds was via lo-fi bootlegged cassette tapes, which were usually off microphone and fuzzy with crowd noise. Some could now be described as 'atmospheric', but in the main they were painful to listen to and sounded like they had been recorded by a toilet brush.

Facebook arrived with even greater self-confidence in 2006 and brought with it a membership of over twelve million US college users. The northern soul scene quickly sensed that it, too, could be used to connect with friends both past and present and that it could curate memory banks of the big northern clubs of the past. This was uniquely important to northern soul; people had often travelled hundreds of miles to clubs. Friendships were scattered geographically across the UK, and Facebook acted as the re-connector. Its online events tools allowed new venues to be more widely promoted and old ones to be commemorated. According to Dr Bernie Hogan, research fellow at the Oxford Internet Institute, timing was crucial: 'The world was ready for a shared list of connections that works like a supercharged, definitive phonebook for the digital age,' he claims. More and more events were being organised in the real world, and with the power of social media the scene had become bifurcated. Major promoters were now running competitive business ventures which favoured large-scale events, often big seaside weekenders or statement all-nighters, but they were no longer alone. Much smaller micro-events were being run on a local basis, mostly not for profit. These events often came with a charitable purpose – breast cancer and Alzheimer's awareness, cot death syndrome and so on – or they had a built-in cost-effectiveness with free venues, collector DJs or open-deck nights. For the first concerted time in the history of northern soul, women DJs began to assert themselves, among them Preston's 'Jumping' Joan Livesey, the 100 Club's Val Palmer, Andrea Butcher at the New Crawdaddy Club in Camden, Pat Bleasdale who DJs at events from Warrington to Whitchurch, and Malayka Erpen, a modern rare soul DJ who works across the UK, Europe and the USA. Even the last bastion of northern soul maleness – the fanzine writer's bedroom – has been invaded by Julie Molloy, one of the scene's most consistent female reviewers and critics.

Of the 620 million Facebook groups in existence, one has had more than passing fad value. It's called 'I Used to Go to Stafford All-Nighters' and is a repository of memories, rare photographs and DJ play lists, which has since grown into a popular history project. Led by Chesterfield collector Karl 'Chalky' White, it has become one of the most complete online histories of a nightclub ever, with full audio sets, a picture gallery, podcasts and interviews. The web history of more famous places like Studio 54, Paradise Garage and Chicago's Warehouse pale into insignificance next to 'The Stafford Story'. What began as a labour of love is now a formidable piece of British youth culture history.

Digital innovation has transformed northern soul and may well have saved its life. Online auction website eBay is littered with northern soul singles and memorabilia, some of it of dubious authenticity, and silent auction software like RainWorx and Bidmaster have allowed the northern scene to be at the cutting-edge of record auctioning. Around 6 p.m. every Wednesday, collectors from the rare soul scene gather in a members' forum called 'Rare Soul Man', an online auction hub run by John Manship Records. It is northern soul's answer to Sotheby's, based incongruously in the village of Waltham on the Wolds near Melton Mowbray in Leicestershire. From these sleepy surroundings the site's tentacles reach out to the ghetto music of Detroit, Cincinnati and Philadelphia, and to collectors worldwide. John Manship has been collecting rare soul as long as I can remember and was a regular face during the heyday of the Mecca and Cleethorpes, but he is far from alone. There are more big-spending collectors on the rare and northern soul scene now than at any time in its history. Far from dying, as many have recklessly predicted, rare soul is passionately alive. The internet has enabled not only real-time auction sites but a global network of reputable dealers: Pat Brady, the Leeds-based DJ who gave me my first break as a fanzine writer; Craig Moerer who runs an 8,000-square-foot warehouse in Portland, Oregon; and Anglo-American Records of Todmorden in Lancashire, run by Tim Brown, who bizarrely is also a world expert on zoos. I can only imagine the excitement in Tim's trousers when YouTube launched with a home movie shot in San Diego Zoo. Back in the seventies, when I lived in Rochdale and worked as a railway clerk, I travelled by train into Manchester with Tim, who was then a trainee civil servant. Every minute was spent discussing records, and the only zoo I remember us ever discussing was a big sound back then – 'The Zoo (The Human Zoo)' by The Commodores (Mowest, 1974). Our conversations followed the same daily rituals – gaining and retaining knowledge about rare soul – and since we both had colossal egos the ambitions were gargantuan. Like the restless Ian Levine, Tim wanted to own every soul record that had ever been issued and pursued this mountainous ambition for years to come. I was even more distracted. I imagined myself as the leader of the Rochdale chapter of the Black Panthers, despite being white, ginger and afflicted with eczema. Every weekend at all-nighters another new record had been played, and as our commuter train rolled into Manchester Victoria the music was aggressively analysed, judged and ultimately given a value. As with dancing, dealing and collecting are high-octane and at times deeply competitive pursuits. There is no great love lost between Tim Brown and John Manship; they frequently have digs at each other and argue over the provenance of northern soul records, as if they have discovered the Turin shroud or found Tutankhamen's Y-fronts in a shop in Delaware.

Although northern soul can be an impenetrable scene, it shares many of the same collecting values as art and antiques. The laws of supply and demand dominate and words like 'rarity', 'original' and 'one-off' are used colloquially to describe the most sought-after records, in much the same way as they would be used in more conventional forms of collecting. Provenance is king. Is this record rare, what condition is it in, and what is the back-story that has brought it to the northern scene?

In May 1994, provenance was about to be blown apart. A team of geeks at Hannover's Fruanhofer Institute had formulated a way of compressing audio files and were about to release a file extension for their 'MPEG Layer 3 Audio' protocol, which they decided to call MP3. It was an innovation that would revolutionise music-sharing and reformat the northern soul scene. Suddenly there was a technology that allowed you to listen to and share super-rare records, either directly by email or more likely through specialist forums such as Soul Source, a northern web forum set up by Mike Hughes from Llandudno, a North Wales seaside town with a fifty-year soul pedigree.

The magic of new media has been kind to northern soul and even kinder to me. For twenty years or more, I have been able to hold down a career in volatile industries where unprecedented technologies have ripped up the rule book. At the height of the digital revolution, I was with Channel 4, overseeing independent film and video and working with young filmmakers as they discovered digital filmmaking. I was part of the artless team that launched the company's website channel4.com. It is now a media-rich destination but back then it was a rusty bike pump sending out press releases like confetti into a gale. My work kept me close to new technology. It was a time when many television executives were spooked by new technology and I often sat in meetings with managers worried that TV schedules would disappear, or that, God forbid, people would watch telly when it suited them. The biggest fear was that new sites like YouTube could provide content free, without the need for broadcast licences, and in time would 'distract' viewers from television. As more people watched content online, the cost of buying high-definition digital cameras collapsed. More people were making their own films and posting them online via YouTube or, as quality and creativity came into play, via sites like Vimeo. Rather than fear the new media as many did, northern soul relished its disruptive charms; a subculture so famously focused on the past became part of the cutting-edge future. Films about northern soul began to appear, some of them lovingly crafted on home-editing systems, many of them just video grabs of dancers, DJs and club exteriors. For a scene starved of media and often frustrated by the way it had been poorly portrayed, these small scraps of authentic media were like gold dust, and pointed to better and more substantial films yet to come.

O

Los Angeles is the capital of film and television. Its garish landscape is burned into our consciousness: the palm trees, the red carpets and the gasoline heat shimmering up from gridlocked freeways. The teetering Hollywood sign, desperately hanging on to a hillside fearful it might be dragged down by an all-consuming earthquake, gives Hollywood the thrill of impermanence. I flew into Los Angeles in 1995, having just commissioned a film on the famous LA-based crime writer James Ellroy. His acidic view of the City of Angels had become my inner guide: 'Achtung, motherfuckers. And good afternoon. I'm James Ellroy, the death dog with the hog log, the white knight of the far right, and the slick trick with the donkey dick. I am the author of eighteen books, masterpieces all; they precede all my future masterpieces. They are books for the whole fucking family, if the name of your family is the Manson family.' The film we were making with Ellroy was a reinvestigation of his mother's murder. Her body had been dumped on the San Bernardino Freeway near El Monte, California, by a mysterious assailant who she'd met at a sleazy LA bar called the Desert Inn. Ellroy was only ten when she was killed and the unresolved sexual violence has influenced his work ever since. He was out of town but had sent me a small hand-drawn map of the murder scene near Arroyo High School where his mother's body had been discovered. A work colleague drove with me to the area and we parked up and then walked silently around the neighbourhood, unsure if the trip would in any way enrich the project or was nothing more than prurience. Ellroy's writing has a similar unsettling effect. You are never sure whether he is taking you closer to the unspeakable or using life's dark places as a sales pitch. On the way back to the freeway, we took a wrong turning at Santa Anita Avenue and headed along a faceless strip of land past a 7-Eleven store, Universal Donuts and an unremarkable thrift store, outside of which was a teetering pile of books, rows of second-hand shoes and crates of records carelessly dumped in the piercing sunshine. I begged to be let out of the car and promised to be no more than five minutes. I raced across to the crates. They were crammed with Hispanic love songs, a few Motown singles and, finally, in a box inside the doorway was a seam of such unexpected wealth that I had to take deep breaths to stop hyperventilating. For reasons that had no apparent logic, the box contained a stack of West Coast regional soul records, some over twenty-five years old. It was as if someone wanted them to survive; they were shaded from the sun and protected by moulded polystyrene packaging in a reinforced apple box. It may have been a house clearance sale, or a charity dump by a local radio station, but the records were there for a reason, maybe even a recent death in the local community. Some of the records had the words 'From the Desk of Eduardo' stamped on the sleeves. One of the boxes was a beginner's guide to West Coast soul. There were several records on the Bronco label, the place where the most unlikely romantic, Barry White, started out, including titles by The Versatiles, Johnny Wyatt and Viola Wills. There were records on Boola-Boola including a great Mecca song, 'I Thought You Were Mine' by The Natural Four, but the biggest thrill was finding a stack of records by a master producer of West Coast soul, Kent Harris. Among them were records by one of Hollywood's unknown greats, Ty Karim, including 'Lighten Up Baby' (Car-A-Mel, release date unknown) and 'You Just Don't Know' (Romark, release date unknown), tracks whose reputation stretched back over decades. This was rare soul from the top drawer, a screeching and emotionally strained female vocalist with a intensely gifted voice. Ty Karim had married the talented producer Kent Harris, but with no funding or any great resource they simply got lost in the most heartless and competitive city in the world and their music stayed gridlocked in the side streets of Los Angeles. They had even tried pseudonyms, releasing a song dedicated to Ty's sculpted afro called 'Wear Your Natural Baby' as Towana and the Total Destruction (Romark, 1970).

On the drive back to the hotel, I went into a ranting soliloquy about the unfairness of the music industry and how a singer as gifted as Ty Karim could be unknown in her own neighbourhood, unknown to the world and hidden away in an apple box in a thrift shop. Back in my room, I laid the Ty Karim records down on a chaise longue and spoke to them as if they were human. It was certifiable behaviour but born out of a deep love for her voice. What I did not know was that Ty Karim had died of breast cancer only ten miles from where I had found her records. Poignantly her daughter, Karime Kendra, has since moved to the UK to pursue her own career and find out more about the rare soul scene that had deified her unknown mother. In 2008, she travelled to Cleethorpes to sing some of her mum's songs to a rapturous audience of northern soul fans. It must rank as one of the most complete genealogical journeys in the history of music but you won't see it on the BBC's *Who Do You Think You Are?* They don't do northern soul.

Back at work, the US sitcom *Friends* had become a lifetime hit, generating more value than any other Channel 4 show before or since. Everyday ideas for documentaries or drama scripts set against the backdrop of the northern scene were submitted for consideration. One book landed on my desk; its title *In the Shadow of Papillon* screamed movie, and the subtitle 'Seven Years of Hell in Venezuela's Prison System' pointed to a harrowing account of brutality, prison gangs and nail-biting escape. The authors were Frank Kane and John Tilsley, but what was not clear from the book was that Frank Kane was a pseudonym for a Stoke soul boy called Frank Kaplonek, a face in the pioneering days of the Golden Torch, whose life had tipped out of control. He had made the tragic decision to smuggle cocaine from Venezuela and found out that the corrupt local police were less tolerant of drug dealing than the squad had been in the backstreets of Tunstall in 1971. Frank was jailed in El Dorado Prison, the hellhole that had once been home to Henri Charrière, 'Papillon'.

Channel 4 sent cameras to a major Cleethorpes weekender and BBC Two's *Culture Show* sent economics editor Paul Mason back to retrace his roots on the dance floor of the north, to explain the scene and analyse why it had not only survived but thrived. It was in his eyes evidence of a resilience in the lives of ordinary people defying globalisation and the cold winds of post-industrial change. Shane Meadows captured that era brilliantly. When we first met, he was an unemployed teenager from Mansfield who came into my office to discuss his first short film with a community group from Nottingham. It was the first tentative step on his way to making the multi-award-winning series *This Is England*, set among the second-generation Mods of South Yorkshire. Christine Alderson was a bright young Geordie girl who had been to northern clubs at the Youthy in Newton Aycliffe when she made her first shorts for Channel 4 and then graduated to make the first feature-length northern soul film *Soul Boy*, set in Stoke-on-Trent in 1974. But that was soon trumped in both quality and success by Elaine Constantine's *Northern Soul*, a film that not only emerged from within the scene itself but used digital media to distribute the film beyond what any professional film company could have achieved. Elaine was a soul girl from Bury whose photography had already set her apart as a special talent and she understood enough about how the northern scene worked to realise that a successful Facebook campaign via the soul club network would give her film greater distribution. Special screenings, midnight movie sessions and all-nighters were organised as northern fanatics badgered their local regional film theatres into booking the movie. Her understanding of the underground kicked in and the film became a sleeper hit; defying all expectations, *Northern Soul* became a BAFTA-nominated film in 2015. Aware of the film's underground success, the McCann Erickson advertising agency ran a new-nostalgia campaign for the breakfast cereal Shredded Wheat, featuring a dad called Dave who goes to all-nighters with his son. The advert divided opinion but spoke to the longevity of the scene.

Northern soul went viral, and the smartphone became an accessory to every conversation and every event. Into the midst of this bite-sized culture came 'Northern Soul Girl', an eighteen-year-old northern soul dancer from Bristol called Levanna McLean, who charmingly danced in public places with an effervescence that is hard to dislike. One particular video, in which she dances along to Pharrell Williams' pop song 'Happy' in a Bristol street, became a web sensation and has now been viewed almost two million times. Levanna had discovered northern soul when her mother played her a mid sixties soul song by The Vel-Vets, 'I Got To Find Me Somebody' (20th Century, 1967). It connected more than any other record she had heard. She told her local paper in Bristol: 'For me, when I heard The Vel-Vets I was like, right, you can't stop me, I'm going on that floor now, I'm going to dance, and that was the first time I danced and I probably didn't look that great but no one cares at a northern soul night. Once you're on the floor, that's it, you're the only person in that room.' Yogi Haughton, a Manchester-born soul fan who now DJs from his base in the Scottish Borders, is of the belief that 'Northern Soul Girl' captures a resurgent mood. Despite the inevitable criticism she attracted from recalcitrant diehards, Levanna represents a new energy on the scene. 'I was DJing in Manchester last year,' Yogi told me. 'I was amazed at how many young people were on the scene. They've found it and they bring a new energy. There's a vibe about it that really reminds me of the old days in Wigan, Blackpool, Morecambe.' This new entrant generation, younger and brasher than the survivors on the scene, are passionately engaged in the scene and its origins, but have a healthy disregard for its arcane rules: the chin stroking, the soul police regulations and the grumpy insistence that yesterday was always better.

The purism of northern soul and the religiosity that I grew up immersed in is corroding like old plaster. It now borrows from across the range of African-American music, from the whisky bar

R&B of the fifties to the synth-soul of the eighties and, inevitably, to the gospel house beats of today. But triumphant in the middle of it all is the towering importance of sixties soul and the voices from the shadows. The media is interested again, but I remain unsure that northern soul wants the attention that currently shines on its rituals. It is at its best as a 'secret' underground and should always maintain a healthy distrust of the false promises that the media brings. But the web success of 'Northern Soul Girl' underlines another paradox. Northern soul has stuck loyally to vinyl through thick and thin but uses digital media platforms more instinctively than any other subculture.

Northern soul has always thrived on defiance. It began by defying the laws of the night, stretching youth entertainment into the next day and resisting drug legislation by making proscribed amphetamines part of a bold subcultural statement. It defied almost everything that the commercial marketplace could throw at it, preferring unknown and forgotten records over chart hits and preferring hidden backstreet clubs to the garish discotheques and mainstream nightclubs of the high street. That culture of defiance has continued to the present day where the music of the analogue era has been spread via digital platforms. But, at the very moment when downloading onto mobile devices became the norm, the original currency of northern soul – original vinyl discs – returned with unexpected bite. Last year alone, over forty-nine million newly minted vinyl records were sold in the USA, a forty-nine per cent increase on the previous year, and every indie band worthy of the name released tracks on cool plastic. The northern soul scene contributed to the vintage revolution that brought ever more rare soul into the price range of those who will not pay or cannot afford ever-escalating prices. Paradoxically, something similar has happened to the rare soul scene's other mainstay, amphetamine – once the forbidden pills of the original Mods, and then the holy grail of the all-nighter scene, when burgled chemists and forged prescriptions fed the scene at the Torch and

Wigan. It ultimately gave way to cocaine, to street-wrapped speed and to the ecstasy boom of the rave scene, but recently amphetamine in its purest form has returned yet again as a pill, with amphetamine stimulants like Adderall and Vyvanse emerging on the drugs market as stimulants for the treatment of Attention Deficit Hyperactivity Disorder (ADHD) in children. The ironies are endless, and endlessly fascinating.

One day at Channel 4, as the pace of technological change was threatening to engulf linear television, I had a meeting with a new start-up company led by two energetic young graduates called Nikhil Shah and Nico Perez. They were looking for a grant to help promote their digital music platform, Mixcloud. As they explained who might use the service, I was already ahead of them; it was a radio station for the cloud, in which you the user are the DJ and broadcast to the world. Since its launch, it has been used by Harvard Business School, Barack Obama and *Wired* magazine. Most importantly, it has become a favoured home of northern soul DJs and a place where play lists, obscure sets and podcasts can be uploaded. All of the big northern soul DJs of the high past, including Blackpool Mecca's Ian Levine and Colin Curtis, Wigan's Richard Searling and Stafford's master archivist Karl White, are regular contributors. It is where the Wigan Casino years and the unissued Motown tracks have been championed by Wolverhampton dealer Pete Smith of Planet Records. Mixcloud points to another contradiction at the heart of the scene. Irrespective of northern soul's fixation with the sixties and the up-tempo music of the past, it plays out those fixations via new technology, fearless of the challenges of new platforms and always self-confident about the story it has to tell.

In the late sixties, when the Twisted Wheel was the northern soul scene's best known all-nighter, it would have been inconceivable that the cherished music played on its record decks would become so readily available. Tucked away in an old and decaying part of Manchester, and known only to the Mod cognoscenti and the local police, its reach was limited to whispered word of mouth. Now, you can be the DJ. Or you can be a dedicated follower of rare soul on your mobile phone. Logic says that northern soul should have faded like other UK subcultures but there are more clubs now than there were at the heyday of the scene in the early seventies, buoyed by new acolytes from the scooter scene, second-generation Mods, vintage lovers and overseas fans.

The worldwide web has been kind to northern soul. What was once a scene restricted to cardboard boxes and wooden crates in a few obscure clubs is now a global phenomenon, and the footprint that was restricted to a few hundred miles of the industrial north of England now has worldwide reach. Rare soul all-nighters are regularly held abroad and all-nighters have been held at Berlin's Statthaus Böcklerpark in the shadow of Checkpoint Charlie and the Berlin Wall, and have spread across Europe with successful clubs in Oslo, Hamburg and Rimini. Vibrant soul scenes have sprung up in places that would have been unthinkable when northern soul originated within a hundred-mile radius of Manchester. The Smart Club in Madrid, the Boiler in Barcelona, Soul Shakers in Bamberg, Bavaria, and the remarkable Nude Restaurant in Kobe on Osaka's North Shore in Japan. Provocatively DJs Keb Darge and Butch list Kobe as one of the greatest northern soul clubs ever, up there with Stafford and Wigan. It is a bold claim but unsurprising, given the vigorous way Japanese soul fans pursue their passions. And so the story of a localised cult that became a popular phenomenon returns full circle to where it all began for me, to the place where I first saw Santa Claus and where I cried myself to sleep aching for my dead father to come home. Forty years after the Perth City Soul Club was founded, an old friend and Wigan campaigner called Brian Cantwell decided the time had come for a reunion. There were still enough of us out there, but much had changed in the intervening years. Since its birth at the height of Wigan Casino, the club had ebbed and flowed, spawning a modern soul club called the Beatbox, which played northern, funk and boogie, and was driven by an old friend and local trendsetter Stewart 'Sparky' Clark. Then, as the beats increased it morphed again into the Rhumba Club, one of Scotland's best house music and rave clubs led by Zammo Simpson. The original venue had been a pub called the Plough Inn in Letham, the housing scheme where I grew up, but it had been ploughed into rubble and was long gone. The second venue was in the backroom of a bar called the Corinna, where I had last seen my old friend from the Wigan days, Mac, playing pool before his untimely death. It was closed for renovations. A Facebook group was launched to gauge interest and it had gone mental online, so it was clear that wherever we gathered it was going to be sold out. The decision was taken to move the event to an old working men's social club called the Tulloch Institute, a place that was like the Taj Mahal to me and came overflowing with a fund of personal memories. My first home was right next door, a low-level prefab which had been hurriedly thrown up to accommodate the post-war poor. As a baby, I was taken home from hospital to its freezing bedrooms, and the windows rattling in their asbestos frames played the first recurring tunes of my life. The Tulloch Institute had shaped me emotionally. My dad had been a committee man there before his death and took me to play in the empty corridors as endless meetings unfolded behind heavy doors. Each year there was a Christmas party for the kids when Santa came stuffed and burly through the doors, staggering about in 'workies' boots' and reeking of Dewar's whisky. The question was not did Santa exist, but could he survive cirrhosis of the liver?

Although I was too young to know it at the time, the Tulloch was built to host a northern soul club: it had a sprung wooden floor, a cheap bar, grumpy regulars who looked on in disbelief, and a precarious trestle table at the door. It sold raffle tickets, it was cash-in-hand, and a box of crumpled fivers was preciously guarded at the door. We converged from all corners of the globe carrying worthless credit cards to a land of cash only. People flew in from abroad, others travelled north from their new homes in England, and many more came from Glasgow and Edinburgh. My overpowering worry was that it would be a *danse macabre* and reveal us all to be near to death: grey, jowly and for ever trapped in a nostalgic past. But that proved to be only partly true. Many of the new and hopeful facets of northern soul unfolded. The host DJs, who often play at the Tulloch, go by the distinctive name of Kasbah v. Beat Surrender, and came to northern soul via punk, power pop, ska and 2 Tone; even their name hints at the great dub clashes of the Jamaican dance hall. They brought with them music fans from wider subcultures including the scooter scene and second-generation Mods. Brian Cantwell, the tireless organiser, took to the decks and played a relentless set of Wigan Casino oldies that ricocheted off the walls at a fearless pace. One of the DJs, former neighbour Tracy McFarlane, had flown in from her home in Majorca and took to the decks as the club's first female DJ. James Marlborough, a younger DJ who was not even born when most of the records he was playing were first big, went into his box and flashed a couple of records on the classic Wand label. It was a fleeting moment to him but a gesture of sheer joy for me. Wand was special. It was the New York home of Maxine Brown, Chuck Jackson and ultra-rare northern sounds like Walter Wilson's 'Love Keeps Me Crying' (Wand, 1966). It is a label with a proud history and its modest profits helped to fund Martin Luther King's march to freedom. To see a younger man collecting such a sublime label in my own backyard was reassuring and spoke to the renewed resilience of northern soul. A few months later, Britain was devastated by floods, and the River Tay broke its banks. Low-lying housing schemes to the north of the city were deluged, but in an act of northern soul self-preservation James ignored the floating furniture, the soggy carpets and the advice of the emergency services, lovingly carrying his record box and Lambretta scooter up the stairs to the safety of his bedroom. It was an act of mindful obsession which I wholly endorse.

To balance out old wars, I broke with nostalgia and played a set of rare modern northern (or what the scene now refers to as 'upfront'), periodically clearing the floor as tumbleweed drifted across the lacquered floor. But it was such a special floor. I had crawled across it as a child. It is where I had excitedly wet myself when chocolate eggs were handed out to the kids on Easter Sunday. It was the social club where my mum and dad would go to drink, smoke and dance in their younger days as I lay in a prefab through the hedge in a wooden cot. It was where they had taken me as an infant to my first family wedding. I had slid across its polished floor in my stocking feet the day after my dad's funeral. It was home.

The reunion of Perth City Soul Club was one among many reunions in a scene that celebrates itself more than any other subculture, but like the myth of Janus, northern soul has two faces, both shaped in the acrimonious years of the seventies: one face looks back and is fixated on the old ways; the other looks forward to soul music underplayed and overlooked. When I finally left to catch the midnight train home to Glasgow, carrying my record box as if it held gold, frankincense and myrrh, I walked through a car park still thronged with old Mods and young Turks, unable to fully rationalise why a scene that should have died years before was in such rude and uncompromising health. Curiosity and a deep emotional longing to look back took me on a detour to the hedgerow where the old Hillyland prefabs once stood. I looked over to the garden that my dad had been so painfully slow to dig and mentally surveyed the place where I had once slept. I stood and stared for ten minutes or more, asking questions that could never be answered. Leaking out of the sound system was the bouncing rhythm of 'Love Is Like An Itching In My Heart', a record once recorded by The Supremes but covered by many other unknown soul singers who came hopefully in their wake. The version that was playing was by Jenny and the Jewels (HIT, 1967), a fast turnaround cover version on a quick cash-in label sold via the now defunct Woolworths chain across America. The session musicians paid by the hour would never gain the fame or wealth of Diana Ross, but the song's obscure origins, relentless beat and nagging chorus line makes it classic northern soul. The lyrics say something about my own life – and the itching in my own heart. I wish I had stopped my dad going to work that day. I wish I had known him much longer in life. Much longer.

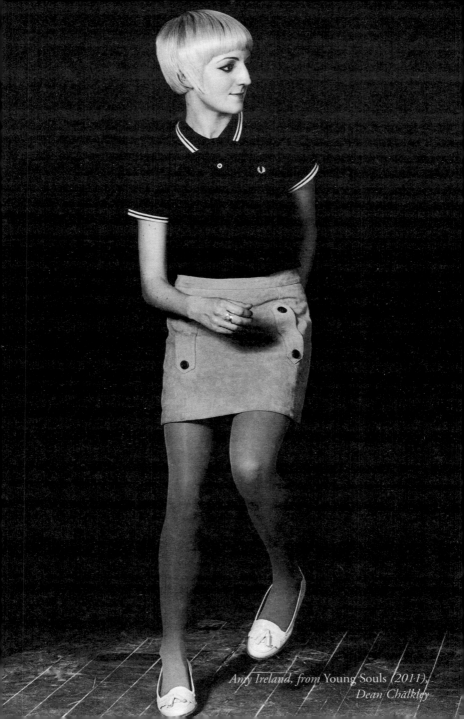

Amy Ireland, from Young Souls (2011),
Dean Chalkley

GLOSSARY OF TERMS

Arctic – a Philadelphia-based soul label founded by radio station WDAS DJ Jimmy Bishop and a forerunner of what became the Philly sound. Best known for its distinctive penguin trademark.

badges – woven badges were often issued as a membership gift at major clubs. Originally sewn on Mod blazers in the late sixties, they became icons on the side of holdalls or on T-shirts. In the seventies, they eventually passed into cliché, only to be resurrected as new local clubs opened up.

boot – a boot is short for bootleg, an illicit pressing of a rare record where the money never returns to the artists; sometimes called a pressing.

backdrop – a backward move in northern soul dancing and a byword for the scene's athleticism.

Beachcomber – a venue within the Wigan Casino complex which was mostly open in the early morning to prevent soul fans drifting into the town and attracting the attention of the police.

Birch – a motorway service station on the M62 between J18 and J19, used by northern soul fans as a stopover on the way to all-night venues. The forerunner of the rave convoys of the eighties.

blazers – popular with Mods and with the northern soul cognoscenti who went to the Twisted Wheel and the Torch. Dying away by the height of Wigan Casino, they sometimes came with coloured braiding and a soul-club pocket badge. In the late sixties, Mods also wore the soulful striped caps of the English public school system. They faded away and were finally killed off by regulations requiring crash helmets.

blueys – a nickname for the pharmaceutical amphetamine Dexamyl, which was light blue in colour.

bombers – sometimes known as 'black beauties'; another amphetamine drug.

Catacombs – a cult club in Wolverhampton set inside an old dungeon-like venue. Broke many rare records and set the standard for the hidden environments revered on the northern scene.

chalkies – the brand name for the amphetamine Tenuate Dospan and the most commonly available amphetamine on the northern scene. The poor man's drug and a substitute for amphetamine capsules. Ssometimes known as 'tombstones', their similarity to slabs of chalk gave them their most common name.

Cleggy – nickname for the east Lincolnshire coastal town of Cleethorpes, and all-nighters at Cleethorpes Pier and the Winter Gardens.

collector – the generic name for the tribe who collect rare records on the northern scene. Collectors often find the records that are either lent, sold or fed to DJs. Collectors frequently have a specialism, e.g. collecting UK issue records, collecting Detroit labels, white demo promotional records or even Canadian issues.

cover up – a rare record was often 'covered up' to disguise its true identity and protect a DJ's unique access to the sound.

crack-up – a term used to describe someone or something that induces amphetamine paranoia.

cranking – injecting drugs, which became more common from 1970 onwards.

crossover – a term with many meanings in soul music. It was originally a term for music that 'crossed over' from the old R&B charts into the pop charts but with the emergence of new sounds at the Stafford all-nighters, the term came to mean music that crossed over the decades – sixties to seventies – and usually rare or forgotten sounds cast at a slower pace than traditional stompers.

Cybermen – a gang of rare soul extremists mainly from the Preston area who were key figures at Stafford all-nighters and often wore insane head-gear; they were a mocking commentary on the rare soul scene.

demo – an advance copy of a record usually supplied to DJs in the USA and UK markets, short for 'demonstration copy'. Demos often came in the form of a white label. Other terms include DJ Copy, Radio Station Copy, Advanced Copy. In America the term 'promo' for promotional copy was commonly used.

div – an ordinary person not cool or informed enough to be on the northern scene.

dobber – sheer beauty or perfection, tinged with uniqueness. The term refers mostly to rare records and would not be used indiscriminately for other objects such as shoes or shirts.

Emidisc – the most popular brand of blank acetate discs in the seventies. When a rare record was near impossible to source, secondary DJs or collectors would buy an Emidisc copy, to allow them to play a top sound. Emidiscs were individually 'cut' or 'carved' by a machine, as opposed to the mass pressing of a commercial release. In later years, they were sometimes known as 'carvers', a term derived from a surviving carving company Vinyl Carvers of Brixton, which also serves the 'dub-plate' reggae market.

find – a find is the term used by collectors when a rare record is discovered.

glove – black leather gloves worn by northern soul fans in the early seventies. Derived from America's Black Power movement and the 1968 Olympics protest. Some northern fans also wore black berets. The idea may well have come from an album cover – *Soul Stomp* – featuring Motown star Earl Van Dyke, sporting a beret he had bought in Paris on the Motown European tour 1965, years before the Black Power movement. Black wooden chokers featuring the black glove were also worn around the neck by both men and women in the early seventies.

KTF – an abbreviation of the northern soul slogan 'Keep the Faith', it began to appear more frequently in the era of social media.

matrix – the matrix number refers to the details carved or stamped into a record in the manufacturing process. It is in the area of the record known as the run-out groove, and is often used to determine whether a record is original or a bootleg.

Mecca – the Mecca Leisure Group owned clubs and bingo halls across the UK. Several northern soul clubs were held on Mecca-owned premises, but the term is usually used to refer to Blackpool Mecca where DJs Ian Levine and Colin Curtis shaped the scene in the seventies.

Mr M's – a small club-within-a-club at Wigan Casino which played mostly older sixties records and was much loved by traditionalists. Mr M's was named after Wigan's managing director Gerry Marshall.

minter – a term of admiration for a mint record with no scratches or diminution of quality.

mither – a northern word for pestering or annoying someone; often DJs would complain that someone was 'mithering' them to play a specific record.

modern – a generic term for post-sixties records which have influences from funk, disco and the new synthesised production techniques of the seventies onwards.

oldie – a record played in the early years of the northern soul scene, or generically a record that the dancers are already familiar with.

Pendulum – a famous Manchester club in the early seventies held in the Manchester Sports and Social Club Centre.

popcorn – a retro dance scene in Belgium with some similarities to northern soul. The scene took its name from the Popcorn nightclub near Antwerp, which was named after the James Brown song 'Mother Popcorn'.

pressing – the generic term for a bootleg or reissued record, not the original.

Ric-Tic – a revered Detroit record label eventually acquired by the Motown Corporation; a nightclub called the Ricky-Tick in Windsor near London was also a famous R&B club where The Rolling Stones first played.

Riker – the pharmaceutical company that manufactured the amphetamine Durophet. Some northern soul diehards had the tattoo 'Riker-Liker' on their arms.

Risley – a remand centre near Warrington where those arrested with drugs offences were held on remand. It is now a Category C men's prison.

rolled – an equivalent word for being mugged. Individuals or small gangs would physically threaten people and steal their money, drugs or records.

Shrine – one of the rarest soul labels ever. Shrine was a sixties soul label based in Washington DC. Its logo was based on the shrine of John F Kennedy at Arlington Cemetery.

sixties newie – a deliberately anachronistic term which refers to sixties soul records discovered or played long after the sixties were over and new to the scene.

SKF – the initials of the pharmaceutical company Smith, Kline & French who manufactured amphetamines. Now part of the pharmaceutical conglomerate GlaxoSmithKline. Like 'Riker' some northern soul fans had the initials 'SKF' tattooed on their arms or hands.

snicket – a Yorkshire word for a narrow alleyway; many northern soul clubs were inevitably up a snicket.

squad – abbreviation of the drug squad.

stomper – a furious up-tempo record with big instrumentation, which dancers effectively stomp to.

Styrene – a plastic used in the manufacturing of records, especially those produced on the West Coast of America; it was thinner than the more well-known plastic vinyl.

upfront – a catch-all term used to describe DJs who played modern sounds stretching to funk and rare groove.

vinyl – the dominant plastic used in manufacturing records.

Yate – a town in south Gloucestershire which hosted a popular northern soul all-nighter, overlapping with Wigan and Cleethorpes.

INDEX

'A Change Is Gonna Come' 190
'A Little Piece Of Leather' 54
'A Long Walk To DC' 190
'A Thrill A Moment' 59
AABB (Above Average Black Band) 7
Abadi, Ivor 23
Abadi, Jack 23
Abadi, Phillip 23
Abbey, John 61
Ace Records 250, 251, 252
acid house 148, 244
acid-jazz scene 246
The Admirations 255
African seamen 17
African-American music 4, 49, 56, 59, 73, 77, 79, 86, 182, 188, 269

'Afternoon Of The Rhino' 73
'Agent Double-O-Soul' 28, 58
Aiken, Ben 49
'Ain't No Soul Left In These Old Shoes' 56
The Alan Bown Set 24
Alderson, Christine 276
Alexander, Arthur 248
'All Turned On' 127, 195
Allanton 165–71, 228
Almond, Marc 74, 112–13
Alston label 89
American Bandstand (TV) 91
Amos, Dave (aka Papa Stone) 6–7
Anarchy in the UK (magazine) 144
Anarchy in the UK (tour) 142–3
Anastasi, Phil 79
The Andantes 197

Anderson, Carol 60

Anderson, John 46, 86, 89, 94, 132, 135, 243

Anderson, Paul 'Trouble' 243

Anderton, Cyril James 13–17, 19, 22, 29, 38–40, 80–2

Anderton, Gillian 80

Andrews, Simon 98, 113

'Angel Baby (Don't You Ever Leave Me)' 53

'Angel Doll' 220

Angelic Upstarts 119

Angelou, Maya 1

Anglo-American Records 35, 198, 262

The Animals 30

'Another Day' 183

The Apollas 49

Apollo Theatre (Harlem) 49

Appleyard, Dave 141

Arctic label 279

Armstrong, Jimmy 184

Armthorpe Pit Club 164

Arnold, P P 108

The Ascots 183

Ashibende, Tim 222

'Ask The Lonely' 59

Astley, Rick 136

The A-Team (TV) 73

Atomic Weapons Research Centre (Aldermaston) 20

auctions 181, 196, 198–9, 260, 262

The Avengers 92

The Avengers (TV) 2

Average White Band 6–7

Ayoub, Ken 93

'baby boomers' 19

'Baby Cakes' 252

'Baby Have Mercy On Me' 220

'Baby I'm Still The Same Man' 136

'Baby Love' 257

'Baby Reconsider' 37, 192

'Baby Walk Right In' 53

'Back In My Arms Again' 59

Back To The World (album) 104

'Backstreet' 28

badges 279

BAFTA awards 268

Baker, Butch 11, 158

Baker, Hylda 119, 216

Bali Hai (bar) 133

Ball, Alan 216

Ball, David 74, 113

Bananarama 136

Bankhall Mine (Burnley) 164

Banks, Darrell (aka Darrell Eubanks) 47, 52, 53, 185

Banks, Tony 107, 108

Barnes, JJ 59–60, 126, 219

Barnfather, Martin (aka Soul Sam) 88, 97

Barnsley Catholic Club 174

Barnsley Miners' Forum 156

Barton, Laura 79

Bass, Fontella 217

Batiste, Rose 126–7, 130

Batley Art and Design College 117

BBC 21, 27, 192, 224, 259

Beachcomber Holiday Park (Cleethorpes) 150

Beachcomber (Wigan) 70, 90, 104, 279

'beat clubs' 17, 19

Beatbox 273

The Beatles 20, 95, 187

Beaulieu jazz festival 21
Bedford Head (pub) 245
Beeching cuts 140
Begbie, Francis 'Franco' 7
'Behind A Painted Smile' 107
Benatar, Pat 217
Benn, Rt Hon Tony 161
Benstead, Dr John 82–3
Bentley, Julian 33
Berry, Andrew 38
Berry, Dave 107
Beta Chapter fraternity 182
Betty Wilson and the 4 Bars 184
Bevin, Ernest 106
Bicknell, Mark 145
Bidmaster 262
Bierkeller (bar) 113
Big City Records 222
Big Frank and the Essences 214
Billboard (magazine) 95, 192
Billboard Top 100 chart (US) 7,
    113, 191
Billups, Eddie 203
Bilston Glen 167
Bin Lid club 109, 110, 121
Birch (service station) 280
Birmingham Times 201
Black Britain 241
The Blackbyrds 179
Black, Cody 244
Black Echoes (newspaper) 99, 144,
    165, 221, 236, 243
Black Magic label 193
Black Nasty 135
Black Panther Party 190
Black Panthers 78, 263
Black Power movement 34, 45, 58,
    71, 78, 190

Blackburn Rovers FC 226
Blackpool 16, 86, 125–7, 128–9,
    148
    Mecca 39, 50, 67, 77, 86, 87,
        104, 125–37 *passim*, 194
Blackpool International Soul
    Festival 150
Blackpool Tower 126, 129
blazers (Mod) 110, 129, 155, 279,
    280
Bleasdale, Pat 261
Blitz club 240
'Blow Your Whistle' 89
'Blowing Up My Mind' 135
Blue Cat Records 71
Blue Rooms (Sale) 75, 80
Blues & Soul (magazine) 26, 31, 50,
    54, 61, 68, 148, 179, 226
Blues Mafia 188
Blues Workshop 6
blueys 280
Bob Dylan 187
Bob Wilson and the San Remo
    Quartet 127, 195
Bob Wilson Sounds 195, 252
The Bodysnatchers 241
Boiler (Barcelona) 272
Bolan, Marc 74
Bolton vii, 50, 68, 76, 97, 148,
    163, 165, 216, 217, 260
bombers 71, 280
'The Boogaloo Party' 5, 110
Boola-Boola label 266
bootlegging 37, 44, 70, 111, 136,
    191–9 *passim*, 212, 225, 226,
    251–2, 260
Boreham, Mr Justice 121
Bostock's (market stall) 108

'The Bottle' 241
Bowie, David 8
Bowie, Roscoe 183
Bozeman, Marjorie 53
Bradford 22, 103–4, 108, 113,
    117–8, 132, 161, 165, 169,
    178, 222
Bradley, Keith 226
Brady, Pat 112, 144, 244, 262
Brandon, Bill 200, 202
Brassed Off (film) 162
Bratton, Joanne 126
Bremner, Stuart 129
Brent, Pete 'Tamla' 107
Brewster, Bill 55, 76, 110, 141
Brick, Chris 240
Brick, Sue 239, 242
Bridlington 126, 139, 150, 162
Brighton 128, 146, 238
Brill Building (Broadway) 77
Bristol 98, 269
Britt, Mel 135, 255
Broadmoor Hospital 122
'Broadway Sissy' 183
The Broken Wheel 35
Bronco label 266
Brooks, Claston (aka Danman)
    119
Brown, Dr Lorraine 188–9
Brown, James 7, 22, 243
Brown, Maxine 104, 252, 274
Brown, Tim 35, 50, 130, 185, 198,
    228, 262, 263
Browner, Duke 46, 47
Brownstone Records 243
Bryant, JD 180
Brynmor Jones Library (aka 'the
    Liquorice Allsort') 9

Buchan, Acky 168
Bullock, Aaron 53
Burke, Keni 148
Burke, Solomon 246
Burke, Steven 'Papa Burky' 119
Burn, Gordon 103
'Burning Sensation' 227
Burning Spear 119
Burns, Johnny 7
Burrell, Kenny 198
Burton, Chris 34, 51, 54, 60–2
Burton, Malc 159
Bus Palladium, Paris 20
Butcher, Andrea 261
Butler, Billy 20
Butler, Jerry 92, 104, 183, 197,
    258
Buttle, Butch 174
Buttle, David (aka Mighty Bub)
    155–62, 167, 172–4
Buttle, Elsie 161
Buzzcocks 193
Bye, Haydn 169
Byrd, Professor Donald 179
Byron, Lord 125

Caesar, Imruh 104
Caesar, Pogus 104
Caesar, Steve 76, 98, 104, 112–14,
    237, 241, 244, 251
Café Francis 39
Caister club 112
Cal Green and the Specials 214
Caledonian Soul Club (Glasgow)
    169
Callas, Maria 95
CALM (charity) 229
Camden Palace 241

Cameo-Parkway label 91
Campaign for Nuclear
    Disarmament (CND) 20, 21
Campbell, Herb 195
Cannon, Ace 158
'Can't Get Over These Memories'
    94, 190
Cantwell, Brian 272, 274
Cappello, Michael 39
'Car Wash' 137–8
Carlin, George 177
Carlton, Carl 244
The Carltons 183
Carlton club (Warrington) 75
Carlton Inn (Morecambe) 147
Carne, Jean 94
Carolina beach scene 245
Carroll, Ted 250
The Carstairs 131–2
Carstairs List 132
Carter, President Jimmy 189
The Casanovas 255
Casbah club 78
Casey, KC 89
Casino (Shaw) 98
Cat in the Hat 243
Catacombs Club 34–5, 105, 108,
    141, 248, 260, 280
Cats club 162
Cavern 20
Cavernes (Bradford) 117
Center Studios (Hollywood) 196
Central Pier (Morecambe) 146
'Chained And Bound' 202
chalet party 149
chalkies 47, 48, 149, 280
Chambliss, Robert 200
Chandler, Gene 93

Channel 4 93, 145, 173, 201, 223,
    224, 260, 264–71 *passim*
Chapman, Colin 139–41, 145
Chapman, Mary 139–41, 145
charitable events 173, 261
Charles, Ray 248
Charles, Sweet 243
Charly label 248
Charrière, Henri 'Papillon' 267
Chateau Impney 36–7
Cheatham, Oliver 215
The Checkerboard Squares 195–6,
    252
Checker, Chubby 158
'Cheatin' Kind' 94
Checkpoint Charlie, Berlin 272
Chelsea School of Art 143
The Chemical Brothers 254
Cher 217
Cherwell (newspaper) 238
Chess Records 20, 23, 52, 251
Chesterfield 160, 161, 195, 261
Chicago Roadshow 142
Chicano low-rider scene 245
'Child Of The Streets' 201
Chitlin Circuit 78
The Chosen Few 92
Christian Police Association 40
Chuddy (Bradford) 169
Chumbawamba 114
Cider with Roadies (Maconie) 93
'Cissy Strut' 183
Clark, Alice 11
Clark, Ian 'Clarky' 221, 247, 248,
    251
The Clark Sisters 179
Clark, Stewart 'Sparky' 273
Clarke, Tony (aka Ralph Thomas

Williams, Ralph Williams,
  Ralph Ferguson) 51, 52–3,
  217
The Clash 142
'Classical Gas' 73
Cleckheaton 110
Cleethorpes 5, 67, 76, 106, 109,
  112, 126, 127, 128, 138–42,
  143, 144, 145–6, 149, 150,
  156, 159, 172, 245, 259, 262,
  267, 268
  Return to Cleethorpes (events)
    150
  Winter Gardens 142, 146
Cliff, Jimmy 24, 119
Cliff Nobles & Co. 52
Clifton Hall (Rotherham) 159, 190
Clone Zone 38
Clouds (Edinburgh) 94, 167, 170
Clough, Brian 114
Clowery, Ian (aka Matchie) 76
Club 70 (Batley) 110
Coal, Crisis and Conflict (Winterton
  and Winterton) 160
Coates, Graham 141
Cockburn, Tommy 216
Cokell, Les 39, 139
Coco and Ben 260
The C.O.D.'s 159
Coe, Alexander (aka Sasha) 254
Collins, Geoffrey (aka Bootleg
  King) 191–2
Collins, Lyn 243
'Come On Train' 67, 241
The Commodores 134, 263
Communist Party (US) 188
Compass Club 36
Concorde (shop) 6

Conley, Arthur 109
Constantine, Elaine 268
Contempo Records 61
Cook, Little Joe 73
Cook, Michael 'Mick' 159
Cooke, Sam 37, 190
'co-pro' 253
Corinna (pub) 8, 273
Cornelius, Don 196–7
Cornet (pub) 237
Cosgrove, Stuart
  birth 3, 272
  childhood 3, 3–4, 5–6, 273
  collecting 202–4, 221, 243,
    265–7
  cousin's death 238
  father's death 3–4, 272, 273
  girlfriends 1, 18–19, 31–2, 44
  overseas travel 177–91, 243,
    265–6
  teenager 1–3, 5–6, 9
  university 9–11, 79, 144, 179,
    241
  work 145, 173, 223–4, 224,
    235–6, 243, 264–8, 271
cover up 280
Cozens, Randy 245–7
'Crackin' Up Over You' 36
crack-up 280
cranking 85, 281
Crass 119
'crate-digger' stores 222
Crawford, Carolyn 246
'Crazy Blues' 56–7
Cream 95
Creative Funk label 134
Crewe 66
Crisp, Quentin 39

Croasdell, Ady (aka Harboro Horace) 150, 172, 213, 246, 248–50
Cromwell, Oliver 14
Crown Hotel (Glenrothes) 167
Cruikshank, Jimmy 'Crooky' 7–8
'Crying Over You' 47
Culture Show (TV) 268
Cummings, William 184
Cunliffe, Ian (Cunny) 74–5, 231
Curtis, Colin 51, 88, 99, 131, 133, 148, 271
Curtis, 'Dandy Dave' 209
'Cut Your Motor Off' 135, 140
Cybermen 72, 166, 248–50, 255

Dade label 89
Daily Express 238
Dakar, Rhoda 241
Dalton, Chris 141
The Damned 119, 142
The Damned United (Peace) 114
dance contests 75–6, 104, 173, 259
dance style 32, 72, 75, 76, 77, 93, 112, 131
Danger High Voltage (album) 90
Daniel, Jeffrey 197
Daniels, David 61
Darge, Keb 76, 166, 212–14, 216, 241, 245, 249, 272
'Darkest Days' 37
Date label 187
Davidson, Billy 148
Davies, John 162–3, 164
Davies, Lorraine 72, 98
Davis, Angela 190
Davis, Carl 57

Davis, Charles (aka Nolan Chance) 55
Davis, Melvin 185
Davis, Paul 31
Davis, Terry 245
Day, Alan 51
Day, Jackie 214
The DC Blossoms 180–1, 203
Dean, Christopher 77
Dean, Snoopy 88
Decca Records 246
deep funk scene 245
'Deep In The Heart Of Harlem' 78
Dees, Sam 92, 200, 201–3
Dekker, Desmond 119
The Delrays Incorporated 87, 135
Del Rio (café) 107
Del-Larks 189
Demob 239–40
Dene, 'Farmer' Carl 36
Dennison, Andy 168
DePierro, Tom 197
Derek B 243
Deroys Sound Studio 226
'Destination Unknown' 87, 135
Detroit 24
Detroit Emeralds 71
'The Detroit Sound' 195
Detroit Symphony Orchestra 127
Dewhirst, Ian (aka DJ Frank) 76, 108–11, 118, 131, 134, 141, 193, 194, 196–7
Dewsbury 109–10, 117, 120–1
Diddley, Bo 23
The Differences 186
Dillon, Pete 33
Dimond, Colin (aka Colin Curtis) 54

Dingwall, Alan 19, 22, 28–9
Dirtbox 241–2
DJ History 129
dobber 3, 178, 281
'Do I Love You (Indeed I Do)' 99,
    196, 197–9, 259
'Do The 45' 31
Dobson, Mark 'Butch' 164, 174,
    215, 222, 249, 254–5, 272
Doctor Buzzard's Original
    Savannah Band 137
Do-Dos 9
Dome (Morecambe) 147
'Dominique' 6
Donald Jenkins and the Delighters
    214
Donovan, Jason 136
'Don't Cry Sing Along With The
    Music' 251
'Don't Let Him Hurt You' 181
'Don't Turn Your Back On Me'
    171
Dors, Diana 39
Dorsey, Lee 5
'Double Cookin'' 195, 252
double-deck turntables 106
'Do-Wha-Diddy' 135
Doyle, Arthur Conan 235
Dr Who (TV) 86
Dramatic and Music Performers
    Protection Act (1971) 192
The Drifters 28, 30
drug squad 22, 28–9, 33, 39, 61,
    82, 85, 133, 144, 160, 216,
    217, 283
Drugs (Prevention of Misuse) Act
    (1964) 22
'The Duck/Love Runs Out' 111

Dudley Zoo 196
Duke Records 23
Dumfries Boys 216
Dunn, Fraser 169
Dyson, Andy 253
Dyson, Clifton 185–6
Dyson, Ronnie 215

Eagle, Roger 23, 24–5, 30
Earl's Heath Youth Club
    (Dewsbury) 109
Earnshaw, Howard 119, 145
Earth Rocker sound system 119
Earth, Wind and Fire 88
East Coast Connection 88, 135
eBay 262
Ebor Suite (York) 84
Eddie Daye and the Four Bars
    181
Eddie (DJ) 35, 137–8
Edinburgh 94, 149, 167, 170–1,
    179, 216, 228, 274
Edwards, Donald 112
Edwards, Lou 135
Elbert, Donnie 53
Ellis, Martyn 51, 58, 68
Ellis, Tony 245
Ellison, Lorraine 68
Ellroy, James 265
Elson, Frank 61, 226
Emidiscs 226, 281
Empress Ballroom (Blackpool) 150
Empress Ballroom (Huddersfield)
    119
Empress Ballroom (Wigan) 15–16,
    40
'The Entertainer' 52
Erpen, Malayka 261

Evans, Ernest (aka Chubby Checker) 92
Evening Standard 21
'Everything's Gonna Be Alright' 108
Evison, Caesar 216
Evison, Dave 72
Evison, Mary 216
The Exciters 135
Exit Centre (Glenrothes) 167

The Face (magazine) 164, 247
Facebook 260–2, 268, 273
Factory Records 17
Falcon Centre (Barnsley College) 173
Falcon Manor 39
The Fall 193
Fame, Georgie 24, 107
The Fantastic Four 59, 171
Fantasy Records 252
fanzines 144–5, 236, 261
Farlowe, Chris 54
Fat Fish label 37
'The Fat Man/Working At The Go-Go' 158
Fats Domino 158
The Fawns 184
Federal Bureau of Investigation (FBI) 191
Federal Theatre Project 189, 199
Fenton, Eddie 211
Ferguson, Dave 258
'Festival Time' 37, 127
'Fever' 220
Fields, Lily 134
Fishwick, Ian 68
'Five Minutes' 186

Flack, Roberta 179
The Flamingos 5, 110
Fletcher, Sam 214
floating (dance style) 76–7
Floyd, Eddie 107
Fonteyn, Margot 95
'Footsee' 92–3
Ford, President Gerald 189
'Forget About Me' 246
Foster, Eddie 198
Fountain, James 241
Four Tops 8, 59, 218, 221
Franklin, Aretha 74
Franklin, Boby 88, 134
Franklin, Fran 216
Fred Wesley and the JBs 243
Free Angela (album) 190
'Free At Last' 170
'Free For All' 36
Freeman, Roy 46
Frith, Simon 77
'Function At The Junction' 237
Fused (album) 73

Gadsden, Walter 200
Gagarin, Yuri 3
'Gangnam Style' (video) 260
Gardiner, Ernest 61
Gardner, Don 94
Garrett Crew 221
Gateside Colliery (Cambuslang) 167
Gavin, Martin 169
gay community 38–40, 87, 91, 130, 133, 136, 183, 197
Gaye Snr, Marvin 219
Gaye, Marvin 60, 218, 219–20, 252

Geddes, Norah 239
Geddes, Phil 238–9
Gedewicz, Michael (aka Michael Geddes) 239
Geno Washington and the Ram Jam Band 24
George, Judge Ronald 220
George Mason University 188–9
The Georgia Prophets 220
Gerry and the Pacemakers 20
'Get It Baby' 74
The Gilder youth club 110
Ginger and Eddie 35, 137
'Gino Is A Coward' 58
'Girl In Trouble' 184
Gladys Knight and the Pips 220
Glasgow 20, 54, 66, 126, 132, 165, 166, 169, 201, 274, 275
Glenrothes 167, 214
Glitter, Gary 70
God Squad 15
Godin, Dave 25–6, 31–2, 50, 130, 142, 145, 231
God's Cop (Prince) 14
Golden Torch 1, 11, 34, 54, 55, 58, 62, 90, 106, 110, 157, 217, 267
Golden World label 59
Goldmine (Canvey Island) 112
'Good Feelin' (video) 260
Good Groove (radio) 243
The Good Old Days (TV) 119
Gordy, Berry 59, 60, 181, 191, 198
Gordy, Raynoma 181, 191
Gorman, Freddie 58
The Gospel According to Dave Godin (fanzine) 26, 145, 231

The Graham Bond Organisation 24, 247
Granada Reports (TV) 224
Granada Television 95–6, 222, 231
Grand Records Ball 106
Granger, Gerri 150
Grapevine label 243
Gray, Barry 98
Gray, Dobie 37
Greater Manchester Police 13–15, 80, 81, 231
Greatest Hits (Four Tops) 8
Green, Al 200
Greene, Laura 71
Greenhof, Derek 157–8, 160, 172–4
Greet, Dave 194
Gregory, Ronald 105
Gregory's Girl (film) 201
Griffey, Dick 197
Grimethorpe 162, 164
Grimethorpe Colliery Brass Band 162
Grindall, Geoff 72
The Groovettes 214
Grundy, Bill 142
Guardian 79, 119, 151
Guarnori, Steve 247
Guess, Lenis 11, 55
'Guess Who Loves You' 181

Hacienda 17, 38
Hair (musical) 251
Halfway to Paradise (TV) 201
Hamilton, Leo 112
Hamilton, Marybeth 187
Hamilton, Roy 36
Hampton, Charlie 183

Hancock, Ken 162
'Handwriting On The Wall' 250
'Happy' 269
Hardiman, Ernest 22
Harehills Middle School, Leeds
    112
Harkins, Lenny 169–70
'Harper Valley PTA' 187
Harris, Bill 134
Harris, Kent 266
Harris, Major 56
Harrison, Joan 85
Harrods 238
Hatcher, Willie 244
Hatfield Main Colliery 157
Hathaway, Donny 179, 182
Haughton, Yogi 72, 269
'Have Love Will Travel' 141
Hawaii Five-O (TV) 94
Hawaiian Eye club 141
Haywood, Leon 37, 192
'Head Over Heels' 244
'Headline News' 59
'Heartaches And Pain' 94
Heath, Edward 156
Heathcote, John (aka Hector;
    Hecta from Selecta) 192
Heaven club 91, 136, 138
Heinemann, Otto K E 56
'Help Me' 29
Henderson, Jocko 170
Hendrix, Jimi 28–30, 95, 192
Hennigan, Guy (aka 'Guy from
    Skipton') 72, 164, 166,
    211–15, 222, 249
Herbie Thompson and Black Nasty
    135
Hernandos (aka Hernie's) club 33

Heroes club 38
'Hey Boy' 180, 203
Hibbert, John 83, 85
Hi-Fi club 122
Higgins, Michael 168, 229
Highland Room (Blackpool Mecca)
    50, 77, 133, 137, 151
Hill, Jacqueline 115
Hill Street Blues (TV) 73
Hilton Hotel (Blackpool) 149
Hipkiss, Jerry 195
Hirst, Damien 242
'Hit And Run' 130
HIV/AIDS 40, 197
Hogan, Dr Bernie 261
Holloway, Loleatta 94
Holt, Sandy 76
Hooker, John Lee 107
Horne, Jimmy Bo 171
'The Horse' 52
Horseshoe club 248
Hot Wax Records 36
Houston, Thelma 197
Howlin' Wolf 5, 23
Hudson, Bill 200
Hughes, Mike 264
The Human Beinz 92
Human League 193
'Hung Up On Your Love' 131
'Hungry For Love' 127
Hunter, Herbert 189
Hutch, Willie 111
Hutchinson, Michael 90
Hutton, Bobby 150
Hydes, Robert 120
'Hypnotized' 49

'I Believe In Miracles' 243

'I Can't Help Myself (Sugar Pie, Honey Bunch)' 59, 221
'I Can't See Him Again' 89
'I Can't Stop Loving My Baby' 49
'I Cried My Life Away' 215
'I Don't Know What Foot To Dance On' 140
'I Got To Find Me Somebody' 269
'I Got What You Need' 87–8, 134
'I Had A Good Time' 245
'I Have A Dream' 190
'I Have A Girl' 171
'I Just Can't Live My Life (Without You Babe)' 49–50
'I Just Can't Speak' 171
'I Miss My Baby' 130
'I Need You' 134
'I Never Knew' 198
'I Thought You Were Mine' 266
I Used to Go to Stafford All-Nighters (Facebook group) 261–2
'I Was Born This Way' 87
'I Was Born To Love Her' 189
'I Won't Be Coming Back' 180
'I Won't Let Her See Me Cry' 214
i-D (magazine) 247
'I'd Think It Over' 214
'If I Had (One Gold Piece)/Huh Baby' 181, 220
'If You Ask Me (Because I Love You)' 231
'I'll Always Love You' 184
'I'll Give You Just A Little More Time' 214
'I'll Never Forget You' 171
'I'm Gone' 189

'I'm Gonna Live Up To What She Thinks' 171
'I'm On My Way' 77, 79
'I'm Slowly Molding' 244
'I'm Spellbound' 47
'I'm Still Loving You' 59
'I'm Your Pimp' 134
'I'm Yours' 184
immigrants 17, 104–5, 109–10, 239
The In Crowd (Ritson) 51
In Search of the Blues (Hamilton) 187
Industrial Commercial Plastics 192
Ingleneuk club 6–7
'Inside Bedford Stuyvesant' 78
'Investigate' 56
The Invitations 51, 93
Iqbal, Dr 44, 48
IRA bombs 83, 238–9
Isaacs, Gregory 119
The Isley Brothers 29, 30, 107
'It Really Hurts Me Girl' 131
'It'll Never Be Over For Me' 173
'It's The Same Old Song' 59
ITV 122, 224

Jacaranda club 20
Jackson, Chuck 8, 252, 274
Jackson, Frank 225, 228–9, 230–1
Jackson, Millie 68
The Jackson Sisters 243
Jackson, Walter 183
The Jam 246
James Barnes and the Agents 170
James, Etta 248
James, Villmore 112
Japanese Mods 259

'Jaws' 137
Jay, Norman 243
jazz-funk 106, 112, 117, 179, 209, 210
Jazzy Jeff 165
'Jealousy' 178
Jebb, Tony 51
Jeffries, Bob 148
Jenkins, Diane 134
Jenny and the Jewels 276
'Job Opening' 189
JoBoxers 240
Jockey Boy Restaurant 200, 202
Joe 90 (TV) 94
John Manship Records 262
John Mayall's Bluesbreakers 24
John Rowland and the Jazz Unit 18
John and the Weirdest 94–5, 190
Johnny Thunders and the Heartbreakers 142
Johnson, Jim 146
Johnson, L J 142
Johnson, Lorraine 200, 202
Johnson, Lou 46, 108
Johnson, Rozetta 202
Johnson, Syl 104
Johnson, Tony 74
'The Joker' 158
Jones, Bessie 203
Jones, Bob 149
Jones, Gethro 76
Jones, Gloria 34, 74, 113
Jones, Linda 49–51, 58, 62, 68, 251
Jones, Rosey 141
Jones, Tamiko 47
Jr Walker and the All Stars 24
Juldane label 182

'(Just A Little) Faith And Understanding' 253
'Just Ask Me' 55
'Just Like The Weather' 55
'Just Out Of My Reach' 201
'Just Say Goodbye' 171
'Just The One I've Been Looking For' 245

Kane, Frank (aka Frank Kaplonek) 267
Kardomah café 21
Karim, Jawed 259
Karim, Ty 266–7
Kasbah v. Beat Surrender (DJs) 274
Kaufman, Rt Hon Gerald 161
Kay, Alan 257
KC and the Sunshine Band 89
'Keep the Faith' (KTF) slogan 282
Keighley 57
Kellett, Gaz 72, 166, 216, 249
Kendra, Karime 267
Kendricks, Eddie 220
Kennedy, President John F 181
Kent Records 150, 248, 250–2
Kerr, George 49
Kesey, Ken 249
The Kibbos 67
Kilt club 164
King, Ben E 28, 107
King, Carole 77
King, Jeff 192
King Jr, Martin Luther 181, 190, 274
King, Pete 137
King, Rodney 222
King Mojo club 30

King Records 244
Kirklees Borough Council 116–17
Kiss FM 243
Klooks Kleek 246
Knack Bar 6
Knight, Gladys 218, 220
Knight, Robert 208
Kool and the Gang 88, 223
Koppel, Martin 178
K-Pop anthems 260
KSOL radio station 195
Ku Klux Klan 200

La Conca D'Oro café 107
La Ronde 117
LaBelle, Patti 183
Labour's Red Wedge movement
    241
'The Ladies Choice' 88, 134
Laika (dog) 3
Lance, Major 54–7, 61, 89
'Landslide' 51, 52, 217
Lantern club 150
LAPD 222
Larkin, Philip 10
Laster, Larry 49, 171
The Last Poets 78
Lavette, Betty 150
Law, Colin 167, 168
Lawson, Pete 25, 145, 166, 185,
    224–32
Lawson, Robbie 227
Le Beat Route 247
Lee, Laura 47, 59, 126, 127
Leeds 33, 71, 103, 104, 106, 107,
    110, 111, 112, 113, 115, 118,
    122, 144, 165, 193, 262
Leeds Central Infirmary 114

Leeds Central Scooter Club 122
Leeds Central Soul Club 34,
    104–13, 114, 117, 122, 196
Leeds Mecca 104
Leeds Polytechnic 74
Leeds Poorhouse 115–6
Leeds Service Crew (Leeds United)
    107
Leeds United 25, 114
Leeds Warehouse 112, 115
Lees, Edwin P. (shop) 217
Left Wing Coffee Bar 18, 21, 23
Legend, Tobi 77, 78
Legerton, Harold 80
Lemon Tree 130
Les Chansonettes 181–2
'Let Me Be Your Full Time
    Groover' 200
Letham 3, 273
Letham Community Centre 7, 8,
    211
Levan, Larry 95
Levine, Ian Geoffrey 39, 50, 55,
    86–91, 129, 130, 131, 133–8,
    142, 148, 151, 181, 260, 263,
    271, 282
Lewis, Jesse 201
Lewis, Louise (aka Miss LL) 226
Library of Congress 188–90
Lifeline Soul Club 253, 259
'Lighten Up Baby' 266
'(Like A) Nightmare' 197
Lil Louis 165
Limelight club 39
Lincoln, Paul 18
'Linda' 183
Linda (from Derby) 44–5
Linton, Mark 168, 241

Little Beaver 90
Little Girl Blue/Jazz As Played In An Exclusive Side Street Club (album) 247
Little Lisa 221
'Little Love Affair' 254
Little Mick (Ormskirk crew) 231
Little Richard 57
Littles, Hattie 60
Live Experience 1967–68 (album) 192
Liverpool 20, 225
Livesey, 'Jumping' Joan 169, 229, 261
Locarno club (Coventry) 136
Loma records 49
London 15, 18, 19, 25, 26, 31, 54, 66, 74, 95, 98, 100, 104, 109, 119, 121, 122, 130, 133, 136, 138, 140, 143, 144, 150, 174, 179, 192, 210, 212, 213, 223, 224, 227, 234–255, 283 *passim*
'Lonely For You Baby' 203
'Lonely Lover' 219
'Long After Tonight Is All Over' 77
Long, Shorty 237
'Looking For You' 108
Lord's Day Observance Society 16, 80, 82, 90
Los Angeles 265–7
Lothian, Andy 7
'Love Don't Grow On A Love Tree' 90
'Love Has So Many Meanings' 134
'Love Is Like An Itching In My Heart' 275

'Love Keeps Me Crying' 274
'Love On A Mountain Top' 208
'Love You Baby' 135
Lowes, Alex 148
Luigi, Steve 107
Lulu's café 107
Luxury Soul Weekender 149
Lydon, John 142

Mac (friend) 45–5, 47–8, 273
McCadden, Dave (aka Dave Purdy) 145
McCann Erickson 268
McCants, Junior 244
McCarthy, John 241
McCarthyism 188
McCoy, Van 58
McCrae, George 89
McCrae, Gwen 89
MacDonald, Jayne 113–15
MacDonald, Wilf 114
McEvoy, David 61
McFarland, Jimmy 219
McFarlane, Tracy 274
McGahey, Mick 147, 156, 167, 171
McGriff, Jimmy 22
McGuire, James 45–8
McGuire, Nettie 47–8
McKay, John Andrew 19, 26–8
McKenna, Pete 69
McKune, James 187–8
McLaren, Malcolm 143
McLean, Levanna (aka 'Northern Soul Girl') 269
McLeod, Glenda 221
McLusky, Sean 240
McMullan, Ian 'Macca' 230

McNeely, Big Jay 214
McNeir, Ronnie 148
Mablethorpe 139
Maconie, Stuart 93
Madame Jojo's 245
Madison Avenue advertising
    industry 77
Madonna 254
The Magicians 253
'Magic Touch' 252
The Magnetics 171
Magnet Tavern (Boston) 139
Major Lance Live At The Torch
    (album) 61
'Make My Love A Hurting Thing'
    184–5
Malcolm X 2, 190
Manchester 11, 13–40 *passim*, 43,
    44, 45, 48, 54, 61, 66, 69, 70,
    72, 74, 75, 80, 81, 82, 84,
    105, 107, 108, 118, 121, 128,
    129, 135, 137, 139, 140, 147,
    149, 160, 173, 179, 215, 217,
    218, 224, 231, 258, 260, 262,
    263, 269, 271, 272, 282
Manchester City FC 137
Manchester Corporation Act
    (1965) 27–8
Manchester Evening News 18, 27
Manchester Tiffany's 218
Manchester United FC 25, 137
Mancuso, David 39
Mandela, Nelson 170
Manfred Mann 30, 135
Manifesto (magazine) 246
Manship, John 141, 198, 245,
    262–3
Mardi Gras club 20

Markham Main Colliery 164
Marlborough, James 274–5
Marsh, Derrick 226
Marsh, George 161
Marshall, Gerry 67, 99
Marshall, Tony 211
Martha and the Vandellas 59
martial arts 76, 212
Martin, Gaynor 260
The Marvelettes 220
Mason, Mike vii, 7, 93
Mason, Paul 93, 223, 268
Masters at Work 149
matrix 282
Matthews, Freddie 157
Maunkberrys 243
Maxwell, Holly 8
May, Derrick 165
Mayfield, Curtis 57, 104
'Me at the Zoo' (video) 259
Meadows, Shane 223, 268
Mecca (entertainment chain) 86,
    133, 211, 282
Mecca (Blackpool) 5, 39, 50, 67, 77,
    86, 87, 88, 91, 99, 104, 113,
    128, 131, 132–8, 142, 148, 151,
    180, 181, 182, 190, 194, 209,
    215, 217, 260, 262, 266, 271
Mecca (Leeds) 104
Mecca (Sale) 45
Meechan, Snitcher 7
Meikle, David 54
Melia, Ian 'Mel' 69, 230, 231
Mental Pack (Letham gang) 7
Mercer, Billy 250
Mercer, Willie 146
Merry Pranksters (Ken Kesey et al)
    249, 250

Mersey Beat bands 20
The Meters 183
Metro (Mod club) 33
MGM Tunes label 108
'Michael (The Lover)' 159
Microsoft Corporation 255
Milk, Sulphate and Alby Starvation
    (Millar) 236
Millar, Martin 236
Miller, Arthur 189
'Millionaire' 252
Mimms, Garnet 108
miners vii, 16, 34, 35, 62, 65, 81,
    126, 156–7, 160
miners' strike (1972) 156–7
miners' strike (1984–85) 160–4,
    168
Minnie Jones and the Minuettes
    244
Minogue, Kylie 136
Minott, Sugar 119
Minshull, Keith 51, 54
Mitchell, Mitch 29
Mitchell, Phillip 36
Mitchell, Stanley 74
Mixcloud 271
modern northern 132
Modern Records 251
modern soul 91
Modernist (Mod) 5–6, 9, 15, 18,
    20–5 *passim*, 29–36 *passim*,
    54, 85, 95, 96, 98, 106–10
    passim, 129, 135, 139, 141,
    144, 147, 155, 157, 162, 191,
    192, 209, 211, 216, 217, 223,
    238, 246, 247, 268, 270, 271,
    272, 274, 275, 279, 280
    Japanese 259

Moerer, Craig 262
Molloy, Dave vii, 72, 93–4,
    216–19, 228, 229, 231
Molloy, Jim 216–17
Molloy, Julie 261
'The Monkey Time' 56
The Montclairs 131
Montgomery, Jack 171
'Moody Woman' 258
Moon, Clinton 201
Moonsong Records 201, 202
Moore, Johnny 187
Moore, Melba 251–2
Morecambe 126, 146–7, 148,
    151–2, 269
Morecambe Pier 146–7, 151
Morecambe Trojans (scooter club)
    147
Moretti, Joe 18
Morley, Eric 133
Morris, Trefor 40
Moss Side 16
Motown Corporation 59, 126,
    218, 282
Motown Records 8, 24, 25, 28, 44,
    59, 60, 73, 89, 94, 107, 110,
    126, 134, 138, 147, 181, 191,
    196, 197, 198, 214, 218–21,
    266, 271, 282, 283
Motown club (Shaw) 45
Moultrie, Sam 184
MP3 263
Mr M's (Wigan Casino) 69, 96,
    99, 282
Murphy, Franklin Delano 214
Murphy, Mary 39
Muscle Shoals Studio 252
Musicor label 251

The MVP's 96
'My Baby Just Cares For Me' 247
'My Block' 78
'My Guy' 28, 191
'My Heart Needs A Break' 49
The Mylestones and Little Leroy
    158

Napoleons club 38
'Nasty Rock' 221
National Coal Board (NCB) 157
National Geographic 73
National Irish Club 109
National Union of Mineworkers
    (NUM) 156, 157, 161, 167
The Natural Four 266
'Naughty Boy' 214
Navarro, Tommy 215
Naylor, Steve 137
Negro Units of the Great
    Depression 188
Nelson, Trevor 149
New Century Hall 29
New Crawdaddy Club 261
New, Frankie 'Booper' 75–6
New Romantics 210, 240
New York club 38
The New Yorker (magazine) 115
New York loft scene 39
News of the World 33
Newtown British Legion Club 67
'Night Train' 22
Nightshift (McKenna) 69
Nile Club 17
Nilsen, Dennis 237
'1969' 78
99 Club (Scarborough) 151
Nixon, President Richard 243

NME (magazine) 143, 144, 164,
    213, 225, 243, 248
'No Good Guy' 230
No Irish, No Blacks, No Dogs
    (Lydon) 142
'No More Tears' 203
'No Stranger To Love' 221
'No Time' 94
'Nobody But Me' 92
'Nobody Knows' 190
North Wales 147
North West Tonight (TV) 224
Northern Soul, defined 4–5
Northern Soul (film) 268
'Northern Soul Girl' 269
Notre Dame (club venue) 248
Nottingham 139, 164, 192, 193,
    194, 253, 268
'Now I've Got The Upper Hand'
    203
Nowell, David 71
'Nowhere To Run' 59
Nude Restaurant club (Kobe) 272
Nuttall, Jeff 112
Nutter, Alice 114

Oasis café 21
Occleshaw, Nehemiah 15
O'Connor, James 'Jocko' 170, 228
Office for National Statistics 128
O'Hara, Jim 165–6, 168, 172, 228
Oi! 147
O'Jays 171
OKeh Records 56–7, 135, 187
OKeh Soul Club 57
Old Bailey 121
Old Mecca 106
On the Right Track (Taylor) 138

'On The Real Side' 190
100 Club 150, 174, 213, 221, 240, 245, 246, 248–55
101 Club 248
One-derful! label 31
'The One Who Really Loves You' 28
'Ooo Baby' 183
'Open The Door To Your Heart' 47, 53, 54
Operation Crossbow 224
The Originals 94, 220
Orwell, George 65–6, 96, 99
Oscar Perry and the Love Generators 134
Ostler bar 113
The Other Side of Jimmy Savile (TV) 122
Otley Street Youth Club 212
'Our Love (Is In The Pocket)' 53
'Out On The Floor' 37
The Outsiders 92
OVO (original vinyl only) 37

package holidays 127, 146
Page, Jemma 259
Pages 94
Palao, Alec 252
Palmer, Arnold 83
Palmer, Tony 95–6
Palmer, Val 261
'Papa Oom Mow Mow' 193
Paradise Garage (New York) 95
Paris 20, 193, 282
The Parish youth club 110
Parker of Waddington, Lord 27
Parker, Eddie 135, 189
Parkin, Ben 22

Parrish, Dean 77, 79
Parry, David 163
Patton, Charley 188
Patty Gilson & Tonettes 221
Paul, Clarence 220
Pavese, Cesare 9
Peace, David 114, 122
Peacock Records 23
Pearson, Derek 145
Pender, Julie 72, 90, 216
Pendulum 45–7, 68, 72, 75, 105, 260, 282
Pennington, Barbara 136, 142
People Records 243
Pereira, Ian 'Pep' 141, 260
Perez, Nico 271
Perry, Oscar 87
Perth 6–9, 45, 95, 237
Perth City Soul Club 8, 272, 275
Philadelphia International 88
Phillips, Brian '45' 31
Phillips, Esther 171
Phoenix Dance Company 112
'Pick Up The Pieces' 7
Pickens, Tyrone 74
Pickett, Wilson 5, 7, 30
Pier (Cleethorpes) 67, 104, 105, 112, 138–42, 143, 144, 145–6, 149, 150, 159, 182, 190
Piller, Eddie 248
Pink Floyd 30
Planet Records 271
'Please Let Me In' 60
'Please Operator' 73
Plebeians café 18, 21, 22, 35, 248
Plough Inn 273
The Pointer Sisters 88, 109

Poitier, Sidney 52
Poke (DJ) 141
Polkemmet Colliery 168
Pollard, Ray 184
Polmont 8
Pop, Iggy 144
popcorn (dance scene) 283
'pop-up' approach 35
Popovitch (cosmonaut) 4
Postil, Leland Michael (aka Mike Post) 73
post-punk scene 193
Pountain, Ady 222
POW WOW 253
Prestatyn 126, 147, 149
Primos club 112, 115
Prince, Michael 14
The Prophets (aka The Georgia Prophets) 181, 220
'Psychedelic Soul' 73
Public Services Vehicle (PSV) Club 17
punk 89, 95, 96, 114, 119, 143–7, 163, 193, 223, 229, 237, 241, 250, 274
'Purple Haze' 29
Purple Haze 71
purple hearts 22, 71, 85
'Put Your Arms Around Me' 73
Pye, Freddy 81

Quadrophenia (film) 98
'Quick Change Artist' 55, 108

Race Records 57
Rachman, Peter 22
Radcliffe, Jimmy 77, 78
Rae, Brian 30

Railway Tavern 246, 247
Rainbow Cottage 67
RainWorx 262
Raith, Stuart 26, 229, 250
Ralph's Records 43–4
rare groove scene 243, 245
'Rare Soul Man' (forum) 262
Ravensbourne College 143
Ray Avery's Rare Records 37
'Reaching For The Best' 135
'Real Humdinger' 60
'Reclaim the Night' (marches) 121
'Red Rave Party' 241
Red Riding quartet (Peace) 122
Redding, Otis 5, 7, 252
'Reference Back' (poem) 10
Reid, Brenda 135
Reid, Clarence 90
Reid, Jamie 144
Reivers, Olivia 120
Relf, Bob 136
religion 5–6, 15, 17, 30, 34, 40, 61, 80, 104, 117, 226
Reno 17
'Rescue Me' 217
Return to Cleethorpes (events) 150
Revilot Records 53
Rhumba Club 273
Richardson, Irene 123
Ric-Tic Records 58, 59–60, 126–7, 219, 283
'Ride The Vibe' 182
Riker 44, 283
Riker-Liker 44, 283
Rimmer, Dave 145
Ring, Robert 120
Risley (remand centre) 283
Ritson, Mike 51

Ritz (Manchester) 137, 215
Roach, Dean 154, 164
Road Runner cartoon character 45
The Road to Wigan Pier (Orwell) 65–6, 96
The Rockford Files (TV) 73
Robb, John 151
Roberts, Kev 68, 134, 150, 178, 198
Robertson, Othello 95
'Rock Your Baby' 89
Rockefeller, Governor Nelson 214
rockers 108, 129
Rodriguez, David 39
Ronstadt, Linda 7
Rooney, Herb 135
Roosevelt, President Franklin Delano 214
Rory Storm and the Hurricanes 20
Roscoe and Friends 183
Ross, Diana 217, 276
Rounce, Tony 245, 248, 250
Rowland, Mark 133
Roy C 24
Royal Birkdale Golf Club 83, 85
Royce, Rose 138
Rudie's club 161
Ruff Cut Soul Club 165
'Running In Another Direction' 136
Rushton, Neil 137, 196
Russell, Gary 168
Russell, Ken 96
Russell, Saxie 73
Russell, Stuart 36
Russell Club 17
Rylatt, Keith 24, 109

Rytka, Helena (aka Helen) 105, 115–21
Rytka, Rita 105, 115–21

St Charles' Roman Catholic School (Leeds) 115–16
St Ives (Cambridgeshire) 138
St Johnstone FC 237
St Louis Union 26
Saint (Manhattan club) 138
St Martin's School of Art 143
St Theresa's (children's home) 116
Sale Mecca 45
Samantha's club (Sheffield) 159
San Remo Golden Strings 37, 127
Sanchez, Roger 149
Sanremo Song Festival 127
Saunders, Larry (aka Prophet of Sound) 190
Savarese, Tom 39
Savile, Jimmy 106–7, 122–3
Saxe, Phil 31
Scala Cinema 240
Scarborough 126, 127, 139, 150, 151, 161
Scargill, Arthur 161
Schifrin, Lalo 137
Schofield, Paul 111
The Scene club 21
'Scots Corner' 216
Scott, Rick 141
Scott-Heron, Gil 241
Scottish Soul Weekender 149
'Sea Cruise' 158
Searling, Richard 46, 50, 68, 91, 94, 95, 100, 137, 148, 150, 181, 189, 194, 217, 220, 243, 260, 271

Seditionaries (shop) 144
Selby, Brian 192
Selectadisc shop 139, 192–5
Selwood, Richard 36
'Send Him Back' 88, 109
'Seven Day Lover' 241
'Seven Days Is Too Long' 217
Seven Stars club 45
Sex Pistols 142–3, 146
Sexton, Anne 203
Sexual Healing concert tour 219
Shades of Soul (magazine) 145
'Shadow Of A Memory' 245
Shah, Nikhil 271
'Shake And Bump' 88
'Shake Off That Dream' 203
Shakes, Trevor 243
Shalamar 196–7
The Shalimars 109, 197
Shard, Rod 218, 220
The Sharonettes 193
Sharp, Barrie 243
Sharp, George 222
The Sharpees 31
Sharpley, Anne 21
Shaw, Dave 97, 98
Shawel, Pastor Stephen 179
Sheffield 30, 93, 120, 140, 159,
    223, 231
Sheffield Wednesday FC 93
Sheldon, Sandi (aka Kendra
    Spotswood) 57–8, 135
'She'll Come Running Back' 255
Shelley's Laserdome 254
Shelvington, Paul (aka Shelvo) 137
Sheridan's club venue 253
The Sherrys 73
'Shoorah! Shoorah!' 90

The Show Must Go On (album) 201
Shrine Records 180–1, 184, 191,
    204, 220, 283
Shrine Soul Club 168
'Signed Miss Heroin' 201
Sim, Debbie 241–2
Simone, Nina 247
Simpson, Andy 178
Simpson, Zammo 273
Sinclair, Stephen 237
The Singing Nun 6
Singleton, Eddie 181, 191
Sioux, Siouxsie 250
Sir Clarence 183–5
Sit Down! Listen to This! (Eagle) 24
Situationist movement 144
Sixties Mafia 212–13, 214, 249
'sixties newies' 213
6Ts Rhythm and Soul Society
    245–6
Skegness 128, 139
SKF 44, 47, 283
'Skiing In The Snow' 51, 93
skinheads 7, 9, 96, 102, 107, 110,
    162
The Skullsnaps 134
Slim, Memphis 107
'Slipping Through My Fingers' 252
slum housing 9, 17, 22
Small, Millie 24
Small Faces 30, 246
Smart Club (Madrid) 272
Smith, Curtis 199
Smith, Doris 230
Smith, Hunter 104
Smith, Jimmy 22
Smith, Kenny 135
Smith, Mamie 56

Smith, Mick 247
Smith, Pete 271
Smith, Tony 227, 238
Smith, Kline & French (SKF) 44, 47, 283
The Smiths 213
Smithsonian Museum 188, 190
Smokey Robinson and the Miracles 24
'So In Luv' 95
Sobers club 135
Social and Reform Club (Grimsby) 35
The Sociology of Rock (Frith) 77–8
Soft Cell 74, 113
Soho 18, 21, 239, 245, 246, 247
Solar Records 197
'Some These Days I'll Be Gone' 188
'Somebody Help Me' 214
Sons of Nature 182
Soo Catwoman 144
'Sophisticated Sissy' 183
Soul Bowl Records 46, 94, 95, 132, 135, 243
Soul Boy (film) 268
Soul City (shop) 25
Soul Galore (magazine) 145
Soul Hole 136
Soul Not Dole 154–5, 164
Soul Searchers 88
Soul Shakers (Bavaria) 272
Soul Sounds label 192
Soul Source (forum) 264
Soul Survivors (Winstanley) 69
Soul Train (TV) 196–7
The Soul Twins 55, 108
Soul Underground (magazine) 145

Soul Up North (magazine) 119, 145
Soulful Kinda Music (magazine) 145
Sound Stage Seven label 195
Sounds (newspaper) 246
Soussan, Michael 'Simon' 111, 136, 193–8, 212, 252
South Wales 157, 240
Southport 66, 82, 126, 148–9
Southport Soul Weekender 148
Southworth, Gis 229, 250
Sowter, Mary 72
Sparkle 93
The Spellbinders 28
Spence, Stuart 146
The Spencer Davis Group 24, 30
Spencer, Linda 44
Spin Inn 32
Spinning Disc 106–7
Spinning Wheel 122
Springsteen, Bruce 187
Sputnik 2, 3
Stafford 5, 36, 100, 164, 166, 171, 207–12 *passim*, 214–20 *passim*, 221, 222, 223, 224, 228, 229, 236, 238, 240, 244, 249, 251, 253, 261, 262, 271, 272, 281
Stainthorpe, John 122
Stalker, John 17, 22, 28, 29
'Stand By Me' 28
Stanhope, Tony 'Stan' 250
Stanley Woodruff and the 'US' Trio 182
The Staple Singers 190
Star and Garter pub 108
Starlight Rooms 246
Starr, Edwin (aka Charles Edwin

Hatcher) 8, 28, 30, 58, 59–60, 61, 107, 126
Staten, Patrinell 254
Staton, Candi 202, 203
Statthaus Böcklerpark (Berlin) 272
Stax label 8, 53, 71
Stevens, April 109
Stewart, Rod 247
Stock Aitken Waterman 136
Stoke Sentinel 211
Stoke-on-Trent 253, 268
Stokes, 'Loveman' Ronnie 215
stomper 52, 91, 131, 137, 156, 158, 173, 193, 215, 247, 281, 283
Stone, Henry 89
Stone, Joss 90
Stone, Sly 195
'Stop And Take A Look At Yourself' 109, 197
'Stop Her On Sight (SOS)' 59
'Stop In The Name Of Love' 59
The Story of Northern Soul (Nowell) 71
Straddling, Glenys 110
Strange, Steve 240
Street, Judy 111
Stringfellow, Peter 30
'Strings A GoGo' 195, 252, 253
Stubbs, Levi 8
Stuffed Olives club 38
'Stupidity' 246
Styrene 284
Sub Club 165
suedeheads 7, 11, 162
'Sugar's Never Been As Sweet As You' 221
Sullivan, Amanda 242

Sullivan, Chris 240
'Summer In The Parks' 88, 135
'Summer of Love' 148, 240
Sun Festival 147
Sunday Entertainments Bill (1971) 81
Sunday People 22
Sunday Times 199
The Superiors 109
The Supremes 24, 58, 59, 181, 275
'Suspicion' 220
Sutcliffe, Peter (aka Yorkshire Ripper) vii, 85, 102, 105, 106, 111, 113, 114, 115, 118, 120–122
Sutherland Road Community project 253
Swallow, Detective Constable 82
'swallows' 72
'Sweet Soul Music' 109

'Tainted Love' 34, 74, 113
'Take Me In Your Arms (Rock Me A Little While)' 59
Take That 136
Takumao 259
Talk of the North (events) 138
Talk of the North (magazine) 134, 144
Tartan Army 95
Tasker, Barry 46, 260
tattoos 44, 56, 222, 232, 283
Taurus Soul Club 111, 118
Tavares 137
Taylor, Ginger 35, 137–8, 141
Taylor, Jill 114–15
Taylor, Johnny 245
Taylor, Leroy 183

Taylor, Little Eddie 245
'Tear From A Woman's Eye' 220
'Tearstained Face' 203
'Tell Him' 135
The Temptations 8, 24, 220
Tereshkova, Valentina 4
Terrell, Tammi 73, 252
Tex, Joe 92
Thatcher, Prime Minister Margaret
    40, 160, 163, 242
'That's Just What You Did' 171
Theatre Bar (Blackpool Winter
    Gardens) 150
'Theme From Joe 90' 94, 98
'There Was A Time' 93
They Call Me Mister Tibbs! (film)
    52
They Too Arise (Miller) 189
'Think It Over Baby' 214
This England: Wigan Casino (TV)
    96
This Is England '90 (TV) 223, 268
'This Love Starved Heart Of Mine
    (It's Killing Me)' 219
Thomas, Carla 179
Thomas, Don 67, 241
Thomas, Dylan 207
Thomas, Evelyn 136, 142
Thomas, Rufus 5, 183
Thomas, Timmy 90
Thorley, David 209, 215, 221–2
3 before 8 77, 79, 159, 170
Three Coins café 21
The Three Coins (venue in Leeds)
    107
'Three Rooms With Running
    Water' 78
'Time Will Pass You By' 77, 78, 79

Titov 4
TK Records 89
'To Win Your Heart' 47, 127
Today (TV) 142
Todd, Rick 141
Tolliver, Kim 140
'Too Darn Soulful' (website) 259
'Too Late' 57
Top 100 Mod Songs 246
Top of the Pops (TV) 69, 93, 96
Top of the World Club 5, 36, 100,
    210–12, 224
Torvill, Jayne 77
'Touch My Heart' 58
'Tow-A-Way Zone' 134
Towana and the Total Destruction
    266
Trainspotting (film) 7, 236
Trevino, Lee 83
The Triumphs 56, 109
Troggs 68, 217
'Try Me For Your New Love' 244
Turing, Alan 43
Turner, Ike and Tina 30
'Turning My Heartbeat Up' 96
Twain, Mark 155
The Twans 89
12 West 39
Twink (DJ) 111, 118
'The Twist' 92
Twisted Wheel 11, 12, 15, 18,
    20–37 *passim*, 38, 39, 44–6,
    51–4 *passim*, 74, 75, 78, 80, 81,
    87, 106, 108, 125, 127, 129
Two For The Price Of One (album)
    57
2i's café 18
Typhoon Yolanda 245

UCATT (Union of Construction, Allied Trades and Technicians) 161–2
'Um, Um, Um, Um, Um, Um' 56
'Unsatisfied' 108
Up the Junction 66
Upnorth Weekender 148
'Uptight (Everything's Alright)' 59
'Uptown Festival' 196
'Uptown Saturday Night' 134
US Polaris base (Holy Loch) 20

Valentino 87
Varner, Don 203
VaVas 50, 68, 148, 260
The Velvelettes 218, 220
Vel-Vets 269
Venn Street 111, 118, 119
The Ventures 94
The Versatiles 266
Verve label 108
The Vibrations 56
Vice (magazine) 93
The Vikings 6, 7
Villa Records 195–6, 252
Vimeo (website) 264
Vincent, John 88, 141
Visage 240
The Vonnettes 58

Wag Club 240, 247
Wagstaffe, Steve 164
Wakefield Unity Hall 35
Wakes Week 126
'Walk Like A Man' 187
Walker, Jr 24, 73
Walker, Lesley 240
Walker, Mike 96

Walker, Ronnie 134
'Walking In Rhythm' 179
'Walking The Duck' 109
Wall, Pat 10–11, 31, 32, 44
Wallace, Governor George 201
Walls, Alan 167, 170
Walls, Steve 167, 170
Walsh, Councillor Mary 121
Walsh, Maureen vii, 109, 110, 112, 121, 122
Walwyn, Steve 114
Wand Records 251, 252, 274
'Wanting You' 109
Ward, Singing Sammy 60
warehouse parties 241–2
Warner Brothers 49
Washington DC 177–91
Washington, Baby 244, 248
Washington, Dinah 174
Washington, Gino 'Whirlpool' 24, 58, 107
Washington Go-Go 88
Washington Post (newspaper) 182
Waterman, Pete 136
Waters, Muddy 23
Watley, Jody 197
Watson, Johnny 'Guitar' 57
Watson, Romance 215
Watson, Tom 83
WDAS radio station 170, 279
'Weak Spot' 136
'Wear Your Natural Baby' 266
Weaver, Carlena 178
'Wee Oo I'll Let It Be You Babe' 226
weekenders 129, 147–50, 162, 172, 259, 261, 268
Wells, James 136

Wells, Mary 28, 191
Welsh, Irvine 7, 236
Wensiora, Jimmy 222
Wesley, Fred 243
West Hampstead 246, 247, 248
West Indian Club 118
Weston, Kim 59
Westwood, Vivienne 143, 144
'What' 111
'What Took You So Long' 182
'What Would I Do' 109
The Wheeltappers and Shunters Social Club (TV) 159
'Where Does That Leave Me' 205
'Where Is The Love' 90
White, Barry 266
White, Graham 'Docker' 37
White, Karl 'Chalky' 160, 261, 271
White, Ted 74
Whitfield, Norman 138
Whitley Bay 126
Whittle, Steve 96
The Who 30, 246
Widdison, Pete 247
Wigan 15–16, 65, 66
Wigan Casino 5, 7, 15–16, 34, 40, 50, 53, 66–100 *passim*, 104, 105, 106, 112, 113, 118, 121, 127, 139, 141, 146, 148, 150, 151, 157, 160, 167, 181, 193, 194, 198, 201, 211, 216, 222, 223, 225, 227, 239, 245, 249, 251, 252, 254, 255, 271, 272, 274, 279, 280, 282
Wigan Observer 84
Wigan's Ovation 93, 96
Wigan Pier club 99
Wigan Rugby League Club 81

Wigley, Rob 210
Wilde, Gary 129
Williams, Clarence 57
Williams, Jerry (aka 'Swamp Dog') 232
Williams, John 99
Williams, Joyce Elaine 52
Williams, Larry 57
Williams, Mason 73
Williams, Pharrell 269
Willowgarth High School 162
Wills, Viola 266
Wilson, Andy 84–5, 188
Wilson, Bob (footballer) 194–5
Wilson, Bob (the White Ramsay Lewis) 195–6
Wilson, Frank 99, 196, 197–9, 259–60
Wilson, Greg 99
Wilson, Prime Minister Harold 258
Wilson, Walter 274
Winding Wheel 160
Wingate, Ed 126–7
Winsford Civic Hall 255
Winstanley, Russ 67–9, 74, 80, 87–8, 91–4, 97
Winter of Discontent (1974) 81
Winter Gardens (Blackpool) 150
Winter Gardens (Cleethorpes) 142, 146, 151
Winter, Ian 162
Winterton, Professor Jonathan 160–1
Winterton, Professor Ruth 160–1
Wired (magazine) 271
Wisdom, Bobby 250
Wishart, Shirley 212

Withers, Dave 72, 97, 218–23
Witherspoon, Jimmy 5, 23
Womack, Bobby 200
Wonder, Dickie 190
Wonder, Stevie 30, 59, 179, 220, 246
Woodcliffe, Jonathan 141, 198
Woods, Chuck 7, 217
Wooler, Bob 20
Worthington, Frank 111
Wright, Betty (aka Bessie Regina Norris) 88–91
Wright, Terry 154
Wyatt, Johnny 266
Wynder K Frog 24

The Yardbirds 30
Yate 98, 215, 222, 284
Yates, Leslie 80
Yellow Pages directory 186, 199
'Yes It's You' 243
YMCA (Glenrothes) 167
Yorkshire Evening Post 33
Yorkshire Post 112, 116

Yorkshire Traction Sports and Social Club (Tracky) 158
'You Beat Me To The Punch' 28
'You Can Have Watergate Just Gimme Me Some Bucks And I'll Be Straight' 243
'You Hit Me Like TNT' 51
'You Just Don't Know (What You Do To Me)' 92, 266
'You Left Me' 255
'Young Hearts Run Free' 202
'You're Gonna Make Me Love You' 57, 58, 135
YouTube 259–60, 262, 264
'You've Been Gone Too Long' 203
'You've Got To Try Harder' 134
Yuro, Timi 173

Zazou (film) 112
Zeigarnik Effect 4
'The Zoo (The Human Zoo)' 134, 263
Zoot Money 24, 247
ZTSC label 44–7